DATE DUE

OCT 1 8 1978			
OCT 1 0 1978			
NOV 2 9 1978			
NOV 1 9 1975			
JAN 7 1981			
JAN 5 1981			
MAY 2 7 1981			
MAY 1 8 1981			
NOV 1 7 1991			
AUG 2 9 1995			

THE WAYWARD GATE

THE WAYWARD

GATE

science and the supernatural

PHILIP SLATER

BEACON PRESS : BOSTON

Beacon Press books are published under the auspices
of the Unitarian Universalist Association

Published simultaneously in Canada by
Fitzhenry & Whiteside Limited, Toronto

Printed in the United States of America

(hardcover) 9 8 7 6 5 4 3 2 1

Library of Congress Cataloging in Publication Data

Slater, Philip Elliot.
  The wayward gate.
  Bibliography: p.
  1. Occult sciences.   I. Title.
BF1411.S57   133   77–75445
ISBN 0–8070–2956–4

to melita

druid, gypsy, pirate,
until you are me
and I am you

*. . . the gate to the psychic world is never
quite where it's supposed to be.*

CONTENTS

SCENES FROM A MARRIAGE WITH SKEPTICISM

When you're standing on the North Pole, which way is East?
—Melanie Gaster

It's hard for me to pin down the moment when I first began to take alternative realities seriously. I know I started out as a rather extreme skeptic and materialist, and remained that way until I was well over forty. While many people have altered their world view in response to powerful drug experiences, my own early encounters with psychedelics left me attitudinally untouched. Starting in 1952 I had a number of LSD trips over a two-year period, but while they were interesting and increasingly pleasurable, they brought about no blinding revelations. In those days there was no psychedelic culture, no milieu for defining the experience as anything but a pharmaceutical adventure. Many of my trips took place in a mental hospital as part of a research project, and the experience tended to be defined clinically rather than mystically. Wandering about a disturbed ward on acid was thought to put you in closer empathic contact with patients. I never noticed that it did, but since I'm rather resistant to most mind-altering drugs, and hadn't learned in those days to compensate for this defect, I probably wasn't the best possible test case.

For ten or twelve years after that period I had nothing to do with drugs at all. Leary came to Harvard and left again without my being moved to give psychedelics another whirl. It was only in the mid-sixties that I became at all interested in drugs again, and then only to get high occasionally. Since 1970 I have had psychedelic experiences that were much more powerful, but by that time the important changes had already occurred.

The first changes were rather specific. For about twenty-five years I've been leading experience groups of one kind or another. My leadership style has been under continual evolution during that period, from a kind of pseudo-Rogerian group-discussion approach, through eight or nine years of the frozen-faced oracular style that many psychoanalytic group therapists affect, to the more active and responsive mode of the eclectic encounter-group leader. I like to think that improvements in quality have matched these stylistic changes, but I know I lack the natural gift for instinctive responsivity that really fine group leaders have. I think I made every mistake enthusiastic beginners can make leading encounter groups, for example. Yet I keep struggling with it, for the simple reason that I get more pleasure from doing it well than from any other occupation.

This is by way of underlining how important it's been to me during the past ten years to learn, painfully and haltingly, and with many reversals and relapses, to rely on a more responsive and intuitive approach to leading groups. People who need to exert rational control over their world are very slow learners.

It was around 1965 that I first became aware of the innovations of the encounter group movement. The psychoanalytic approach I'd been using seemed sterile, dishonest, and ineffectual, and I was intrigued by the daring and creativity of the newer methods. For a long time it was just a matter of changing techniques, then of changing my whole style and approach, and finally of realizing how much I'd have to change as a person to be the kind of group leader I wanted to be.

An intellectual turning point also occurred in 1969, at a symposium in which I finally absorbed, at a visceral level, the idea that I was part of a system—not a detached observer, initiator of action, or recipient of transference. This meant that both my acts and my emotional reactions were not entirely "mine," but grew out of an organic process that everyone created together—that I was simply one organ of a living system, that my twitches (whether "rational" or not) were the twitches of that system and hence could be used to diagnose it, and that when I inhibited and falsified those twitches in order to preserve my dignity I was starving the system of information.

From Gregory Bateson I learned the fatuity of thinking of people as separable units. My second piece of learning in that symposium came from Warren Brody: it was the importance of trying to maintain some congruence between (a) the content of what you say and (b) what you're doing while saying it. A liberal professor, lecturing five hundred students on the evils of capitalistic exploitation, represents one kind of incongruence. Sitting around in a plastic, smoke-filled hotel room, discussing Man's insensitivity to his environment, is another. When one can attain some kind of congruence, however—when the medium and the message are one—the effect is very powerful. In my experience, professional people have the greatest difficulty in achieving or even recognizing congruence—I don't really know why. Perhaps the splitting of process and content is something that's taught in all graduate schools.

It took a couple of years for these insights to have any salutary effect on my behavior—in or out of groups. And it was another two years before I developed any interest in psychic phenomena. Yet I feel these changes were important in creating a receptivity to ideas that had bored or re-pelled me prior to that time. They helped me think of my-self as other than my ego—helped me focus less on inner cerebrations and more on action and process. They gave more weight to relationships rather than *things*, energy rather than matter, experiencing rather than manipulat-ing. This made it a lot easier to see possibilities formerly closed off by the rectangular rigidities of rationalistic thought.

I had always felt a little bit open to the idea of psychic healing. I could accept these seemingly miraculous occur-rences because they had already been "translated" via psychosomatic medicine. Since doctors had managed to trace at least a few of the ways emotional forces can change the functioning, shape, and even the structure of the body, I could assume that the rest would some day be found.

I think I didn't realize how far these events had out-stripped any conventional scientific explanation. It was clear to me that the standard testimonials of faith healers, whether faked or not, were not particularly unusual—that most doctors, if pressed, could recall miraculous spontane-ous recoveries from their own experience. Before I realized that this contradicted many other beliefs, I knew to my own satisfaction that massive bodily changes could oc-cur, for good or for evil, without physical intervention of any kind.

As I became more familiar with body-oriented therapies, like bioenergetics and Rolfing, new oddities occurred. I saw people's life histories reconstructed, sometimes with daz-zling specificity, by someone merely looking at their bodies. I saw memories elicited by pressing certain muscles. I saw the color and shape of tissue alter in response to the ex-pression of feeling. I saw chronic symptoms of decades' duration disappear overnight.

These events were by no means mysterious. They usually made very good sense in terms of everyday wisdom. But increasingly I realized how much they diverged from tra-ditional medical assumptions. So when I began to hear of acupuncture cures, of Edgar Cayce, of auras and energy bodies, I found it easier to entertain these notions.

It wasn't until around 1973 that I found myself particularly *interested* in psychic phenomena. Freed from all intellectual tasks for a while, I discovered that the only books that interested me fell in the "occult" category. I began to understand what people like Castaneda were saying.

I'm still not sure what happened. I can still think in the old way, but it hasn't helped me figure out how I learned to think (a little) in the new one. I know that the trick is to detach yourself from your mind or ego—not permitting it to be the unquestioned despot it usually is for most of us. I have the feeling that most people go through two kinds of event: (a) a gradual mental process (it can be physical, as well) of restructuring your viewpoint—rearranging your basic assumptions; and (b) some sudden illuminating experience. These can occur in either order or simultaneously.

I suspect that the sudden illuminating events are personal and idiosyncratic and have little meaning when told to someone else. Rather than belabor the reader with accounts of ineffable experiences, I'd rather spend the time doing what I think I can do better—spelling out some of the gradual mental rearrangements that make such experiences more likely to happen and easier to understand when they do. In large part, then, this book is directed to the ego. I'm not interested in blowing the mind with accounts of extraordinary events, or challenging it with paradoxes, or asking it to surrender itself to some external authority. The purpose of this book is to persuade the ego, in its own language, to enlarge its repertory of experience: to rule more democratically, more wisely, more openly, more richly. I want to convince the despot that it's ill-informed—that its own desperate need for control has strangled its information channels, that the result of this anxious vigilance is the impoverishment of its own experience and of the whole kingdom, and that its understanding of the universe is wildly erroneous.

The Wayward Gate

Most books on alternative realities do some of this—that's what books are for. Perhaps what's unusual about this effort is that I'm not writing as someone who's "been there," and is trying to describe the view from the other side. I've had many wonderful experiences, but none that in and of themselves would tempt me to believe in any system of reality besides the familiar three-dimensional burrow that Western science has dug for us. I've never been definitively out of my body, or seen into the future, or participated in a clear-cut telepathic event, or seen a spirit, or experienced the oneness of the universe. I'm as thoroughly mired in our everyday world as anyone I know. I'm somewhat embarrassed to admit that I've arrived at an appreciation of alternative realities through some sort of intellectual process.

This puts me in the awkward position of writing for an audience that's probably more "advanced" in the subject than I am, but I've noticed over the years that people who move slowly also have much to teach. The traveler who dashes ahead to see the rainbow misses the flowers that grow along the roadside, and vice versa. People who have had some sort of nonworldly experience often leave it completely unintegrated with the rest of their lives, and most of those who devour Castaneda's books treat them as they would a fascinating novel about the Middle Ages. Changing a world view is a gradual and difficult process, and I can't help feeling that the experience of a plodder might contribute something to it. Although our mental horizons are continually being extended these days, the extensions tend to occur in dramatic bursts—in isolated spasms. Science incorporates what it can, while the rest of the new information lies about in scattered heaps. Our thinking about "nonordinary reality" is incoherent and contentious. New theories are improvised, while old ones—much the worse for thousands of years of heavy wear—are pressed into service despite their conspicuous disrepair. Science is pitted against spirituality, East against West, and most of us stumble through each day equipped with a junk heap of contradictory theories, all of which we firmly believe and just as firmly disregard. While I have no ambition to create a new world view for the twentieth century, I think it would be helpful to build a few bridges between ordinary and nonordinary ways of thinking about experience; to reduce the discordance between our ways of treating material and spiritual reality. I personally would prefer not to have to change vehicles when dealing with these different kinds of events. To speak of a psychic or spiritual realm is only a verbal convenience, a convention. There is no such "realm," just as there is no "material realm." There is only experience, and it would be nice if some day we could develop a language that applied to all of it.

Naturally my reasons for writing this book aren't entirely altruistic. I like writing my ideas down and arranging them in some kind of pattern. I like to find out what I "know" from time to time, and I discover this in the act of writing. Most of all I need to communicate with my own internal despot and convince him to make further concessions to the oppressed masses, whose gradual betterment has only whetted their appetite for more freedoms. For me this book is one more internal Magna Carta.

I had many internal debates about writing this book. One qualm, as I've mentioned, was that it seemed pompous to offer myself as a kind of guide when I'd had so little experience in these matters. But then I reflected that anyone can be a guide since we've all been somewhere that someone else *hasn't* been: We're only pompous if we think this makes us special. If I go South for a month and you stay in the North, then I can be your guide to the South when you go. But I'm not special because I went South—when I come back North I'll need you as a guide to fill me in on what happened when I was away. Everyone's always accumulating experience that might be useful to others. If I travel to Rome alone I'll see more new sights than a busload of tourists on a guided tour, but although the bus tour equips me less than the solo trip for being a Roman, it equips me more for being a good tour guide or camp director or housemother. Experience in itself is of equal value: We like to divide it into categories and then fight over how to rank those categories.

These thoughts about the value of experience produced another qualm: if nothing is more valuable than anything else, why do anything? The idea seemed paralyzing. Yet I know from long experience that whenever I feel paralyzed with indecision I'm attaching exaggerated importance to myself and my actions. A thing can only be of value *to someone*. When we leave off those last two words it's just a shorthand way of saying "to a lot of people." So the fact that nothing is of greater *absolute* value than anything else needn't paralyze me in the least, since there are all kinds of things that are more valuable to *me*. The trouble starts when I translate my own urgings into a principle—when instead of standing in one corner of the universe saying, "I'm this person here, who likes eggs," I become God, standing everywhere in the universe saying, "eggs are good for everyone, and that's why I subscribe to them." *I pretend no longer to have any motives*. "Objectivity" is the search for a uniform totalitarian standard, for the "objective" person is motivated primarily by a desire to be God.

CHAPTER 1

THE NARROW EYE

> There never has been an explanation that did not itself
> have to be explained.—Charles Fort

Sixty years ago Charles Fort was busily collecting data on
bizarre happenings. It didn't matter much in what *way* they
were bizarre—a rain of blood, a blizzard of spiders falling
on the Alps, young girls igniting fires without matches, odd
disappearances, UFOs, poltergeists—he loved them all. He
proposed ridiculous theories to explain these events and
then showed with brilliant and hilarious incisiveness that
his crackpot hypotheses were better supported by the evidence than the desperate improvisations of scientists.

Fort was a strange man—a fierce and humorous skeptic
fighting whimsically on the side of "superstition" against
scientific piety. He liked to refer to his array of awkward
facts—culled by the thousands from scientific journals,
where they lay ignored year after year, each shrugged off
as an isolated incident—as "the damned." He argued that
nothing could claim reality except by excluding something
else, and predicted that some day his army of "accursed tat-
terdemalions" would achieve respectability at the expense
of contemporary science—becoming the "sleek angels" of a
new intellectual establishment. Much of what we now call
"real" would become "unreal" for a time. But the "damned
won't stay damned," he insisted, and "salvation only precedes perdition." Hence at some *still* later day, he argued,

his redeemed damned would go right back to damnation
again.

The first stage of Fort's prediction is already coming
true. Every paperback store seems to have a shelf full of
books on "the supernatural"—most of them made up of
material pilfered from Fort's own books—and more and
more respectable intellectuals are approaching the "occult"
with serious intent.

In the fifties psychologists and sociologists used to write
papers explaining why people persisted in thinking they
saw and heard things that were contrary to scientific
dogma. I suppose in some dusty place people are still writing those papers, but the trend now is quite the other way.
The walls are crumbling and the damned are escaping
through every crevice. Never, since Science first began to
enforce its rule that certain kinds of events must not be
treated as real, have there been so many challenges to that
rule.

But what on earth do telepathy, psychic healing, UFOs,
psychokinesis, the Bermuda Triangle, ancient astronauts,
Atlantis, astrology, Yogic self-mastery, clairvoyance,
biofeedback, auras, astral projection, and so on, have in
common? Why does an interest in one so often open an
interest in the others? Some are plausible theories, some
are observed phenomena difficult to explain. Some are
steeped in magic and religion, some more akin to science
fiction. Some fit quite comfortably within conventional scientific ideology, others require a complete transformation
of that ideology. Some deal with what seem to be "material"
phenomena, others with what seem to be "spiritual" ones.

Most conventional scientists have no trouble with this issue. For them, what ties these things together is ignorance
and superstition. Others see real scientific potential in one
or another area and strive earnestly to differentiate their
particular interest from all others. Men like Hynek, Michel,
and Vallee, for example, want to get other scientists to take
seriously the volumes of hard data on UFOs. These men
try laboriously to separate good reports from "crackpot"

reports, and would be heavily discouraged to have anyone link UFOs with psychic phenomena. Similarly, many scientists want to study telepathy in the laboratory but see astrology and astral projection as hogwash.

I'm with the full-blown reactionaries in one respect—as usual they have a good instinctive sense of what goes together. For example: Communism, pornography, communes, ethnic pride, fluoridation, women's liberation, socialized medicine, drugs, gay liberation, and Buddhism are all an assault on individualistic capitalism and they, at least, know it. In the same way, UFOs, telepathy, and the other interests I listed above all assault and affront a certain way of looking at the world—a way that has dominated conventional science for centuries.

I can vouch for their communality. Ten years ago I wasn't the least interested in any of them. Some of the labels made me faintly nauseous. (Some still do—the term "astral projection" arouses a massive skepticism, while "out-of-the-body experience" leaves me unruffled.) Now I find myself fascinated by almost all of them.

What they share is that they've been shut out by scientists for threatening certain dogma—the importance of cognitive mastery of the world, the doctrine of individualism, the doctrine of gradual and peaceful evolution, and so on—doctrines that have less to do with the way the world is than with the way scientists have to behave to become scientists.

Accepting the reality of some items on the occult bookshelf wouldn't really overturn the scientific way of looking at things. UFOs propelled by unknown methods could easily exist. Atlantis could very well have once stood in mid-ocean without shattering anything more than a single somewhat shopworn theory. Some psychic phenomena might be explained by as yet undiscovered physical forces. After all, Einstein's theories would have seemed superstitious nonsense in the eighteenth century.

Science has a lot of flexibility still, and is itself approaching questions that threaten to revolutionize it: attempts to deal with black holes and other oddities of the universe are propelling physics into ideas that overlap the psychic realm quite considerably. Physics today is where it was just before Einstein shook it up—complacent but puzzled, about to be turned on its ear, forced to deal with utterly unacceptable ideas, but still possessing great capacity to adapt.

But when we look at the total onslaught, coupled as it is with a burgeoning interest in Eastern religious and esoteric traditions, it seems clear that more is at stake for science than a major theoretical revision, or even several at once. The underlying world view of science itself is being abandoned. Science is in the position that organized Christian religion was in two centuries ago: it must either stamp out the intruding world view, share the stage with it, or be cast into a secondary and ineffectual position. I think it's already too late for the first outcome, while science is too resilient to fall into the third. Stage-sharing will be an awkward and painful process, and one of my goals in writing this book is to soften it.

Why is this happening right now? Could Castaneda's books have been bestsellers twenty years ago? People have never stopped being fascinated with the supernatural, but these books came from the heart of academia. They were made popular by intellectuals, not by readers of the *National Enquirer*. What has changed in twenty years?

But this question demands a prior one: why were science and psychoanalysis so popular during the *preceding* decades? Every system tends to assume its own truth and offer special explanations for the perverse popularity of "untruths," but I feel unwilling to give any system this special status. No system succeeds because it's "true"—it succeeds because it *delivers* in some way. Science, capitalism, psychoanalysis, and other systems that overvalue the functions of the human ego, delivered mightily for a period of time and have, for some reason, stopped delivering, just as the Church of Rome and feudalism stopped delivering in an earlier century. I leave the explanation to historical analysts.

One of the most pressing forces for change right now, to

me at least, is a sense of urgency about the tininess of the small corner of reality we're aware of—a sense of how little we see and hear and know, and how vast the dimensions, not of space, but of what immediately impinges on us.

Lyall Watson points out, for example, that while the entire electromagnetic spectrum ranges in wavelength from a billionth of a centimeter to millions of miles, only a tiny slit of this—between 380 and 760 billionths of a meter—is visible to us, while many other forms of energy are not visible at all. Robert Ornstein cites research on the eye of the frog showing that it discards all the stimuli available to it except for four kinds of differences: (1) fixed contrasts, that show the general shape of the environment (light sky, dark water, darker lily pad); (2) sudden moving outlines and (3) sudden decreases in light, both of which signal approaching predators; and (4) a special sensitivity to small dark objects close to the eye, which enables the frog to catch bugs (Ornstein, pp. 21–23). Except for these little bits of information that help the frog stay alive, it's blind as a bat.

And so are we. The difference between us and the frog is just one of degree. We see a tiny fragment of reality—one that allows us to master our physical environment—and little more.

Knowing how little we can see (or hear, or smell, or feel, or taste, or sense)—knowing how little the frog sees and why it sees what it does see—tells us something important about our understanding of reality.

What we mean by "reality" is not what exists.

Reality is merely what we *need*.

Therefore, if our concept of reality is changing, it's because our definition of what we need to survive is changing.

We are like frogs about to be removed from the pond, perhaps forever, and taken to a place where "food" is not flying insects, and "predators" are not flying birds. We need a whole new set of sensory equipment, and a brain to match.

The universe is flooding in on us too fast. We sense that

conventional science is moving too slowly, clinging to its millpond discriminations when the millpond is about to be dried up. The world will implode before science works itself out of its rut by its own techniques.

But how do we get out of our tiny sensory and conceptual box? How can we learn to see beyond what we can see?

The method is simple. We just did it with the frog. Instead of expanding our awareness we shrink it, imagining ourselves with less instead of more. Then we think how we would distort the world this way. Then we extrapolate.

Plato taught us this method of pulling ourselves up by our own psychic bootstraps—transcending our own awareness by using our imagination—in his oft-quoted Parable of the Cave (*The Republic*, Book VII). The parable has a lot of prisoners chained up in a cave with their backs to the light, seeing only the shadows thrown on the wall. The prisoners imagine that the shadows of objects are the objects themselves. When one of the prisoners is released and brought into the sunlight he is blinded and confused for a long time but later realizes the pitiable plight of his fellow prisoners. He scorns their skill in observing shadows, but he himself does so poorly at it when he first returns that they think him blinded by his journey, which, in a sense, he is.

The uses to which Plato puts this parable are less important than the technique itself. He says explicitly that the cave is the world of sight. In other words, he makes a distinction within our known experience (shadow versus "reality") and then extrapolates that distinction into unknown experience: shadow is to our reality as our reality is to "true" reality. Ornstein uses this same method with the vision of the frog: frog vision is to our vision as our vision is to what's really there to be seen.

This is the only way we know to expand our perspective except through inspiration, intuition, or revelation. We could make a lot more use of it than we do.

The Narrow Eye

THE NEED FOR NEW MAPS

Scientists as a group are strongly wedded to their instruments and techniques, and tend to pay heed only to what can be mechanically registered. It has been said that a scientist is a person who will believe in the existence of the moon only after viewing it through a lens of some kind.

When I say that psychic phenomena are being taken increasingly seriously, then, I mean by scientists and their fellow travelers. Ordinary people have always taken them seriously, because most people have had experiences of this kind. But skeptics have always demanded that such events submit themselves to laboratory conditions as a prerequisite to being considered real.

This presents difficulties. It's a little like trying to study musical genius by setting a famous pianist down to play scales in a laboratory, on a dummy keyboard with electrodes attached to his hands and feet. As Ornstein points out, emotionality is of primary importance in telepathic communication (pp. 222–223), yet most research has been based on the use of neutral symbols. Studies that have taken emotionality into account typically yield more dramatic results.

Acceptance of the reality of telepathy would force a drastic revision in our concepts of communication. Acceptance of the reality of UFOs would revolutionize our ideas of gravity and propulsion. Acceptance of precognition would upset all our notions of time, and so on. But the most revolutionary change of all would be forced by acceptance of the idea of an "energy body" ("astral body," "soul," "spirit," or whatever) distinct from, and *detachable from*, the material body. At present there is simply no way that scientific thought could bend to absorb this stimulus. An ironclad laboratory demonstration that an out-of-the-body event could influence material reality as we know it would undermine some of science's most fundamental assumptions.

The Wayward Gate

As yet, such demonstrations have been uncertain, infer-
ential, and circumstantial. No one will be convinced by
them who doesn't want to be, but they're suggestive
enough not to be ignored altogether. We're living in an
odd moment in history.

Whether real or imaginary, the ability to leave the body
has been fundamental to esoteric traditions throughout
history. It lies at the root of shamanistic healing, of some
oracular traditions, of much sorcery, and many mystical
cults. Much of Castaneda's apprenticeship with Don Juan
was spent preparing for highly controlled out-of-the-body
experiences. Indeed, if we are to believe what Castaneda
tells us of Don Genaro, that roguish gentleman has
achieved more conscious control over his energy body than
any human being for whom we have comparable information. Amateurs in this field, such as Robert Monroe and
Oliver Fox, report great difficulty in establishing such control. Fox never seemed able to control where he was going
or in what form, while Monroe could do so only with
enormous effort.

To read any of these accounts is to be plunged into what
seems like a chaotic dreamworld. For every faint thread of
communality in the experiences there are a dozen diver-
gent, unique, and unintelligible variations. How can we
navigate this territory? Not everyone is so fortunate as to
have a Don Juan to interpret his or her experience. Some
have been able to find some sort of map among the many
Eastern traditions. But most Westerners interested in the
psychic realm are just blundering around as best they
can—alienated from scientific thought and uncritically absorbed in an undigested potpourri of non-Western traditions.

We need bridges from our Western training to this very
uncomfortable domain. A phrase like "chaotic dreamworld" reveals how uncomfortable it is—a phrase like that
is a way of giving up before you start, dismissing the unknown as having no meaning. Much is being written now to

overcome this strangeness—Castaneda, Weil, Ornstein, Tart, Monroe, Pearce, and many, many others are trying to map the new territory from a Western vantage point. This book is another effort in that tradition.

THE EMPEROR'S ELIXIR

PART I

Once upon a time, on a planet less citified but more civilized than ours, there lived a great emperor. Like all great rulers he was troubled by headaches, due to the pressure of grave responsibilities, which he refused to delegate.

The planet, called Fettacenza on local space charts, was luxuriant and untroubled by internal strife. Life was comfortable and pastoral: people moved around very little, lived in simple houses in a benign climate, and had absolutely no understanding whatever of the importance of tragedy.

But if the emperor had few worries, they seemed all the more burdensome by contrast. His biggest vexation was nothing more than a surfeit of birds, yet it drove him nearly to distraction.

The Wo birds were even pretty—gold with purple markings and green eyes—but they had extinguished most other birds on the planet and they bred like rabbits. Since they had no natural predators they simply increased until their food supply—mainly flying insects—was endangered. They were a nuisance.

Since the birds were noiseless, could fly at incredible speeds, and never landed except in the highest treetops, they were almost impossible to catch or kill. They were always diving close to the ground to catch insects, and people never knew when they were going to be startled out of their wits by having one swoop soundlessly by. The emperor was particularly vexed, first because his luxuriant palace gardens were infested with the birds; and second because everyone expected him to do something about it.

Every other Tuesday a Wo-bird committee met, and a semiannual symposium brought experts from all over the planet to pool ideas. Millions were spent in research—mostly on the offspring of a pair of mutant Wo birds who couldn't fly. As with cancer and heart research in our country, major breakthroughs were announced every year just before funding time, but nothing much ever came of them.

Finally one day the emperor, suffering from a particularly excruciating headache, flew into a rage. He fired all his researchers, canceled all future conferences, and stomped off to his tower to sulk. In his misery he tripped ascending the stairs, and stumbled against a door he had almost forgotten. It said "Wise Man" on it, and the ruler remembered that years ago he had hired an elderly adviser in the tradition of his forebears, but had never consulted him.

Muttering fatalistically, the emperor pushed open the door and walked the narrow corridor to the wise man's apartment. He listened at the door a moment and then knocked.

"Who is it?"

"The emperor," said the ruler with some impatience.

"Go away!"

"What do you mean, 'go away'!" the emperor screamed indignantly.

At that the door opened, and spewed forth a little old man with wild kinky hair and red eyes.

"What do *you* mean," he shouted, "coming here and upsetting my reveries after twenty-seven years! Twenty-seven years without a single request, or even an invitation to dinner. Why did you bring me here if you weren't going to use me?"

"I'm sorry," the emperor muttered. His head throbbed worse than ever.

But the wise man was just warming up. "I don't mind so much being away from my loved ones—the food is good and my apartment's comfortable—but a man needs to feel useful. I've studied every royal crisis since I've been here—read old books, brainstormed with myself, drawn diagrams—I even wrote a ninety-page report on the Minister of the Interior's fall into corruption and how to prevent future such—I could go on for hours——"

"Please don't." The pounding was becoming unbearable.

"——but none of it was used. I could have saved you days, weeks, *months* of worry! Did you put me up here just to be an ornament? I have skills, knowledge, *wisdom*! Why don't you ever *consult* me?"

"I'm consulting you *now*, you kinky-haired kvetch! If you're so wise tell me how to get rid of these headaches!"

"Oh, that's easy," said the wise man, restored at once to total equanimity, "the headaches come from the Wo birds."

"Then would you tell me," the emperor begged, with desperate reasonableness, "how to get rid of the Wo birds?"

"You can't get rid of them," replied the wise man, "I've studied the problem at length and any attempt to destroy them will only make matters worse. But-I-have-an-answer!" he shouted quickly, to ward off another explosion from the emperor. "Since you can't get rid of them" (he slowed down again to recapture the dramatic effect), "the only solution is *not to see them*."

He paused meaningfully, but the emperor merely stared at him in sullen noncomprehension. The wise man froze his enthusiastic smile in place and settled down to wait him out.

"All right," said the emperor, finally jarred into action by the silence. "How is this magic to be accomplished?"

First Tale

"I have developed in my laboratory an elixir which renders a person incapable of seeing any object moving faster than forty miles per hour. Since the Wo bird and a few insects are the only living things on our planet that travel faster than that, the loss will be very small and the gain very great."

Fettacenza had no flying vehicles, and surface transportation was slow. Rapid transit was restricted to underground trains, which seldom ran and never encountered each other. The emperor realized that the plan could work under current conditions of planetary placidity.

"You'll still be able to see everything else," continued the wise man, "except our satellites and the odd meteor."

"Our satellites!" exclaimed the emperor. "You mean——?"

"Yes, the moons will become entirely invisible."

This was more serious. The two rapidly circling moons of Fettacenza—one pink, one blue—were the most dazzling physical feature of the planet and the subject of much poetry.

But pain is an impulsive tyrant. The emperor glared at his wise man resolutely.

"Give it to me now," he ordered, "and a couple of aspirin while you're at it."

Months passed. The emperor lived ecstatically for a while, free from headaches. He and the wise man became friends and spent many a pleasant evening together. Knowing the emperor well made it easy for the wise man to smile owlishly as his leader began to drift bit by bit into his old irritability.

"You're missing the satellites," he ventured one night, during a moment of abstracted silence.

"It isn't that," the emperor grumbled. "It's the constant *talk*. People still complain about the birds and expect me to remedy a condition I'm not even aware of. I don't know which is worse, hearing poets get saccharine over the moons or receiving delegations bitching about the bloody

13

birds. I'm not sure you did me a favor giving me that elixir. Of course I appreciate getting rid of the headaches," he hastened to add, "but I may get them back if people don't stop running off at the mouth about things I can't see."

"I anticipated this," said the wise man sagely, "and have prepared a solution. Actually, it was part of my plan all along, but I wanted to let nature take its own course."

The emperor stared at him with the sour wariness of one who has proven predictable.

Oblivious, the wise man continued, "One of the main advantages of power, sire, is the ability it confers to generalize one's miseries."

The emperor perked up. He loved to be called "sire."

"If it offends you that others can see what you cannot, then why not give the elixir to everyone? No irritating conversation, no bird complaints—all problems vanish in one fell swoop."

"But will it be permanent?"

"One swallow of this elixir not only restricts your sensory range for a lifetime, it also alters the genetic structure so that none of your descendants will be able to see rapid movement either."

The emperor considered. It was a grave responsibility to restrict the vision of an entire planet forever. Still, people never stopped complaining about those demented birds. Weren't they really asking for it?

"However would we do it? You can't just go around giving glasses of water to fifty million people one at a time."

"It's very simple, really. The elixir is very strong and not difficult to manufacture. In a few months we'll have enough to saturate every source of drinking water on the planet. Given the interconnectedness of Fettacenzan waterways, lakes, and underground streams—so troublesome in the Era of Pollution—a few strategically placed tons of elixir and we'd have everybody speed-blind in a month."

"But what if the people object?"

"Oh, you don't tell them, silly. You simply say that we've

found a nontoxic repellent that drives the Wo birds away without killing them."

"What about the moons?"

"You announce tomorrow that an obscure elderly astronomer (I have a man for the job) predicts their disappearance within six months, due to the interposition of a layer of cosmic dust which will be captured by our planet and go into a lower orbit."

"Will they believe it?"

"People will believe anything if it comes from high enough authority. Especially when attached to a prediction that comes true. After all, that's the basic principle of science, right? Your theory is correct if you can predict events with it. A silly premise if you go into it very deeply, but convenient to our purposes. Anyway, all the imperial astronomers will denounce the theory until it proves 'correct.' Then they'll fall all over themselves revising and rationalizing and reinterpreting the event to fit their own theories. It doesn't really matter what they come up with— the satellites will be just as gone."

A smile spread over the emperor's face. He experienced the rare and delicious anticipation of one who is about to fool all of the people all of the time.

A WORLD IMBIBES

It all came about as the wise man had said. The prediction of the satellites' disappearance was greeted by the imperial astronomers with the terse derision scientists reserve for odd tidings from outside their fraternity. They said there was no basis for such a prediction and that the old astronomer was a senile publicity seeker.

A month later the old man repeated his prediction and offered some confusing new arguments to support it, thus forcing the imperial astronomers into a more energetic rebuttal. They expressed amazement that the emperor would pay so much attention to the ravings of a notorious lightweight, instead of consulting those especially qualified.

15

The Wayward Gate

They hinted at corruption. And each and every one, to their subsequent collective embarrassment, concluded his statement with the same spirited literary flourish—a remark to the effect that the old astronomer was "throwing cosmic dust in the eyes of the emperor and the public."

Three months later the old astronomer conveniently died, reviving the whole controversy only a month before the event was to occur. Since the emperor had already announced an imminent solution to the Wo-bird problem, the stage was set.

All went according to plan. Wo birds and satellites disappeared from the entire planet over a period of about three weeks, giving rise to joy, terror, astonishment, and grief. The dead astronomer was immediately reinstated in the public regard, and aspiring scholars began poring through his utterly undistinguished writings in an eager search for additional pearls. Fourteen doctoral dissertations on his work were begun that year—the first trickle in a sustained flood.

Although the imperial astronomers dismissed it as mere coincidence, the simultaneous disappearance of the Wo birds and the moons aroused the suspicion in every untrained mind that there was some relation between the two vanishings. Wild theories were advanced, some of them perilously close to the truth, and the emperor became worried that a credibility gap had been created. With the wise man's help he issued a statement suggesting that the two events *were* related—that the ascending birds had blundered into the cosmic dust and been destroyed.

That wasn't the end of the matter, however, since the imperial astronomers had shot the cosmic-dust theory full of holes. They pointed out that such an occurrence would produce many other effects besides blotting out the two moons. Why didn't the dust darken the sky, change the weather, burn up in the atmosphere? For a time they proliferated alternative hypotheses of bewildering inconsistency—most of them as transparently ridiculous as the cosmic-dust theory itself.

First Tale

Then one day a young astronomer named Ascius, watching his little daughter Emma make light spots on the ground with a mirror, had an insight. He decided that the two moons had never really existed, but were merely reflections cast upon the sky by the sun's rays bouncing off the two gigantic canals that circled Fettacenza—both of which were miles wide and had metallic beds. The Wo-bird repellent, he reasoned, had created a light-filtering film on the surface of the canals, blotting out the illusory moons.

The Ascius theory was an immediate hit, and soon replaced the dust theory in all but the deepest recesses of academia. It was plausible, accounted for certain anomalies in the orbit of the moons, and held out hope for their return. Some people were scandalized at the idea that the satellites had been a mirage, but their current invisibility made counterattack difficult. The theory was publicized brilliantly, great emphasis being given to its humble domestic origin, and Ascius was an overnight success. The wise man, seeing the superiority of Ascius's theory, gave it discreet support. He realized that giving the people a moral victory over the emperor would blunt their paranoia. He and the emperor, publicly chagrined at being shown up, were privately elated at the windfall.

The imperial astronomers, tired of an issue in which they had come off so poorly, were delighted to retire once again to their own research. Contenting themselves with a few academic papers showing that the Ascius theory was contradicted by as many as twenty-three hard celestial facts, they withdrew altogether from the public arena.

The intellectual community as a whole, however, had received a real shot in the arm. In addition to the spate of papers on the Ascius theory itself, there were dozens on the man, his intellectual history, and the process of discovery: "Moon over My Emmy: the Role of Serendipity in Scientific Progress," "Smoke Before Ascius: A Survey of Pre-Ascian Reflection Theories," "The Family of the Genius—Help or Hindrance?" to name just a few.

The Wayward Gate

Hardest hit by the Ascius theory was the Fettacenzan priesthood. The established religion on Fettacenza—born in the Era of Pollution—had a strong ecological bent, somewhat oversimplified through centuries of sclerosis and decay. It centered around a handful of crabbed and punctilious deities, who punished ecological misdeeds with ferocious celestial whippings.

Over the years the priests had become subservient to the emperor, but a few were bold enough to suggest that the disappearance of the moons was a divine punishment for driving off the Wo birds. Before the Ascius theory came out it looked like a major religious revival was underway—as more and more Fettacenzans turned to the church for meaning in the confusion of the times.

The Ascius theory struck at the heart of this renaissance. Not only was the idea of ecological punishment robbed of force, but the reality of the moons—center of much Fettacenzan religious ritual—was called into question.

The priests, however, had one weapon: according to the Ascius theory, the "moons" should reappear when the Wo-bird repellent was completely dispersed—a matter of a few years. Secure in their ignorance, the stubborn priests sat down to wait.

CHAPTER 2

EXPLAINING IS CONTROLLING

Behind every mirror is a window.—Stella Denova

The other day I remembered, with some amusement and a little embarrassment, that while I was in college I used to jot down notes for a projected work entitled "The Return to Reason." The notes went where most of what I write goes (not enough, according to some) and the project was happily aborted, so it's hard for me to remember what I was all fired up about at the time. I recall vaguely that I thought eighteenth-century rationalism had been abandoned prematurely—that the welfare of humanity could best be advanced by assembling facts and tying them together according to principles of logic. True, I had never discovered anything myself through this procedure, but it didn't occur to me to connect my own experience with what I was thinking about abstractly.

The essence of what we call rational thought is leaving out things—gut sensations, feelings, impulses to act. It excludes all information that might be troublesome, arguing that if I leave out the most complicated and turbulent regions of reality I can better understand the rest.

The Wayward Gate

The most important thing it leaves out is the thinker—his or her unique location in the universe, with its associated urges, feelings, and motives. Rational thought pretends that it doesn't reside in a person—that it's cosmic, unemotional, and unmotivated. This delusion is its fundamental defect. To paraphrase G. Spencer Brown: being "objective" about myself means that I have to split myself into a part that sees and a part that's seen; but what I see is therefore only partly me—to see myself as an object I have to make my seeing part distinct from the rest of me, and since by doing that I'm falsifying myself, I will elude myself.

When I engage in rational thought I pretend that I'm detached from the springs of action in the universe—that I'm outside, looking on. But I can never be outside. I'm a part—creator and product—of all I see. When I put my energy and thought in one place I withdraw it from another; the world reacts to that and changes me. The first question you should ask of any "objective" person—doctor, critic, scientist, economist, psychiatrist, judge, bureaucrat, psychologist, sociologist—is: "What do you *want?*" Only after they've answered that question to your satisfaction can you afford to listen to what they have to say. Usually you have to ask the question repeatedly. Usually they don't know.

Intellectual life is by nature parasitical, for it sucks its energy from other people's actions and feelings. Consider, for example, how many pale and frigid minds have been fueled by the witless adventures of a handful of Greek thugs? We need to remember that *the main purpose of thought is to avoid risk*. This is its greatest strength and its greatest weakness as a form of human action.

FLATTENING REALITY

It used to be important to me to explain and interpret emotional events, but today my passion for this has waned a little. Most explanations seem designed to rob such events of their novelty, wonder, and life—to translate something fresh into something hackneyed—to numb all experience with familiarity. I can't recall who first pointed out that the word "explain" means literally to *flatten out.*

Seeing a UFO, for example, is a dramatic experience. People usually try hard to make it look like something familiar, and when the evidence overwhelms them they're often very frightened. Suppose an airline pilot sees a bright red light approaching his plane at enormous speed from the right. His copilot also sees it. They swerve to avoid it, shaking up the passengers, some of whom also see the glaring object, which now stops in midair and makes a right-angle turn. It follows them for awhile, then suddenly makes an abrupt vertical ascent, disappearing from sight in a few seconds. During the time the object is close by, the plane loses radio contact. Air Force ground controllers pick up the object on radar and dispatch planes to pursue it. Two pilots see it and follow it for a while, but then it disappears suddenly. At the same moment it disappears from the radar screen. Meanwhile, an engineer driving his car along a desert road sees a huge egg-shaped mass, glowing like a neon sign, straddling the road ahead. As he approaches it, his lights abruptly go out and his motor dies. He notices lighted windows in the object. Suddenly it rises vertically, stops, and then disappears at great speed. He calls the police, who have already received dozens of similar calls. A patrol car spots the object, which is lighting up a large area with an enormous search light. Viewers are overwhelmed with awe at the power and strangeness of the craft, which stops in midair, hovers without noise, can reverse direction instantly, and gives off enormous heat.

The Air Force is ready, however, to interpret the engineer's experience. The good gentleman's eyes simply deceived him: what he saw was a weather balloon, while what the pilots saw was the planet Venus, having a bright night. Or else the other way round; it really doesn't matter. Poor

The Wayward Gate

Venus has been blamed for UFO sightings even when she was well below the horizon, and weather balloons when there were none in the vicinity.

I've always been fascinated by the fact that the Air Force always blames Venus for these celestial pranks. I assumed at first that the practice was *invented* by the Air Force in the late forties. I was astonished, therefore, when I came across the wry comment made in 1923 by Charles Fort, on the "now standardized explanation that, when a luminous object is seen in the sky . . . it is Venus . . . exciting persons, unversed in astronomic matters, into thinking that a strange object had visited this earth" (*New Lands*, p. 91). If it moves around too much, he adds, astronomers say it was a fire balloon. How little things have changed in the one hundred twenty-five years since this habit began!

Have you ever wondered why one specific planet was elected as the culprit in these episodes? Why Venus alone is seen as capable of abandoning its fixed position in the sky and leaping about in such peculiar ways, altering size and shape? Is it just military lack of imagination that allows no other celestial body to jump about? Or is there a hidden romanticism behind that tired bureaucratic reflex? Do secret fantasies of love goddesses, leaving their exalted thrones to dally with mortal men, throb still in the numbed psyches of the Pentagon? Perhaps Venus looms large in their explanations because they're sometimes called in the middle of the night to make them.

Words like "objective" and "rational" are often used to imply a lack of emotionality, but I would be the last person to deny the feelings of rational thinkers. On the contrary, I think it's vital that we recognize the emotions that govern this need to be "objective"—to analyze, distinguish, and categorize. Foremost among these are anxiety, fear, and tension: some driving uneasiness keeps the mere appreciation of an experience from being satisfying. Some tremulous mistrust, some nervous perturbation, some clammy dread, some fluttering alarm gives rise to our unwillingness

22

simply to give our hearts to life—our need to draw back and stare and reckon and order our existence. A thought, after all, is just a deed running scared, and "rational," "objective" thought is the most frightened form of thinking.

An explanation or interpretation is usually a negation of experience—a way of shutting it out. Since we don't like to have to create new categories for new experiences, we sometimes chart an unexplored terrain by superimposing on it the map of a familiar one—like pasting a French road map over the empty chart of Antarctica. This saves us the trouble of exploring: we know what to expect from Venus and weather balloons; we don't know what to expect from a UFO.

DREAMING

Dreams give us another example. Dreams have overawed humanity throughout history, yet very few attempts have been made to confront the dream world on its own terms. People never tire of trying to *interpret* dreams—to redefine them in some way that seems familiar to waking life. No one agrees about what dreams mean, but everyone agrees that they don't mean what they say. But what if they *do* mean what they say? What if the statements "I dwelt in marble halls," or "I talked to my dead grandmother" required no more interpretation than "I walked to the drug store and bought toothpaste"?

It's an arbitrary custom, after all, that makes us assign more reality to waking life than to dreams, and it isn't clear that it's useful. The Senoi of Malaya, famed for their involvement in dreaming, have no illness, no crime, no mental illness, no civil strife. They treat their dream experiences as having equal weight with waking life, and as being intimately connected with it. For the Senoi, waking reality is a construct, molded by the mind from the raw materials of dream reality. The Senoi don't interpret dreams so much as act on them. Someone injured in a dream, for example, is given a gift on waking (see Stewart, pp. 161ff.).

The Wayward Gate

The difference is one of respect. Freud respected dreams as having personal meaning for the dreamer, and even this was an improvement over conventional scientific scorn. But Freud lacked any respect for the dream as a reality in and of itself, without translation. For to interpret a dream is to say it's unreal—a mask for something else, not an actual event of its own. This is in keeping with traditional psychoanalysis, in which patient and analyst agree to disrespect their own relationship—to pretend that what happens between them is just a series of projections on the patient's part, with the analyst serving as a mere stand-in for the patient's parents, without any personality of his own. In both cases the experience itself is invalidated, and reclassified according to the analyst's conventions.

The Senoi treat dreams as another domain of life—not just a source of psychological clues, to be acted on only in waking life. Action must be taken within the dream itself, and children are taught early how they should behave in dreams. Dreams, for example, must always be followed through to a conclusion, no matter how frightening, menacing, or incestuous they may seem. The dreamer must never retreat or wake up in the face of danger. He or she must always advance, calling, if need be, on friends for help. Dream spirits are seen as susceptible to the control of the dreamer—helpless unless the dreamer is afraid. The dream always leads to some creative gift if followed through to the end: a song, a dance, a poem, an artistic design, an invention. The culture of the Senoi is continually enriched through these dream encounters.

But one doesn't merely use dreams to enrich waking life. One also behaves with integrity in waking life in order to facilitate one's dream career. Fair dealings, cooperativeness, clean and open conflict, and reparation of injuries—whether "real," dreamed, intentional, or accidental—ensure a healthy dream life.

This is a far cry from Freud, or even the timid obscurities of Jung. Psychoanalysis is like trying to carry on a love af-

Explaining Is Controlling

fair by telephone. There's so little living and so much talking *about* living—so much investment in rational control of the universe.

RATIONAL CONTROL

In the old days I took it for granted that thinking preceded action. People who lived life as an experiment, people who actually tested reality instead of sitting around talking about "reality-testing," people who "acted-out" (a term psychoanalysts apply to those more bold, energetic, and cheerful than themselves)—these people were always a little disturbing to me. They moved too quickly, changed directions too fast, expressed themselves too forcefully. They seemed too "emotional," too "impulsive." They made scenes. They got into scrapes, and instead of learning to be more cautious, they just seemed to have fun getting out of them again. I always wanted to slow them down, get them to "understand themselves" and protect themselves better. They made me nervous. I felt irritated at them a lot and wanted to control them. And yet I didn't like being the cautious, uneasy bystander, either.

Every so often I would burst through the accumulated encrustations of that caution and live out a period of joyful and intense impetuosity myself. During these periods I found that things "went well." Complexities dissolved, dangers evaporated, incautious leaps proved strategic. It was a way of being that seemingly had its own order.

Trouble came from tangling up the two modes. In my impulsive state I seemed to be in a kind of intuitive harmony with the world. I felt sure that everything would "work," and it did. In my far more lengthy periods of reserved intellectualism, on the other hand, little was lost because little was ventured. But while frantically erupting from my cocoon, and even more as I would begin slowly to lose my nerve and sink back into it, I made grievous and painful errors that injured myself and others.

The Wayward Gate

It was a long time before I thought of those risk-taking periods as containing any system of control. Today, although obviously it's still important to me, rationality seems a bit simpleminded as a way of maintaining one's equilibrium—sort of like painting-by-numbers.

Rational control is an emergency mechanism—like a state of martial law or an iron lung. Having lost the capacity to breathe or govern myself I employ a mechanical substitute. But if I never discard the substitute I'll never find out if I can still breathe spontaneously. If everyone were in iron lungs we might even forget that spontaneous breathing is possible. Like the iron lung, rational thought is a device we call into play when we're thrown off balance in life and need help while we find our way back to the point where we can breathe naturally.

Imagine life as a complicated dance. When we're thoroughly "into" the dance we don't have to analyze it in order to participate in a creative and harmonious way, no matter how rapid and intricate it becomes. But occasionally we're distracted, get self-conscious, lose confidence, trip, collide with someone, get out of synchrony with the rest. At such times we may mentally step out of the situation, look around, and try to figure out where the dance is going and where we fit in. Like children jumping rope, we adjust our timing for a few turns and then, when we're back in tune, leap in and again relinquish rational control in favor of a more instinctive kind of coordination.

Rational control is a useful and necessary device. But to use it every day is to be off balance every day, and eventually this begins to dislocate the other dancers. Ultimately the entire dance threatens to grind to a halt.

A dilemma arises: rational control is necessary to restore balance, but having become chronic destroys balance and must be abandoned. Yet how can we abandon it when it's most needed?

The dilemma is artificial. Rational control becomes chronic only when we get hypnotized by the complexity of

26

the dance and want to gain some kind of mastery over it—not just over our own part in it but over the whole thing. Instead of just absorbing it, enjoying it, or adoring it, we want to control it, put it to our own uses.

Fortunately, *this wish itself prevents us from understanding the totality of the dance, which transcends so narrow a motive*. All we can do is gum up the dance a bit, introduce a little dissonance — sometimes pleasing and interesting, usually not.

The return to the dance, then, requires only an understanding of one's own place, not of the totality, which is impossible to grasp.

Giving up the habit of rational control requires a kind of heartfulness—a leap of faith. Not a renunciation, nor an assertion of will—these only squander energy in a futile inner struggle to push or "master" oneself—but rather an act of alert excitement, curiosity, and participation. Let me suggest a metaphor:

The water is icy cold, the sun hot, the waves alive, the sea aflame with light. I detest cold water and vacillate a long time. If the water didn't offer something special I'd be quite happy to remain out of it, as friends will testify. But once in a while I really want to go in: my reluctance to experience that horrible shock is in no way diminished, but is balanced by something that pulls me. After much hesitation I finally take the plunge. It isn't my will that gets me there (when will drives me I move grimly), for there is joy as well as fear in my final leap—a reckless casting aside, a hunger for the experience, good or bad, a losing of myself in the environment, of which I am a small but integral part, no more or less important than any other part.

Giving up rational control, even for a little while, feels like that.

"OBJECTIVITY" AS SELF-CONSCIOUSNESS

I said that rational control was a way of getting back in the dance when we'd lost our footing. But sometimes we get dazzled by the intricacy of the dance and forget about getting back in. We want to grasp, to understand, the *whole* dance, not just our own part in it.

Why do we want to grasp the whole dance?

So we can control it, reproduce it, mechanize it, and make sure we never lose our place again. And in order to do this we try to get outside ourselves, to be "objective," to transcend our little space-time slot and see the Whole Dance from the *point of view* of the Whole Dance.

But our attempt is doomed at the start. *We can't adopt this point of view because to do so we would have to lose our motivation to grasp, and if we lost that motivation we wouldn't be engaged in the whole silly business in the first place.* We can't fully comprehend something that doesn't share our need to comprehend.

We can't have a viewpoint other than our own, and even if we could we can't adopt the viewpoint of the Whole Dance because it has no viewpoint. By definition it's everything and everywhere. To get our heads in the place of the Whole Dance, as some mystics do, is to lose all viewpoint, all motive, all desire, all sense of self. At this point the Whole Dance can be *experienced*, but it can't be grasped or used or reproduced or controlled because all desire to do so has been lost.

My wish to understand "objectively," in other words, is inherently subjective. It comes from my particular position in the dance—nine thousand and thirty-third whirler from the left, spinning on one of those bumpy places that make people lurch every so often. Lurching gives me a desire to grasp that the dance as a whole doesn't share. The most grandiose, "objective" theory in the world, in other words, is just a complicated personal effort to find one's own place in the dance.

It's easy to detect a lurching dancer—the clearest sign is a lack of joy—what we usually call "depression." It comes from taking yourself too seriously to dance. Psychiatrists say that depression comes from anger or hurt that isn't discharged, but this is just another way of saying the same thing. For why *isn't* it discharged? Always out of some enlarged sense of superiority: "I'm *above* anger," "I'm too noble to complain," "I won't waste my anger on him," "Let her come to me, she knows that she's hurt me," "A real man doesn't cry," "A real lady doesn't raise her voice," and so on. If you accept the fact that you're just a human being you laugh when you're tickled, cry when you're hurt, yell when you're offended. Sometimes you look pretty, sometimes you look silly—it's all part of the dance. But some people put on airs and refuse to react. They're so concerned with how they look that they hardly dance at all. They're so vain in their shyness that they think the other dancers just want to watch and criticize.

People lurch when they become self-conscious about what they're doing. As soon as they look, they falter. Instead of dancing they're comparing themselves to something in their heads. But comparisons are meaningless. If I'm more courteous than you, you're more honest than I. If I'm more modest than you, you're more self-respecting than I. If I'm more prudent than you, you're bolder than I. If I'm more elegant than you, you're more natural than I. If I'm more stoical than you, you're more passionate than I. If I'm more frugal than you, you're more generous than I. It's all pointless, since the nearer I am to one "virtue" the farther I am from some other one.

Of course, from another point of view even lurching is just part of the dance, and so is stepping outside the dance, and so is trying to analyze and control the dance, and so is being too vain to dance. They're all dances. Ultimately there's no way not to be dancing. There's no way to be lurching or stumbling or standing outside trying to grasp the dance. You can *imagine* that you're doing all those things, but in reality they're all part of the dance—you're just dancing. The real question, perhaps, is whether we feel that grasping is a pretty part of the dance or an ugly part.

Certainly it's an aggressive part: The use of the word "grasp" itself expresses a kind of mental imperialism. Now in politics, imperialism sooner or later leads to war, and the same is true in thought. Intellectual conflicts arise when we inflate an impulse into a policy—when we move from saying, "I feel like dancing," to saying, "It's good to dance." The first is subjective, human, limited to a single location in time and space: "I feel like dancing right here and now." But the second statement, "It's good to dance," is infinite and eternal, inflated and unbound. Freed from the mouth that spoke it, it struts and swaggers all over time and space looking for a fight. It doesn't have to look long, either, for there are a million other greedy statements trying to gobble up the same infinite territory: "it's good to work," "it's good to eat," "it's good to fast," and so on.

There's world enough and time for all my impulses—they come and go like lights dancing on the water. But when I extend an impulse outward from its own moment into the future and into the past, it collides with other impulses. This wouldn't happen if it were simply expressed in its own time, leaving other moments to other impulses.

A policy is simply an impulse turned gangster.

MOBILE BALANCE

But what do we do to maintain our equilibrium when rational control is relinquished? One alternative is what I call mobile balance. It involves trusting your internal harmony with the earth, feeling your way, reacting fully, committing yourself to people and situations, allowing yourself to sort things out through trial and error. It's riskier, but more pleasurable. Rational control is detached, risk-free, but in a state of mobile balance you can lose. You can also "lose yourself" in things, which is another way of saying you can lose the need for rational control.

The difference between rational control and mobile balance can be illustrated by an example from the world of male-female relationships. Traditionally, men in our culture have been trained to be detached and "rational," while women were trained to be responsive and emotional. This has often led to a rather uncomfortable division of labor in relationships, in which women have expressed all the couple's feelings and men have done all the analyzing. Now suppose the couple begin to get into conflict: she expresses her upset while he interprets and analyzes it (since he's out of touch with his own feelings and hasn't expressed any, he sees nothing else to analyze), thereby provoking her to further frenzy which he feels an even stronger need to control by interpretation and analysis, and so on. Now if he's anywhere near as smart as he pretends to be he'll pick up this division of labor and realize that this is what's getting them into trouble. At this point he has two choices. He can share his insight with her, but this will just perpetuate the division of labor—nothing will have changed (this is why traditional psychotherapies, which limit themselves to talking *about* experience, are so ineffectual). He is still doing the analyzing and interpreting. Change will only come about if he *acts* on his insight (instead of talking about it), and begins expressing his own feelings (by this time she will have had the insight, anyway). In doing so he begins to rely on the dynamic of the relationship to create its own balance. If it's fundamentally a good one and the feelings are expressed clearly (which takes some practice), a strong sense of balance will be achieved without all the verbiage.

All of us rely on mobile balance in play, or in almost any physical activity—you can't learn to ski or ride a bicycle through rational control. But it's only in the last few years that I've been able to trust it in situations where I held any responsibility. I was surprised to discover how much better it worked than rational control, and both delighted and relieved to find that another balancing mechanism really exists, whether I understand it or not.

There's nothing mysterious about mobile balance. A human being is, after all, an organism—self-regulating, self-corrective, and all the rest. It's designed to balance itself. It's only our "rational" notions of how it *ought* to feel or respond that gum up the mechanism.

We usually talk about being "intuitive" when we drop rational control, but this is only half the story. Relying on "intuition" ceases to be mobile balance if you cling to it in the face of negative feedback. The other half of mobile balance is a willingness to commit yourself to trial and error. You haven't relinquished rational control unless you're willing to make a mistake—make a fool of yourself. Mobile balance ends when you say "I goofed." At that point you've left the scene and are into postmortems—that is, rational control. So long as you're in mobile balance there aren't any goofs, there's only feedback and a new response.

The problem is that we're most aware of using mobile balance in games, and games have built-in stopping places. If I'm playing tennis and hit the ball in the net, that's the end of that point—perhaps of the match. But in life the game never ends until death—it has no frame. My stopping places are completely arbitrary—I make them up. I say, "that's the end of that play, and I blew it." But this is meaningless, for each act leads merely to another: I do something, a response comes back, I do something else, another response comes back—why should I call any one of them a "goof"? I try something, and its effect is different than what I expected. I say it "didn't work." But if I respond to that effect, producing a new effect, and so on, it's meaningless to say it "didn't work." So long as I remain in the here-and-now everything "works." *I can't "lose" until I've declared that there's a specific game and that it's over.* Otherwise it's just one experience leading into another.

Human beings tend to seek equilibrium, like all organisms. Put a bunch of them together and they'll bump around until they achieve it. Unfortunately, we have all kinds of ideals and dramas in our heads, and they trigger off signals that light up, saying "failure," "despair," "humiliation," or whatever, when certain kinds of negative feedback occur. We then retire to the sideline and rail against ourselves or the world. It's always fascinating to watch people trashing themselves for not doing something when they're still in a position to do it. Or doing something that hurts them over and over again because they think it *ought* to work, even when the world keeps signaling them to try a new direction.

Bumps can be painful, of course, and it's understandable that we would want to use rational control to avoid them. And rational control is enormously valuable in situations where we seem likely to encounter bumps from every direction. For the most part, however, the only way to avoid big bumps is by encountering little ones. It's often said, for example, that a toddler with no bruises on its body is overprotected.

Yet the goal of science often seems to be to avoid all bumps. It doesn't succeed, of course, but the precautions are extraordinary. Why is there such fear of making mistakes? Don't we learn from mistakes? Do we really want to anticipate and avoid all possible errors? The science of immunology suggests that science as a whole may be endangering itself by this excessive caution. If it never makes little mistakes it can't immunize itself against big ones. The scientific method, with its extraordinary cautiousness, is a way of protecting us from feedback. In the long run it can only lead to grievous error, since it allows us to proceed on the same track for a long time without any correction. While it's true that certain errors are avoided through caution, *the errors that have not been anticipated will be all the more cataclysmic.* Current ecological alarms hint at this danger.

The motive beneath the scientific method is fear—the fear of making a mistake. But mistakes produce feedback—the most priceless kind of information. To protect ourselves from this information is to make a suicide pact with the future.

Scientists believe, of course, that the scientific method allows for such correction. The experimental method, for example, is based on feedback, and science displays a ravenous hunger for empirical data. How can I say that it's starving itself of information?

The problem is that *by its very nature* scientific caution

trains scientists to fear certain kinds of information and experimentation, even while hungrily seeking others. You can't base a system on caution without blinding yourself—that's what caution is all about. The despot is in the same situation: since the narrow base of his power necessarily starves him of information he may create an enormous system of spies and secret police to compensate. But it still won't provide him with the information he doesn't want to hear.

The experimental method, for example, may be based on feedback, but there's a stranglehold on how much feedback is allowed to occur. The fear of error leads to such tight controls that results can only reflect the extremely narrow question the experimenter has asked—the information is framed and constricted by his viewpoint and ordinarily can only give him answers he has already considered as possibilities. A chemist, discussing an origin-of-life experiment, once remarked that chemists usually like to control each step of an experiment, setting up a separate operation for each part: heating, cooling, distilling, decanting, and so on. Rarely do they establish a process and just let things happen.

No matter how much information scientists accumulate, they won't learn about those aspects of reality that frightened them into being cautious in the first place.

THE EMPEROR'S ELIXIR

PART II

Decades passed, and the secret of the elixir died with the emperor and the wise man. The Ascius theory lost credence as the insubstantial satellites failed to reappear, but the priesthood did not benefit as greatly from this as they had hoped. It was hard to interest people in whether something invisible was real or not—or in rituals directed toward that invisible something.

HALLUCINATIONS

Meanwhile, generations grew up who had never seen a moon or a Wo bird, and after several centuries people ceased utterly to believe in them. Stories of Wo birds were used to frighten recalcitrant children, while the vanished moons were said to symbolize a pair of mysterious Fettacenzan deities. In reality, there were more Wo birds than ever—the air around Fettacenzan dwellings was never still, but full of draughts and stirrings. Yet this was pleasant in their hot climate, and the Fettacenzans couldn't imagine things being any different.

There were a few holes in the elixir curtain, however. One was a species of domesticated desert animal called *gapers*, who never drank water but manufactured it in their bodies, and hence had not been affected by the elixir. They spent hours watching the birds and trying to catch them, much to the delight of their owners.

A second source of mystery was *Deeps*—a particularly nauseous hallucinogen, popular among affluent youth in the fifth century after the elixir. In actuality, *Deeps* was neither hallucinogen nor emetic, but merely speeded up perception, thus counteracting the limitations of the elixir. Exposed to so much stimulation and movement the Fettacenzan psyche pretty much caved in, and stopped even trying to organize the data it received, while the Fettacenzan stomach, dizzied by the ubiquitous birds, revolted altogether.

Given its unpleasantness, the *Deeps* fad was short-lived. Those who stayed with it were a stiff, religious lot who withdrew increasingly from Fettacenzan society, preferring the company of the Grubfolk, a primitive tribe of mountaineers who created the third gap in the elixir curtain.

There were only a few thousand Grubfolk on the entire planet, living in the mountains in isolated groups, and drinking from small, barely accessible brooks and springs. They were a little slow-witted, had slovenly habits, and lived by an unsophisticated religion that had come down virtually unaltered from the Era of Pollution. Furthermore, they all hallucinated—seemingly the result of a defective gene and centuries of inbreeding. Occasionally they ran amok and raced into town shouting of meteor showers or spaceship armadas, but Fettacenzan townfolk were tolerant of these outbursts. They thought the Grubfolk habitually took some sort of natural drug, and occasionally overdosed. When this happened, the townspeople herded

them kindly into clinics and injected them with tranquil-
izers.

DEAD BIRDS

Every so often, when competition for food was keen, one of
the usually unerring birds would actually brush someone
or strike a glancing blow. This produced an uncanny sensation in the recipient, and led to a number of superstitions
among the more credulous. Some talked of mischievous
spirits, some of hostile impulses that had somehow been
materialized, some of spirits of the dead. One fantasy was
that they were spirits of the mythical Wo birds, seeking re-
venge for their destruction at the hands of the legendary
Fettacenzan emperor, Noly Matonguray. One woman actually sustained an injury severe enough to warrant medical treatment and became the subject of a learned paper:
"A case of Psychogenic Bone Fracture in Conjunction with
Fantasies of the Winged Phallus," by the eminent psychiatrist, Dr. Michael Middelmauss.

But despite these occasional accidents, dead Wo birds
were rarely found, for sick or dying birds normally flew to
inaccessible mountain peaks and died there. The first few
that came to public attention, during the fifth post-elixir
century, were said to be frauds or mutants and of no scientific interest. Their resemblance to conventional descriptions of the mythical Wo bird aroused marked aversion
among scientists—just as the corpse of a dragon would on
our planet. "If there were such a thing as a Wo bird," scientists asked, "why hasn't a serious scientist ever seen one?"

During the next two centuries others were brought to
scientific laboratories, but were either dismissed as
anomalies or recorded dutifully, but without comment, in
scientific reports, where they were soon forgotten. Only
once did anyone attempt to make anything of them: a scientist named Doppelhedder, who had acquired a pair of
birds, wrote a sensational book arguing that the mythical

Wo birds were real. He claimed to have found ancient records proclaiming the imminent elimination of the species, and presented detailed reproductions and descriptions of the dead birds. He hypothesized that the birds had survived by staying at high altitudes, which is why they were never seen alive.

Doppelhedder was attacked with unprecedented vehemence by his colleagues. They pointed out that his ancient "records" were known to be forgeries, since the material on which they were recorded had not been invented until two centuries after they were supposedly written. The scientists suggested that Doppelhedder should avoid trespassing in disciplines other than his own, with which, heaven knew, he was little enough conversant. They asked pointedly what the birds could live on at such high altitudes, and wondered sarcastically whether they normally evaporated at death, since only two had ever been found, if, indeed, even these were authentic, which they doubted. They theorized that Doppelhedder himself had perhaps spent a bit too much time at high elevations.

Although Doppelhedder was successfully ostracized he made a lot of money writing and lecturing for the year or two that his fame lasted, whereupon he retired comfortably and was never heard from again.

THE EPIDEMIC

But scientific ingenuity was sorely taxed one year during the ninth century, when the Wo birds were seized by a flu epidemic. During the peak of the illness the reaction time of a bird would be slowed just enough to cause large numbers of accidents. News media were suddenly filled with reports of mysterious thumpings and the discovery of hundreds of bird corpses. Some people were inclined to link the two events, but scientists scoffed at this: "What possible connection could there be between a dead bird and a sudden pain of unknown origin? Can a dead bird cause a pain? If there is a link, how does it happen that no birds are ever seen when the blow is struck? Nature is full of coincidences: people once believed that rainbows were caused by rain since they so often occurred together, until the great meteorologist Noerr pointed out that (a) it frequently rains without a rainbow appearing, and (b) rainbows occur near waterfalls on cloudless days. This cool logic, for which Noerr was justly famous, ought to be applied to the current craze to avoid our being overwhelmed with prattle about Wo spirits."

There was a lot of talk about "mass psychology," and a sociologist wrote a brilliant book linking the thumpings to current economic conditions which were, as he pointed out, "a thump in the breadbasket."

But the people were not so easily put off. Clubs were formed by victims of bird accidents who wanted to share their experiences and who felt indignant about being considered hysterical. For although the media were at first fascinated and sympathetic, the governing bodies of Fettacenza soon became worried about mass panic and began to enforce a skeptical line. Media accounts became increasingly waggish, and people stopped reporting thumpings except to their close friends. As the epidemic spread the clubs grew stronger and more numerous, and resentment toward the government—fueled by the bad economic conditions—transformed them into a revolutionary movement that swept the old Fettacenzan elites out of power and inaugurated a new era.

The sociologist saw these events as confirmation of his theory of economic determinism and received from his publisher the largest advance in Fettacenzan history to write a sequel about the revolution. Unfortunately for Fettacenzan letters, however, the book was never written: irate revolutionaries assassinated the sociologist by driving an immense bamboo bird beak into his heart. Rumor had it that the assassins were agents of the revolutionary secret police—the Free-Lance Avengers of the People, or FLAP, as they came to be called. They wore gold and purple capes and green sunglasses and spoke in rasping voices.

The Wayward Gate

When the revolutionaries came to power they mounted, as promised, a full-scale investigation of the mysterious thumpings. The commission in charge took fourteen months to complete its research and publish its findings, by which time the epidemic was over and the public had lost interest in the matter. In its 2,000-page report the commission suggested a half-dozen theories, with the majority favoring the mass psychology view. There was also some support for an alternative theory that the thumpings were the result of a disease that affected the vascular system in such a way as to produce the sensation of being hit from without, although actually the "thump" was internal.

THE DENOVAS

It wasn't until the eleventh century after the elixir that interest in the birds was rekindled. Drugs were again popular and anthropologists became interested in recording the legends and rituals of the Grubfolk. It was a period of fascination with the emotional and the bizarre—the "nonrational layers of the human personality," as one eminent psychologist put it. Psychologists were abandoning their experiments with animal learning habits to concentrate on the abnormal, the pathological, and the mysterious. They probed the unconscious endlessly—a million hours of psychotic oratory, half a million dreams, a library of folk tales and fantasies, drug laboratories in every village—searching always for a simple key that would make it all understandable.

This quest for uniformities led one of the more alert psychologists, Sol Denova, to become interested in certain common hallucinations. Denova was puzzled by the frequency with which moons and birds appeared in psychotic fantasies. Was this mass psychology, he wondered? Why did people so often hallucinate the same things? Was it some genetic defect, and if so, how did it get so specific? Or was it cultural, and if so how was it transmitted? In a book called *Lunar Lunacy* Denova traced the unconscious origins

40

of bird and moon images, and showed how they were rooted in deviant childrearing patterns.

Toward the end of his life, Denova's theories altered somewhat, giving more weight to the influence of old myths in shaping the plastic material of unconscious effusions. The mind, said old Sol, as he slipped into the chaos of senility, strives at all times for order and familiarity; when bizarre images race across the screen of our senses, the mind seeks desperately to clothe them with form and meaning, and the nearest garments at hand are often those that already belong to the domain of the absurd—the visions and phantoms of the ancients. When Sol died most people felt that the problems he had struggled with had been laid to rest along with him.

Yet Denova was scarcely comfortable in his final resting place before his theories were challenged by his own granddaughter, Stella—an engaging iconoclast whose popularity was based on the widespread assumption that she was joking (Stella herself was uncertain of this). Stella had no particular wish to undermine her grandfather's prestige—she merely followed her curiosity wherever it led.

What triggered her interest was an offhand remark in one of Sol's papers. Sol was impressed with the fact that *Deeps* users had always been drawn to the Grubfolk, with whom they shared the Wo-bird hallucination. He reasoned that either the two groups were friendly because they shared a vision, or they shared the vision because they were friendly. The first possibility led nowhere, said old Sol, since it still didn't tell us where the vision came from. The second, on the other hand, showed a chain of influence and helped put us on the path: the Wo-bird idea clearly must have diffused from the Grubfolk to the *Deeps* users, since the former had always believed in it, while to the latter it was new. This line of thought was so reasonable that no one had questioned it—the terrain had been mapped and a beachhead established. All that was left was to find out how the idea had started among the Grubfolk.

The Wayward Gate

But young Stella was of a contrary nature. The minute her eyes lighted on the two possibilities she liked the first one better. What could conceivably have drawn elite youth to the Grubfolk *except* a common vision? she asked (not a very pointed query just then, when the Grubfolk were overrun with anthropologists and curiosity seekers).

The theory she advanced instead was so bizarre that only the intellectually frivolous paid attention to it. Suppose there's no such thing as a hallucination, Stella suggested. Suppose everything that anyone has ever seen is really there—has actuality? "We really don't *need* to see these Wo birds, and there must be many other phenomena the sight of which would merely confuse and dismay us. Our sensory equipment is designed so that normally we perceive only what we need to get us through our daily round. Does a mole need to see the shining sky? An oyster can't hear our complex music and wouldn't know what to make of it if she could. Does that mean it isn't real? If her senses were suddenly expanded so she *could* hear it, wouldn't her friends think she was hallucinating?"

Stella went on to suggest that from time to time such expansion of the sensory range *did* occur, giving rise to startling, confusing, and disorienting perceptions. Psychosis, she argued, is not the *cause* of these perceptions but the *result* of it. "A hallucination," she said, in an oft-quoted passage, "is merely a reality we normally don't have to bother with. And psychosis is the conceptual disorganization caused by sensory overload when our usual sensory constriction breaks down."

Fettacenzans smiled at Stella's theory. They knew how much she loved to invert things, and although they admired her wit, the intellectual consensus was that her work was brilliant but flawed.

Alas, we shall never know how it would all have turned out. Two years after the publication of Stella's book, *There's a Wo Bird in My Garden*, an enormous intergalactic caravan, blown off course by galactic storms, made a forced landing on Fettacenza, inadvertently causing mass destruction and loss of life. The remorseful leaders of the caravan, wishing to compensate for the suffering they had caused, left a small group of missionaries to civilize the planet. Meanwhile, to provision themselves with as little rapacity as possible, they took what they knew the Fettacenzans could well do without: the entire Wo bird population for food and the two moons for fuel.

Fettacenzan history abruptly became part of a much larger pattern.

CHAPTER 3

BIASES OF SCIENCE

The description "mass psychology" does partly apply to it, just as would "horizontal ineptitude," or "metacarpal irridescence," or any other idea, or combination of ideas, apply, to some degree, to anything.—Charles Fort

My academic background calls out to me to arrange the biases of science into a set of numbered categories: "the six main biases of science are . . ." I acquired this habit listening to lectures in college, and it was reinforced when I began lecturing myself. Nodding heads would snap erect and pencils move when I began to enumerate categories: the three causes, the four styles, the five approaches, the six types—clearly eligible exam questions. It all comes from believing that people can learn while sitting quietly in their seats.

I used to amuse myself with a little game that I called "Lecturer's Roulette." Whenever I had two related points to make I would announce pompously: "There are *three* basic so-and-so's in such-and-such," and try to come up with a third concept before I'd finished describing the first two. The numbered categories kept them awake; the mental scramble kept *me* awake.

I've always wondered who invented the précis, and how it came about: for what is there in life that corresponds to an outline? Even a skeleton is arranged more elegantly. But if you start by sitting in rows and learning in numbered sequences, you end quite automatically with professional societies and research reports. And if you insist that a scientific paper be arranged into Hypothesis, Review of Literature, Method, Results, Discussion, and Summary, you'll only be able to find out about those aspects of reality that lend themselves to being arranged that way.

To begin with, your hypothesis must in some way fit current conventions. This is reasonable, since it's a lot of trouble to rewire a whole theoretical structure. If we can arrange it so that unconventional hypotheses don't even need rebuttal it's a great convenience. A few years ago, for example, a newspaper article "exposed" a faith-healing church in Oregon. To do this the reporter faked an illness and then wrote an article about the non-cure of her non-disease! This is hardly a fair test, even from a conventional scientific viewpoint, but it would be extraordinarily inconvenient to give every idea a fair hearing. It's like the equal-time problem on television: we give Republicans and Democrats time, but what about the Socialist Labor Party? And if we give *them* time why not the Prohibition Party, the Klan, the antivivisectionists, and every other group that has an opinion on anything? And then who would bother to watch?

Science has the same dilemma. It has to believe that fundamentally it's on top of things—that it has a firm conceptual grip on the universe, with only a few bugs left to iron out. Any really intelligent scientist knows how preposterous this assumption is, but the alternative seems unbearably worse—a million psychotic piebald beggars scrambling over each other to get in the gate and be heard. Like the networks, science can only afford to give a hearing to its own establishment and the loyal opposition—"random error."

When Captain Ruppelt first began to examine UFO reports for the U.S. Air Force he ran into this very problem: sifting through incoming reports to distribute to his various debunking specialists he first withdrew any that mentioned actual landings or spacepeople and threw them in the wastebasket (Vallée, p. 83).

Ruppelt was not a highly prejudiced man. Like most people who have personally investigated UFO reports he ultimately became a cautious convert to the idea of their extraterrestrial origin. Although his job was to rule out this possibility he approached the task with a certain fair-mindedness. Yet all reports of landings and living astronauts were destroyed.

This is a bit illogical. To investigate UFO reports you must at least entertain the *possibility* that they're aircraft of some kind, since this is the conclusion of almost every observer who reports a UFO. Indeed, you can entertain other hypotheses only by ignoring the data and making the gratuitous assumption that the witnesses misperceive or falsify. Virtually all our information about UFOs comes from people who perceive them as some kind of aircraft—if they can make them look like anything else they don't bother to report them. Now, if we're going to investigate things that might be aircraft, it's silly to assume they can't land or have pilots. If you allow for the first possibility you have to allow for the others. But the thought of dealing with reports of "little green men" was too much for Captain Ruppelt. He not only declined to examine the evidence, he destroyed it.

Not logical, but understandable. The mind can only stretch so much at one time, and sometimes this means letting in a spaceship without its pilot. The same thing would happen if a Socialist Labor candidate were given equal TV time with a Democrat and a Republican: the door would be slammed so quickly behind her that a dozen splinter-party candidates would have splintered noses.

Jacques Vallée points out that there are many reports of landings and UFO pilots from highly reliable witnesses. Despite Ruppelt's purge of the evidence, there are enough such reports for Vallée to estimate than an average of fifty landings a year occur on the planet. (Most descriptions of pilots do indeed represent them as little—about four feet tall, with something like a diver's suit on—although never, *never* as green. Cf. Vallée, pp. 12, 129ff., 141ff.) But even Vallée himself excludes many reports out of hand: if the witnesses contradict themselves or change their story, if they meet spacepeople who speak to them in their native tongue, if they report being chosen for some special mission. And who could argue with this selection? Why look at reports that have "hoax" or "delusion" written all over them? It's usually easy to tell the lucid, sincere witnesses from the deluded and the self-seekers, by their brevity, clarity, surprise, and desire to avoid publicity.

It's convenient and important to do this—otherwise we would get lost in confused and limitless possibilities. But it's also important to know what we're excluding. A man could see a real UFO and weave a fabrication around it. He could be psychotic and still have some sort of UFO experience. He could also be sought out by space travelers *because* he was psychotic, or because he wasn't a credible person. When we throw out a whole category of events we're probably losing something we may at some later time want.

What such exclusions ignore is that a bias or distortion can be applied just as well to reality as to a daydream. One of the tip-offs of a crazy, "cultish," fantastic report is, paradoxically, a lack of imagination: A spaceship lands and a beautiful Nordic male jumps out dressed in flowing robes and speaks to the witness in English. How come no spacesuit, we ask, and why is the pilot such a familiar hero-type? *But lack of imagination is the same problem whether we're dealing with reality or fantasy.* If we have no categories for describing what we see, we force it into familiar ones.

Lyall Watson raises the same problem about English ghosts. His skepticism is aroused by the fact that they always wear clothes and behave rather stupidly (Watson, p. 274). But both of these characteristics may be distortions of the observer—they say nothing about the reality or unreality of the ghosts. The English have a reputation both for modesty in dress and for attributing inferior intelligence to those who speak other languages. Whether one actually

47

The Wayward Gate

sees a ghost or merely imagines it, the trappings will be biased in the same way by past experience.

The experience of the Hills (see John Fuller's *Interrupted Journey*) is another example. Driving late at night through central New Hampshire, the Hills saw a UFO close enough to observe windows and faces. They became frightened and drove on, although they had amnesia for a portion of the drive, and arrived home about two hours later than they should have. The wife had repeated nightmares about the incident and talked to friends about it, but the husband just wanted to forget it. Some years later they went to a psychiatrist and over several months they independently recovered, under hypnosis, memories of being taken aboard the UFO, examined, and released—memories that tallied closely with the wife's nightmares.

If we accept the possibility of extraterrestrial UFOs, the Hills' story is perfectly plausible: a scientific expedition is out collecting data and the Hills turn up as samples. It's a bit wounding to our egos to be specimens for a superior civilization, but there's nothing really bizarre about it. The integrity of the Hills is not in question and their struggle to avoid accepting the reality of their experience was long and bitter. Yet there are pieces of the recovered narrative that strain our credulity. The examiners on the craft sound too much like Western physicians—in fact too *many* things sound too familiar. Yet once again, the problem may be not that the Hills are making things up, but that they're pouring the hot metal of a novel experience into familiar molds. Barney Hill acknowledges this at one point, observing that what he first experienced as audible speech could only have been a telepathic communication of some kind (Fuller, 1966). In the same way, Robert Monroe at first interpreted his out-of-the-body perceptions as "seeing" and "hearing."

Life would be simpler if we could just say: "This report is true, that one is bogus." Then we would only need to find one flaw in a report to dismiss it. But truth is more complex than that, and more elusive. Even the most compulsive liar tells the truth some of the time, and the most honest man in

48

the world lies inadvertently whenever he opens his mouth. Every UFO report is part fact, part fiction, for when confronted with a completely new phenomenon we literally cannot see it—all we can see is what it *resembles*.

Science makes a virtue out of this necessity. It says a good theory shouldn't require us to throw out too much of what we already think we know. The word "reasonable" in science means just what it does in law—it means "in accordance with the conventions of the community." We cannot do without some such restriction but we need to be wary when it's tied to a clear-cut prejudice.

ISOLATIONISM

One of science's most ardent prejudices, for example, is isolationism. As Charles Fort pointed out long ago, it makes scientists uncomfortable to think of life on this planet as subject to external influence of any kind. Astrology, for example, has always been a target for abuse by scientists (most of it well-deserved); and the irrational resistance to UFOs and to Velikovsky's work (see below, page 237) is also due in some part to this planetary isolationism. It wasn't so very long ago that scientists viewed meteorites the same way—witnesses were scornfully dismissed as credulous peasants, for how could stones fall from the sky? Before scientists would believe in meteorites they had to be personally deluged with them. But as Fort observed, the door was opened only a crack even then. Once the "reality" of meteorites was established, reports of anything *else* falling from the sky were scornfully dismissed because they weren't of "true meteorite material"! Now that complex organic molecules have been found floating in space, however, Fort's outlandish collection of data may have to be taken more seriously.

Lyall Watson shares Fort's conviction that life on earth is subject to more external influence than scientists want to allow, and, like Fort and Velikowsky, backs up his claims with material provided by the scientists themselves. Watson cites studies showing the effect of the moon on rainfall, potatoes, oysters in laboratory tanks far from the sea, the movements of flatworms, the time of human birth, the time of ovulation, the rate of bleeding, the frequency of certain crimes, and blood chemistry. He also discusses research showing the marked effect on career choice of the position of the planets at one's birth. This research, which has been replicated several times in various countries, and has survived intense scrutiny by scientists and statisticians, is still dismissed out-of-hand by many scientists because it lends support to astrology. Watson also observes that astrological "good and bad aspects" correspond precisely to planetary positions that favor or disturb radio reception (*Supernature*, pp. 20–28, 42–46, 49–62). Astrology is the decayed form of a very ancient science, and although the uses to which it is put today are mostly nonsense, they're no more absurd than the idea that life on this planet is immune to extraterrestrial influence.

Now scientists are aware that other planets and stars have some relation to us, that matter sometimes comes from them to us, that there is certain to be civilized life on many, many planets in the universe, and that cataclysms occur in space. Why are they so upset by suggestions that any of this has relevance to human history? Is it their individualism—their childhood independence training based on the devout American belief in the irrelevance of everyone to everyone else? Or is it the uneasy resemblance these events have to themes from science's old enemy, religion—defeated, but still breathing in its rusty dungeon?

Perhaps it has to do with the issue of control. Frank Brown's research (see Watson, pp. 25–26), showing that remote environmental factors can influence living things, provoked a storm of scientific criticism, partly because it demonstrated the impossibility of maintaining environmental constancy, even in a laboratory. It revealed the fatuity of scientists' efforts to "control" or "hold constant" the flow of Nature.

"Proof" is a favorite word among science-worshiping

Biases of Science

laymen, as if establishing certainty were the keystone of the scientific method. But certainty doesn't exist, and major theoretical revisions in science have been made in response to hunches, rigorous experiments, careful observations, and pure flights of fancy, in roughly equal proportion. When the time is ripe, a theory is adopted: All the bright and open minds seem to know instinctively that it's correct—even though it usually turns out to be deeply flawed a century or so later. How, when, and on what basis scientists decide something is "true" or "real" is as deep a mystery as any theological riddle.

SCIENTIFIC HISTORY: THE MOVING SPHINCTER WRITES

It's commonly believed that scientists have a single standard of evidence that they apply uniformly to all events that come to their attention. This is pure fantasy, as we've seen. Some events get in the door on their own say-so; others arouse a storm of objections and get dragged off to the laboratory to be given the third degree. How an event is treated depends on how subversive a character it is. If it threatens planetary isolationism it gets the third degree— voices steeped in scientific austerity and massive amnesia inform us that nothing is proved outside of a laboratory.

Knocking down the boundaries between humans and other animals used to be considered subversive, but now that they've all come down scientists are pretty relaxed about the whole business, and the requirements of evidence have been correspondingly relaxed. So when Jane Goodall reported that she had seen chimps engaged in what would have to be called toolmaking, scientists around the world began revising their theories (see Van Lawick-Goodall, 1971).

On the word of one investigator.

What if Jane Goodall had seen a UFO? What theories would have been revised? Even if she were an astronomer? The astronomers who have admitted seeing UFOs were told to wash their glasses.

The Wayward Gate

The fact is, there are no universal rules of evidence. There are merely fashions in belief. Hundreds of competent professional observers have witnessed and reported psychic phenomena without making the slightest impact on scientific dogma. On the contrary, the report itself has disqualified them.

Jane Goodall took some films. Had they been films of a UFO, or a psychic healer, or Bigfoot, or the Loch Ness Monster it would have been suggested that they were fakes. Why did no one accuse Jane Goodall of faking her films?

What is it about some events that allows them to be accepted, while others—reported by the same caliber of witness—are rejected? Is it probability? Ask a roomful of people about psychic experiences and most of them will turn up a few. Wherever children aren't indoctrinated with the belief that such experiences are "not real" most people have had many. Psychic experiences are not rare or unusual in the statistical sense.

By contrast, I have never seen a tornado, a volcanic eruption, a total eclipse of the sun, an earthquake, a migration of lemmings, an electron, a quasar, a protein molecule, or a chimp fashioning a tool. Yet I have no trouble at all believing in these things.

When David Graybeard, the first chimp of his tribe to see an ethologist, first saw Jane Goodall, did he think she was "real"? Had he reported her to the other chimps would they have believed him? Not a chance if they were modern biologists imbued with the doctrine of uniformity, which says, in effect, that if something hasn't happened lately it could never have happened in the past and can't possibly happen in the future—surely one of the least imaginative theories ever spawned.

It isn't really a matter of how rare the event is, although scientists usually try to make it appear that way, by treating each occurrence as if it were either a doubtful instance, or the first instance, or both. There's something about the *quality* of certain events that makes scientists want to invalidate them.

Biases of Science

It's estimated, for example, that more than ten million Americans have seen "unidentified flying objects." Ordinary people like to call them "flying saucers" because that's what most of them look like, but this was too vivid for the Air Force. They invented the more acceptable term "UFO" which lends an air of unreality and vagueness to the whole thing. As Jacques Vallée points out, "unidentified" implies that these events don't fit into any existing class of events, although in fact there's a rich UFO typology that the Air Force itself employs privately (manuals for recognizing "enemy" aircraft include silhouettes of the most common types of UFO).

Many of the sightings have been made by experienced observers, often by several independent witnesses. Many witnesses have been scientists. Some have even been astronomers, although members of that discipline have historically been zealous in their opposition to accepting strange sights in the skies. (In 1957 the Astronomer Royal of Great Britain ridiculed the idea that space travel might some day be possible, calling it "utter bilge.") Charles Fort was fatalistic, if unrelenting, concerning the mulish myopia of some astronomers: "Early in our investigations, we learned that the prestige of astronomers has been built upon their high moral character, all of them most excellently going to bed soon after sunset, so as to get up early and write all day upon astronomical subjects" (*New Lands*, p. 192). Yet many of Fort's own UFO examples come from astronomers.

UFOs have been seen in every part of the world. They have been photographed and picked up by radar. There have been sightings by astronauts—a group not noted for hysteria. Sightings in France have been frequent enough on some dates to enable scientists to plot the UFO routes on maps. Many if not most UFO sightings are not even reported for fear of ridicule or censure. Air Force and commercial airline directives expressly forbid public mention of UFOs, and most pilots are gun-shy about the whole topic. Yet of the available reports, most have never even been investigated—the amount of data is simply too overwhelming. While it isn't hard for a skeptic to select a dozen or so cases out of the tens of thousands available and explain them away, they keep piling up, and almost everyone willing to take a serious look at them has been convinced. Often skeptics have had to fall back on raising spurious objections: Why aren't UFOs picked up on radar (they are); why weren't there any sightings before 1947 (there were); why don't they ever land (they do); why haven't any astronomers or other scientists ever seen them (they have); and so on. As many authors have pointed out, there are hundreds of sworn and corroborated statements, careful and detailed, by unimpeachable witnesses, any one of which would constitute the kind of documentation that could single-handedly send a man to the electric chair in a court of law.

The main distinguishing characteristic of the observers is not suggestibility, as some would like to believe, but the fact that they have some reason to be looking at the sky— particularly at night. A great many reports, for example, come from pilots, or from state police on night patrol. This is important to remember when armchair skeptics suggest that the observer made some ludicrous mistake in perception. A pilot and co-pilot with forty years of experience between them are likely to have a pretty good idea what Venus looks like (or a weather balloon, or ball lightning), and any pilot making the kinds of errors that skeptics are willing to attribute to UFO observers is clearly too drunk to fly. To thus disqualify all such pilots would put a heavy damper on air travel, however, since the veteran pilot who has never seen a UFO is a rare bird indeed.

THE SEA SERPENT

The practice of glibly discrediting witnesses when we don't like what they see isn't new. A century ago the same kind of controversy raged over the sea serpent. And just as it's popularly believed that UFO reports come from little old ladies in tennis shoes, most people assume that sea-serpent reports came from drunken and superstitious sailors. In fact, most sea-serpent reports came from experienced captains, who entered them in the ship's log as scientific observations. To do so, however, was an act of considerable courage often leading to merciless public ridicule, and existing reports are merely the tip of the iceberg. Like UFO witnesses, most people who saw sea serpents avoided mentioning it in public.

Charles Gould's comment on sea-serpent reactions could be applied to any rare phenomenon—Yeti, UFO, Loch Ness Monster, Bigfoot, or whatever:

The dread of ridicule closes the mouths of many men who could speak upon the subject . . . When for example, an unimaginative shipowner breaks jests over his unfortunate shipmaster's head . . . we may be sure that an important barrier is put to any further communication on the subject from that source, at least; or when, again, some knot of idle youngsters enliven the monotony of a long voyage by preparing a deliberate hoax for publication on their arrival, a certain amount of discredit necessarily attaches to the monster on the ultimate exposure of the jest (Gould, pp. 262–63).

This is quite irrational, of course, since hoaxes and swindles occur in every field of endeavor. Any branch of science can boast as many hoaxes as any branch of the so-called occult, yet a discovered hoax in science leaves the field itself untouched, while the same discovery in a less conventional field is taken as firm proof that the entire field should be dismissed from serious consideration. The "Piltdown Man" hoax, for example, left the fields of paleontology and evolution unscathed, but a single ESP hoax condemns the whole field to the limbo of "mere superstition." Hoaxes in medical and biological research occur every year, but the funds for such research keep rolling in, while a single UFO hoax permits skeptics to accuse millions of sensible people of "mass hysteria."

The Wayward Gate

This reaction is particularly common among academic scientists and scholars, who tend to be security-minded rather than adventurous—more concerned with avoiding mistakes than with breaking new ground. (I suspect a person who goes through life never having been hoaxed is a kind of intellectual coward.) I have heard academicians dismiss a brilliant theory on the grounds that its author had once been guilty of a factual error—a viewpoint that comes perhaps from the traditional practice of testing students for accuracy of memory rather than for understanding. Scientists are conventionally concerned with details, and laypeople tend, in imitation, to preoccupy themselves with names and dates in evaluating the validity of an experience. Yet in psychic matters it's the deep *emotional* events that come through vividly, with least distortion, while names and dates "are precisely those things that are forgotten first," since "they have the least value psychologically." To the inner self "names simply do not matter" (Roberts, *Seth Speaks*, pp. 445–6). Although science actually proceeds by successive theoretical approximations—by superimposing better and better theoretical maps on an experiential territory—many academicians still operate from day to day with the archaic idea of theory as a tower of blocks resting on a foundation of factual certainties. For such mentalities, one hoax is enough to dismiss the whole subject. I suppose if they ever saw a counterfeit bill they would stop believing in money.

In any case, ridicule is an effective way to shut out disturbing data. When Captain Austin Cooper reported the serpent seen by himself and his fellow officers and crew of the *Carlisle Castle* about a century ago he was lampooned at such length in the newspapers that he vowed never again to play the naturalist. "It is too much to be told that one of Green's commanders can't tell the difference between a piece of sea-weed and a live body in the water. If twenty serpents come on the starboard, all hands shall be ordered to look to port" (C. Gould, pp. 262, 304–05).

Biases of Science

Many who did make sea-serpent reports did so anonymously, as the following newspaper excerpt indicates:

We are glad to see that the two gentlemen . . . have published in the *Zoologist*, a monthly journal of natural history, a careful description of the creature which they saw, and which seems to resemble the engravings of what is called the Norwegian sea-serpent . . . There is such a dread of ridicule in appearing publicly in company with this mysterious and disreputable monster, that we must commend the boldness of the two clergymen in putting their names to the narrative; especially as we observe that other observers have not been so courageous, and that they have been obliged to give some of their information anonymously (C. Gould, p. 282).

Another who stuck to his guns was Captain Drevar, master of the barque *Pauline*, who saw a sea serpent attack and kill a whale in 1875. His observations were entered in the ship's log and he and several of his officers signed a sworn declaration before a magistrate in Pakistan. Like Captain Cooper a few years before him he was ridiculed at length in the London Daily Telegraph—prompting him to remark that: "It is easy for such a paper to make any man, good, great, or interesting, look ridiculous. Little wonder is it that my relatives write saying that they would have seen a hundred sea-serpents and never reported it" (C. Gould, pp. 311–12). One captain went so far as to stay below deck when a sea serpent was sighted, on the grounds that had he seen and reported it he'd have been considered a "warranted liar" the rest of his life. Another refused to make a log entry since "they will say we were all drunk," and asked a passenger not to mention it to the shipping agents. Daniel Webster saw one with a friend but swore him to secrecy to protect his reputation (Heuvelmans, pp. 143, 196, 357; cf. also pp. 33 and 405). The same reluctance muted Bigfoot reports around the turn of the century (Grumley, p. 97). On the other hand, a strong open report tends to bring out these hidden ones. A sea-serpent sighting off British Columbia led an enterprising editor to obtain almost a hundred signed reports of previously withheld sightings.

As usual, local Indians had known of the species for centuries (Heuvelmans, p. 444).

Despite all the scoffing, the *Zoologist* printed many other sea-serpent accounts during the nineteenth century, as did *Nature*, and many eminent naturalists and biologists were persuaded of the monster's reality—including Sir Charles Lyell, Louis Agassiz, Philip Gosse, T. H. Huxley, and D'Arcy Thompson (C. Gould, pp. 276, 287–91, 328–29; Heuvelmans, pp. 24–26).

In some countries, furthermore, there were no skeptics at all. The coast of Norway was for centuries such an active haunt of the sea serpent that fishermen in that country simply considered the monster a part of everyday life—a negative part since it drove away fish. Fishermen used to carry castor and juniper shavings with them, since the serpents seemed averse to the substances. They quite reasonably considered it dangerous to row over coils or concealed parts of the animal, for fear of being overturned, but thought nothing of rowing toward the highest sections and throwing something to make it dive and swim away (Heuvelmans, pp. 108–9). Serpents came every summer, apparently to spawn—in July 1849 a serpent was seen every day in the same part of the sound off Otersoen, sunning itself. A ship's captain and a merchant, interviewed separately, estimated the length of the serpent at about six hundred feet.

Sir Arthur de Capell Brooke summarizes his inquiries in Norway as follows: "In traversing a space of full seven hundred miles of coast . . . accounts have been received from numerous persons respecting the appearance of an animal called by them a sea-serpent . . . When these several relations as to the general appearance of the animal, its dimensions, the state of the weather when it was seen, and other particulars, are so fully confirmed, one by the other, at such considerable intervening distances, every reasonable man will feel satisfied of the truth of the main fact . . ." (C. Gould, pp. 275–76).

Biases of Science

In the summer of 1817 a large sea serpent was seen almost daily in Gloucester Harbor, in Massachusetts. The Linnaean Society of New England made a thorough investigation, interviewing many witnesses using a checklist of twenty-four detailed questions. The written accounts agree very closely (C. Gould, pp. 288–89; cf. also Heuvelmans, pp. 149–154).

Doubtless some sea-serpent observers haven't seen what they thought they saw, and clearly not all have seen the same kind of creature. A large number of accounts, however, agree on several points: The sea serpent is very large—fifty to two hundred feet—and capable of swimming very fast—fifteen to thirty knots. All respectable accounts report the monster to be harmless unless attacked, although naturally an object of fear because of its size (it has been shot at and wounded on occasion). It normally appears only on calm, hot summer days when the sea is glassy—July and August in the Northern Hemisphere, January and February in the Southern. It rarely leaves warm currents, and is rarely seen more than a hundred miles from land. It's usually described as brownish, having a serpent's head, large, transverse mouth, large eyes, long neck, and sometimes as having something that looks like a mane hanging from the back of the head. It is shy and unaggressive, sinking when the wind comes up or if anything is thrown at it. On the other hand, it is playful, shows some interest in boats, and often follows them. It sometimes lies stretched out in the water but more often undulates in folds. Most accounts that describe its motion in detail say that it moves with a vertical undulation, like a caterpillar, not horizontally, like a snake (Heuvelmans, pp. 325–27; C. Gould, passim).

This last peculiarity led Richard Owen, the main scientific opponent of the sea serpent (although better known for his opposition to Darwin), to disqualify it, since all known serpents undulate horizontally. But as Gould points out, this argument evaporates if we simply accept the possibility that the sea serpent is not a serpent, or is one of those anomalous species that tax the taxonomists. Some people have suggested a giant eel, a notion that found some support in the discovery of a six-foot eel larva in 1930—arguing a sixty to seventy foot adult (Dinsdale, pp. 77–78; Heuvelmans, pp. 484ff.)—but this doesn't account for the vertical undulation. Heuvelmans, a zoologist who has written the definitive book on the sea serpent, argues that at least six and perhaps nine different species are involved, five of them mammals (pp. 96–99, 539ff.).

But if the sea-serpent reports were accurate, why do we never hear of any today? Gould observed in 1884 that sea serpents had stopped appearing in the Norwegian fjords around 1850, and attributed their disappearance to the steamship. But he also noted that these waters once abounded with whales—thousands in a single shoal—and that the sea serpent "generally follows the track of whales." Several reports have the serpent attacking whales, others pursuing shoals of grampuses, porpoises, or fish (C. Gould, pp. 263–64, 291, 298, 311–17; Dinsdale, pp. 65, 71, 136, 160, 165; Heuvelmans, pp. 281–2, 286, 386). If the sea serpent fed on whales it wouldn't be hard to understand its having become extinct.

THE SEA SERPENT TODAY

But in fact the sea serpent hasn't disappeared, but only changed neighborhoods. Most of us don't hear about them because an ordinary sighting isn't newsworthy unless a reporter can turn it into a humorous account. Since 1900, furthermore, sea serpents have rarely been seen from ships. All accounts make it clear that the animals normally avoid noise, and whereas sailing ships of necessity strayed widely from narrow shipping lanes, steamships do not. Most sea serpents today, therefore, are seen by small vessels outside the heavily traveled sea-lanes—less often in the Atlantic, more often in the rest of the world. This isn't too surprising—naturalists don't try to study land animals by driving down a busy highway. Wild animals have to be looked for in out-of-the-way places. Despite this difficulty, there were more sightings from 1900 to 1950 than in any previous half century, and there are still more than two a year, on the average (Heuvelmans, pp. 34–5, 40, 325–27). The sixties brought many sightings—some with photographs that match closely the many drawings made by earlier observers. The new witnesses, like the old, include many of the highest repute (Dinsdale, pp. 78–97 and passim).

In 1975 a sea monster was seen in the St. Johns River in Florida (*The Boston Globe*, June 14, 1975). The account is handled in the jocular style that most reporters adopt when confronted by unconventional events, and follows the classic pattern: a detailed (though in this case rather informal) account by several witnesses, greeted with disbelief by people who weren't present, who suggest that the witnesses mistook the object for something else—something that doesn't in the least resemble the perceived object, but satisfies those not present that nothing unusual occurred. There are also the usual insinuations that the witnesses were drunk or otherwise disqualifiable—the headline for the item reads "Could Pinky the monster replace pink elephants?"

Since the reporter doesn't take the event seriously his account is sketchy, but some familiar themes appear. The woman who first saw it, for example, was told by her companions that she "must have seen a school of flying fish." When it surfaced again, only twenty feet from their boat, they were all frightened by the monster although "he didn't look harmful. He was just ugly." And when they reported it to the Florida Marine Patrol they received an equally glib reply: ". . . it had had a lot of calls from people seeing things, and had always told them it was a sea sturgeon, because they get up to eighteen feet long . . . I guess a lot of people have accepted that. But . . . a sturgeon has a long pointy nose, and this thing had a neck and a head . . . it was turning its head around." Finally the scientific expert is consulted and makes the automatic and conclusive judgment; he "insists Pinky has to be a sturgeon—or a tree stump—or maybe a sea cow." He admits, however, that sturgeon are rare in the vicinity and that the other two possibilities don't fit the description, which places him a cut above most armchair skeptics in matters of this kind.

So ends the mystery. Fear is allayed (who could be afraid of "Pinky," or "Nessie," for that matter?); the easily cowed doubt their perceptions; the stubborn are laughed into bitter silence; the monster submerges; and that's the end of this "unique" event. Since it will never happen again no one needs to bother with it—it's just one of those odd loose ends. And when it *does* happen again—here or somewhere else, it will again be a unique occurrence. If we isolate such events we never have to deal with them. We could, of course, treat comets or eclipses in the same way, but these have passed through our mental barriers and been accepted.

LAKE "MONSTERS"

Not only the sea serpent but also its freshwater cousins appear with undiminished frequency. The Loch Ness Monster is the most famous, of course, but there are few lakes of comparable depth in the Northern Hemisphere that don't also boast monster reports: they are found in Sweden, Scotland, Ireland, Canada, and Siberia. Like the sea serpent, the monsters are usually seen on calm summer days, and then infrequently. One retired sea captain who lived near such a lake scoffed at the reports for twenty-seven years before he saw the monster himself (Dinsdale, pp. 21–66). One can't help wondering: if all these sightings are hallucinations, why do they only occur around lakes of extreme depth?

The Loch Ness Monster is now teetering on the edge of respectability. Once scientists can register something on a machine they seem to find it easier to believe in. Photographs alone never convince anyone; if they're unclear or taken from far away they're explained as misperceptions;

while good, clear shots are dismissed as palpable fakes. Scientific skepticism is like Catch-22: "Since there's nothing new, the more distinct your evidence is, the more obviously it's a fraud." A fuzzy blurred photograph is more respectably "scientific" because it's easier to explain away.

But as people with some scientific bent begin to putter around with some sort of equipment, scientists get interested in claiming the new territory for science itself. They send scientific expeditions and obtain evidence that suits them better than the sober testimony of mere laypeople (cf. *The Boston Globe*, November 22, 1975).

But if Nessie gets through the door it will be slammed again at once, for nothing seems more disturbing than the possibility that several of these myths will become realities at the same time. The "Pinky" story, for example, opens with the reporter saying, "The Abominable Snowman has vanished, along with the snows of yesteryear. Nessie of Loch Ness remains submerged, sulking. Bigfoot no longer has footroom in the Northwest because of the tourists. But take heart, monster fans. A brand new one, Pinky, has surfaced . . . ," and so on. Actually, Yeti, Nessie, and Bigfoot were all very much in the news during this period, but there seems to be some kind of unconscious conspiracy to pretend that untoward events of this kind are a thing of the past.

ARMCHAIR IMPROVISATION

Armchair skeptics always claim to have a better view of the object than the eyewitness, and never hesitate to attribute an impressive naiveté to people experienced in their field of observation. But I find myself skeptical of the skeptics: my problem is that their tortured inventions seem more incredible to me than a sea serpent or a non-terrestrial spacecraft. I never saw a star, satellite, or balloon that looked anything like most UFO reports, so I have a hard time imagining an airline pilot making such a mistake. Similarly, I've seen a lot of porpoises and seaweed in all kinds of weather, but never any that looked even remotely like sea-serpent reports.

Usually the armchair improvisations simply disregard some crucial fact in the report. The night Venus is supposedly mistaken for a UFO it happens to be covered by a cloud layer. The alleged weather balloon mistaken for a UFO manages to achieve speeds of several thousand miles per hour and has lighted windows. The long string of sea-weed "lashed into fantastic motion by the surge of the ocean waves," and hence mistaken for a sea serpent, is actually seen in the glassy waters of a windless fjord. As Gardner Murphy observes, "it is almost proverbial in science that *whenever a fresh hypothesis has to be invented to account for every fresh case, it is an indication that the explorer is off the track*" (p. 251; italics mine).

The report of the two clergymen in the *Zoologist* concludes as follows: ". . . as the public will most probably be dubious about quickly giving credit to our account, the following explanations are open to them, all of which have been proposed to me, viz.: porpoises, lumps of seaweed, empty herring-barrels, bladders, logs of wood, waves of the sea, and inflated pigskins! but as all these theories present to our mind greater difficulties than the existence of the animal itself, we feel obliged to decline them" (C. Gould, p. 286).

What is about UFOs, sea serpents, and psychic phenomena that triggers all this strained ingenuity? Perhaps it's that all of them share a dramatic, mythic quality—evoking an image of dark, uncontrollable forces—the kind that deadpan male heroes are always subduing. What will become of the unemotional blond scientist if these murky forces prove never to have been successfully harnessed after all?

Sea serpents are less scary than they used to be before air travel, and the Loch Ness Monster is now licensed for scientific pursuit. The existence of another large marine animal is less bizarre on the face of it than an armadillo or a platypus. (I find it difficult to believe in the armadillo even when I see one face to face.) A hundred years ago sea serpents were as threatening as faith healing, but today the sea is too polluted to be very mythic any more—it's now under human control.

The Yeti is approaching respectability for the same reason, although it's been a long struggle. A zoologist, Edward W. Cronin, Jr., came out in favor of the beast in *The Atlantic* (November 1975). He pointed out that (1) the animal has been reported for 200 years and Himalayan villagers include it matter-of-factly in any list of local fauna; (2) more than forty Westerners, including many of highest repute—competent naturalists and mountaineers, familiar with the area—have sighted the Yeti or its footprints; (3) eyewitness reports are detailed, remarkably consistent, and the Yeti's appearance and behavior are "exactly what a scientist would expect" of a human-sized ape; (4) a plausible fossil antecedent exists in Gigantopithecus, remains of which have been found in exactly the same region, and which closely resembles the Yeti; (5) the narrow, steep, lush valleys between mountains in the Himalayas are virtually unexplored—a "biological sanctuary" for many species elsewhere extinct—and make a logical habitat for the Yeti, which is seen only when it crosses snowy mountain passes to get from one dense valley forest to another. Cronin also observes wryly that "the ability of large mammals to escape documentation by scientists is infamous": The Kouprey, a large wild bison living quite visibly in open savannas in Cambodia wasn't pronounced "real" until 1936, while the mountain gorilla, pigmy hippopotamus, and giant panda—long familiar to "ignorant" villagers— were considered moonshine by scientists for years.

Cronin concludes that "the biases of the scientists involved, rather than any inductive logic, determine the interpretation of the data," since the same evidence produces utterly opposed conclusions. He asks the same kind of question I asked above about Jane Goodall. Why are we so quick to accept the evidence of a new fossil—all the fanciful reconstructions of an animal's behavior, morphology, and ecology from a few bone fragments—and so slow to accept the (comparatively) overwhelming evidence for the Yeti?

Most apes were originally considered fabulous by Western scientists, but this mythic quality has gradually seeped away—King Kong to the contrary notwithstanding. Animals of any kind are less likely to threaten a scientist's feeling of rational control than they used to. But UFOs and cosmic cataclysms are something else again, since they would reduce the scientist's position to one of powerless triviality. So although it's hard to look at the face of the earth and not infer that catastrophes have occurred scientists have strained and grunted mightily to explain them away. Only a few, like Darwin, have had the grace to admit that the data contradict the theory of gradual and peaceful evolution.

Immanuel Velikovsky assembled much of this material in his book *Earth in Upheaval*. He used data from geology, oceanography, and archeology to show how overwhelming the record of catastrophe really was: beaches on the ocean floor, whales on mountain tops, tropical fossils in the Arctic, marine fossils miles high in the Himalayas, caves full of smashed animal skeletons from both polar and tropical regions, hills composed of trees, and evidence suggesting that natural wonders such as the Himalayas and the Mississippi are of relatively recent origin.

One datum that puzzled Darwin was the sea of frozen mammoths and rhinoceri on the arctic coast of Siberia. Conventional scientific theory has it that the ice age moved in slowly over thousands of years, occasionally catching an animal too slow to avoid it. But a weather change that slow wouldn't even be noticeable in one animal's lifetime. These animals were frozen so quickly that dogs ate them when they were thawed out thousands of years later. In the mammoths' stomachs and between their teeth were plants and grasses that do not grow in northern Siberia—indeed, nothing grows in northern Siberia today that would keep a herd of such animals alive. The evidence is that they died of suffocation (Velikovsky, pp. 15–20).

Eminent scientists, who to this day boast of never having read a word of what Velikovsky wrote, attacked him at length, hired a hack reporter to review his work negatively, forced one publisher to suppress his book on threat of boycott, refused to allow him to rebut his opponents in scientific journals, and generally violated every tenet of their own tradition. Only a few, like Albert Einstein, were willing to come to grips with his ideas.

Since the early 1950s, when all this took place, Velikovsky has been largely vindicated—many of his predictions borne out by space probes and other new evidence—and although few of his original enemies have admitted their error, the furor seems to be a thing of the past. But what was it all about? Why was the idea of cataclysmic change so threatening to scientists? Perhaps because scientists have no place when history is "in the making"—that is, when changes are happening so fast that we pay particular attention to them. Scientists need to work slowly to avoid becoming the lackeys of men of action. They want life to stand still and be counted—the mere *idea* of a cataclysm tends to disrupt this orderly and gradual process. For it isn't Nature that evolves slowly and peacefully, but science itself: the theory of uniformity is a projection of academia onto nature.

PATTERNS OF RESISTANCE

Ramón Margalef observes (p. 56) that the "development of a personality involves the use of information to make oneself impermeable to new sources of information . . . everyone knows how difficult it is to make new ideas acceptable to a hard-boiled scientist." It should be apparent by now that this resistance follows certain patterns, regardless of the particular kind of information being resisted—

whether UFO, giant squid, sea serpent, meteorite, Yeti, gorilla, telepathy, prehistoric skeleton, or Bigfoot. The gradual acceptance of such events as real also follows a pattern.

Let's look first at the techniques of resistance, by now quite familiar to us:

(1) *Scientific amnesia*. The events I've described are occasional, and lie outside the conventional scientific understanding of the world. This means that they aren't recorded regularly when they occur, and if they *are* recorded it may be in a different place each time. When a sunspot or an earthquake occurs there is an elaborate recording system waiting to receive the information because scientists are *looking* for these things. Since they aren't looking for sea serpents or Bigfoot in the early stages of such events, each occurrence is an anomaly. There's no context to put it in, and it's easily forgotten since it can't be related to anything.

Hence scientists often argue that events are not real because they have only begun to occur, and therefore must be hallucinations or hoaxes. It was long maintained, for example, that the first sighting of the Loch Ness Monster was in 1934, although in fact the sightings go back hundreds of years. Similarly, a popular scientific myth held that UFO sightings began in 1947 and were an expression of "postwar hysteria," although in fact UFO sightings are at least as old as the written word. Bigfoot sightings are supposed to have started in the 1960s, although they go back to the first white travelers in America and far beyond when we include Native American sightings.

(2) *Discrediting the witness*. This technique and the first one are mutually reinforcing. If you forget that hundreds or thousands of witnesses have seen the same thing and described it identically over a period of decades or centuries, then obviously each witness has a heavier burden of skepticism to overcome. Furthermore, if you ridicule and humiliate a few witnesses you will tend, as we have seen, to

get far fewer reports in the future, which makes scientific amnesia much easier.

The first line of defense in discrediting a witness is to show that he is a foreigner. (If the witness is a woman this is unnecessary since female witnesses are always dismissed as "impressionable" anyway. This would seem to mean that women have minds that are flexible enough for sensory stimuli to make some impression on them. Not all men are granite-heads, however.) The sea serpent, for example, first received major attention among Europeans as the "Norwegian" sea serpent. After the frequent and exceptionally well-documented New England sightings in the first half of the nineteenth century it became the "American sea serpent," and was dismissed by Europeans as an example of "Yankee credulity." One Englishman announced frankly he had never believed in it until he had an eyewitness account from another Englishman (Heuvelmans, pp. 168–178, 218–19). In the latter part of the nineteenth century, however, there were more English sightings than American ones, and now Americans made fun of the "gullible" British. And of course non-Western or pre-modern witnesses receive no credence whatever, being dismissed as "superstitious savages" although many of their reports are quite prosaic and matter-of-fact. Reports of Yeti were ignored until seen by white men; reports of lake monsters, and sea serpents in many areas, were ignored until seen by white men; reports of gorillas, orangutans, okapi, oryx, komodo lizards, and Bigfoot were all ignored until seen by white men; and this is true of thousands of other animals and plants. Yet the accuracy of witnesses is not determined by their location in time or space, nor by racial or cultural background.

If the witness is not a foreigner an attempt is usually made to suggest that he or she is drunk or in some kind of altered mental state. This is usually done by innuendo.

The next line of defense is to maintain that the witness is not a scientist and hence is incapable of seeing anything properly. This is very effective unless the witness *is* a scientist, and it is important to remember that *the "bizarre" phenomena discussed in this chapter have all been witnessed by reputable scientists, some repeatedly.* In this case one simply reverts to the previous argument, maintaining that the witness is obviously crazy since no sane scientist would ever admit to seeing such a thing—another scientific Catch-22.

The last and best defense is to find an ulterior motive for the witness. This technique is frequently used by Philip Klass to debunk UFOs. The only anti-UFO spokesperson I know of who actually investigates cases, Klass does, in my opinion, successfully dispose of a few, but in most of the important cases the reader waits in vain for a convincing disproof, and discovers that Klass feels content if he can merely cast doubt on the report—often by impugning the character or motives of the witnesses. In one case, for example, he points out that the town in which the UFO was reported had been economically depressed and subsequently attracted some tourist interest (Klass, pp. 112–114). A similar argument has been used to debunk the Loch Ness Monster (see Costello, p. 15), and Bigfoot. In 1976 the economically depressed town of Chowchilla, California, became a tourist attraction after a sensational kidnapping, but no one dared to suggest that the kidnapping was a publicity stunt. While hoaxes *have* been perpetrated in an effort to attract tourists, the mere interest of tourists is not enough in and of itself to discredit a witness. If it were, we would have to call the entire space program a hoax.

In another case Klass dismisses a sighting out-of-hand because the witness ate his dinner while the UFO was still in the vicinity (Klass, p. 240). Apparently excitement would have banished food from his mind had he not had some ulterior purpose. By far the most common insinuation is that the witness is seeking some sort of notoriety. No allowance is made for the fear of ridicule. Yet as John Napier points out (p. 88) to see a Bigfoot is "to risk personal reputation, social status, and professional credibility," not to mention one's job.

A special problem arises for the skeptic if there is more than one witness. It's a lot easier, after all, to argue that one person is drunk or hallucinating than to maintain that a whole crowd is. The Loch Ness Monster has often been seen by several people at a time—once quite independently from opposite sides of the lake, once by a large crowd (Costello, pp. 76, 97–8, 102, 142, 148–49). In Siberia a lake monster was seen on land in broad daylight by a group of scientists (pp. 264–66). Sea serpents have been seen repeatedly by crowds of up to 200, appearing every day so that everyone in the vicinity had a chance to come and look. In all there are 150 known groups (in addition to the more than 1,000 *named* individuals) who have witnessed sea serpents. Furthermore, their descriptions have been in close agreement, sometimes with "monotonous" exactitude (Heuvelmans, pp. 36–7, 168–175). UFOs are *usually* seen by many people at once and even Yeti and Bigfoot occasionally draw a small group (Grumley, pp. 106ff.).

But the skeptic is equal to the task. In danger of being outnumbered he retreats behind the shield of language and calls it "mass psychology" or "mass hallucination"— terms which have no real scientific meaning but are simply a way of saying, "I don't care *how* many people saw it— you're *all* crazy!" The most brazen version of this gambit comes from Sir Arthur Keith (famous for being either the perpetrator or the principal victim of the Piltdown hoax), who thought that "the very large number of people claiming to have seen the Loch Ness Monster proved that it was imaginary" (Costello, p. 50). This is still another well-turned Catch-22: the *fewer* people the less credible and the *more* people the less credible.

(3) *Mythification.* A related technique is mythification, in which you introduce a fantastic tone not present in the original reports of witnesses. If someone reports seeing a large animal swim across a lake, for example, you scoff at

"these stories of monsters coming out of the lake and carrying off screaming women." Reporters are of great assistance to skeptics in this regard: a classic postcard rendering of the Loch Ness Monster, for example, has a lamb in its jaws, based entirely on a reporter's invention. Usually, however, mythification is more subtle—skeptics simply fasten on the most dramatic and dubious story and treat all reports as equivalent to this one (cf. Costello, pp. 32–37, 50, 62, 210–17). Philip Klass makes excellent use of this device in his anti-UFO book (pp. 245ff. and chapter 14). He devotes an entire chapter, for example, to cases in which UFOs are cast in the role of brutal killers, although in fact no investigator has ever taken any of those cases seriously. By giving undue weight to crank examples and ignoring most of the more convincing ones he makes his debunking efforts look a great deal better than they really are.

Mythification is used very successfully with reports by non-Western peoples. It is simply assumed that if a Native American or a Sherpa tells of an animal living in a lake or forest, it is mythical. If the report is matter-of-fact and involves no story or legend, travelers and reporters are always happy to fill the gap.

John Napier points out that Bigfoot reports lack any sequences, social purpose, symbolism, wish fulfillment, or meaningful narrative of any kind. For 160 years, at least, we have had dull stories of harmless giants who just walk away when seen. Why not some variation—why not a fierce King Kong once in a while? The very dullness of these reports lends them credibility, as does the fact that the animals are perceived as harmless and mild-mannered. Native American reports of lake monsters or Bigfoot often made it quite clear that these animals were not threatening, but potentially dangerous only because of their great size. They tell of lake monsters that look like "upturned boats" and have dull names like "cowhide." A sea serpent seen repeatedly off Vancouver was even described by observers as "loveable and homely" with "warm and kindly eyes." And despite King Kong, there is virtually *no* sexuality among the Yeti and Bigfoot accounts (cf. Napier, pp. 19–20, 196; Byrne, pp. 31, 72; Costello, pp. 242, 303, and passim; Grumley, pp. 12–13, 66). Reporters are used to making dull stories interesting, however, and where they can find nothing mythic they seldom hesitate to imply it anyway. Artists' renderings of sea serpents for example, favor stormy nights, though the beast is almost always seen on calm, sunny days.

The word "monster" itself is a form of mythification, since a heavily loaded word is being applied to what is simply an animal that hasn't yet been classified. Compare the impact of saying "there's a large unclassified animal in the lake (woods)" with: "There's a monster in the lake (woods)." *The word "monster" in and of itself adds decades to the time it takes to accept an animal as real.* A "monster" is almost by definition unreal—something out of the movies. Before it can be accepted it has to be *de*-mythified, usually by giving it a new name—preferably Latin or Greek. "Dinosaur" sounds much safer than "Terrible Lizard," "Orangutan" than "Wild Man," "Meteorite" than "Stone-Falling-From-Sky," "Komodo Lizard" than "Dragon."

Mythification thus serves as a kind of delaying action until science gets around to staking its own claim. Ninety-five percent of the reports of sea serpents, lake monsters, Yeti, Bigfoot, and so on, are prosaic and unemotional descriptions of harmless animals engaged in routine behavior appropriate to their general type and habitat. By implying that these reports are hysterical, fantastic, and tied to folklore and legend, scientists manage to reserve their presumed monopoly on truth and correct observation, while debunking what they will later "discover" on their own. When scientists themselves begin actively to look for the animal and find it, they congratulate themselves and science, saying, "look here—this mythical monster everybody's been screaming hysterically about is just a harmless old primate (or long-necked giant seal, or plesiosaur, or whatever). Isn't that interesting!" Which means, "isn't it interesting to us scientists and dull to you laypeople"; for science is supposed to be fascinating only if you get into it—dull and forbidding to the uninitiated. What the scientists "discover," of course, is just what laypeople have been seeing and describing accurately all along, but this way science preserves its image as a kind of intellectual Lone Ranger, saving the world from superstition.

Science is a profession, and all professions are inherently anti-democratic. They attempt to make their knowledge inaccessible to all but their own initiated disciples, usually by developing a secret language. This betrays a deep doubt as to their real competence. For if scientists, doctors, and other professionals really believed they were smarter or more competent than laypeople they wouldn't need to mystify their terminology with Latin, Greek, or neologisms borrowed from other fields. All of the anatomical terms for bones, muscles, arteries, and so on, could be translated into English with no loss of clarity, but having to learn a thousand new words before one can even begin to study medicine serves to discourage the curious and uninitiated and enhances the prestige, power, and authority of the expert. The use of Latin terms in medicine, in other words, serves the same function as it once did in the Roman Catholic church.

In any case, the ultimate "discovery" does nothing to impair science's image. Meteorites, for example, are now a *part* of science, though scientists steadfastly pooh-poohed them for decades. Reality is always dull enough to validate the scientific vision. The only thing mythic about all these unknown animals is their inaccessibility. Once captured and studied, a Bigfoot or gorilla or Yeti or orangutan is no more interesting than a baboon or a leopard. A sea serpent is less dramatic than a giant squid or a whale, and the behavior of the Loch Ness Monster is about as exciting as that of a hippopotamus. A unicorn is interesting, an oryx is not. A woman who saw a sea serpent in 1933, a few yards off and as long as the ship she was sailing in, reported: "When I *saw* the beast, and realized I was looking at a creature which was generally supposed not to exist, I had the sensation that it was not so very wonderful after all" (Heuvelmans, p. 439).

(4) *Hoaxes*. The process of mythification is greatly facilitated by hoaxes, since hoaxes are always more dramatic than the real thing. This, in fact, is one way to detect a hoax—realism detracts a lot from excitement, which often tempts the hoaxer to overstep himself. Most hoaxes are easy enough to spot, as Heuvelmans points out, by the "extravagant details" of anatomy, dramatic adventures, and the fact that witnesses disappear on investigation (Heuvelmans, p. 224). But drama has its own power, and *even after a hoax has been exposed, it tends to be included as a central part of the data for that phenomenon*, simply because it's much more dramatic than the careful descriptions of honest witnesses. There is no book on sea serpents, lake monsters, UFOs, or Bigfoot, no matter how sympathetic, that doesn't include a famous known hoax or two, simply because these stories are more interesting to the reader. Perhaps this is only natural—one could even defend it on the grounds that such books try to consider *all* the evidence, for and against, and known hoaxes are powerful negative evidence of a sort. But the problem becomes even more extreme when we come to pictures and photographs, where known hoaxes are always wildly overrepresented—again because they're more mythic and hence more interesting. Pictures by hoaxers get reproduced more than any others (Heuvelmans, p. 226), and although understandable, this helps perpetuate skepticism.

One rather peculiar regularity about hoaxes is that the more blatant ones usually occur just as large numbers of people are beginning to take the phenomenon seriously. (For an interesting interpretation of this trend see Vallée, 1975.) This has been true for the Loch Ness Monster, Bigfoot, the sea serpent, and UFOs (Costello, p. 44; Napier, p. 111; Heuvelmans, pp. 162, 204, 223–4; Vallée, passim). It may also turn out to be true for the acceptance of alternative realities generally (see de Mille, 1976). Sea-serpent hoaxes, for example, are largely concentrated in (1) the

New England period, in the decade following the 1817 Gloucester sightings studied so carefully by the Linnaean Society, and (2) the English period, from 1848–1890. More than a third of all known sea-serpent hoaxes occurred during this latter period—far out of proportion to the number of legitimate sightings. (Unlike the legitimate sightings, which are always concentrated in the summer months, the hoaxes were spread evenly over the whole year. Most of the hoaxers were Americans.)

Perhaps this timing isn't too surprising. Just as a concentration of money attracts thieves, so a concentration of publicity attracts hoaxers. The same timing characterized the Piltdown hoax, which occurred just as evolutionary theory and paleontology were being taken seriously. The only difference between the Piltdown hoax and UFO, sea serpent, or Bigfoot hoaxes is that its author was a sophisticated scientist and that for forty years it worked. The "discoverer" of the Piltdown skull was the subject of some 500 learned papers, and those scientists who saw through the deception were successfully silenced by the weight of majority opinion. The general scientific acceptance of evolutionary theory and much of the paleontological science of the first half of the twentieth century was firmly rooted in the Piltdown skull, which provided confirmation of a theory just when it was needed. Scientific history has since been rewritten, of course, to deëmphasize this embarrassing incident, but it's fair to say that it was the Piltdown skull more than anything else that routed the clerical opposition to Darwin and convinced people that human evolution was a process occurring over millions of years (cf. Millar, pp. 10ff.). As Millar points out, the victory of fossil man, evolution, and uniformitarian theory over biblical and catastrophist theories was based less on new data (of which there was very little, aside from the Piltdown skull) than on the "sheer exuberance" of the proponents and a sudden willingness to redefine old data (Millar, pp. 96ff.). The Piltdown skull was accepted as long as it was needed—

about the time that far more compelling skulls came to light the hoax was "discovered."

At the same time, the success of the hoax was not altogether surprising, considering the tenuous and arbitrary nature of the field—replete as it is with total theoretical reversals, dates set arbitrarily and then shifted by hundreds of thousands of years, "foolproof" tests utterly relied upon and later discarded as meaningless, and arbitrary reconstructions based on minimal data becoming rigid conventions treated as iron fact. Few fields are as helplessly dependent upon fashions in belief, although obviously no science is free from such dependence (cf. Heuvelmans, p. 320).

Amusingly enough, during this same period of belief in the Piltdown skull, newly-discovered paleolithic cave paintings were being rejected as hoaxes because of the exaggerated genitalia on some of the figures (Millar, p. 98). It is in the reasons for rejecting new data that we usually find most clearly stated the prejudices of the old order. Thus the clerical opponents of Darwin argued that if human bones were found in an archeological site it could not be ancient since "we know" that human bones are modern (Millar, p. 21). The same kinds of arguments are used today against UFOs and other such phenomena, as we shall see.

The idea that anyone would crawl for miles into virtually inaccessible pitch-dark caves and work for months under intolerable conditions just to fool someone is reminiscent of similar fantasies about Bigfoot tracks and sightings. There have, of course, been Bigfoot hoaxes, but the anatomical ignorance of their perpetrators makes them quite transparent. Most sightings are too brief and in areas too remote for a hoax to make sense. As Byrne asks, how many men would "travel thousands of miles . . . just for the doubtful privilege . . . of showing himself for a few seconds to some hardworking and rather disinterested woodsman?" (Byrne, pp. 101–2). For a fake footprint to fool Bigfoot hunters, he argues, it would have to be made by a scientist and left in remote woods for someone to find before it rains. It would have to be made with much greater than human stride lengths, by someone carrying hundreds of pounds of extra weight while doing it. The scientist would have to make special devices to mimic the unusual primate toe movements and other peculiarities, and know primate and human anatomy well enough to know how it should be altered (Byrne, pp. 232–242).

(5) *Selecting and weighting the evidence*. Suppose a witness's report survives these first four hurdles and actually finds itself considered as some sort of evidence. We might suppose that having journeyed so far—buffeted by storms, bitten by the watchdogs, insulted by the servants, and harassed by mischievous children—our report would finally be received with courtesy and dignity by the lord of the manor. Isn't it widely advertised that science's house is always open to the weary traveler? Isn't science's hospitality to the Observed Fact legendary? It's true that the householder needs to be cautious these days about wandering rogues and impostors, but shouldn't a respectable and sober traveler get a fair hearing?

Unfortunately, the traveler's trials and misfortunes have only begun. Whatever insults and scorn the dogs, servants, and children have overlooked, the proprietor now offers. Like everyone else in the world, science wants to hear what it wants to hear—no more, no less. It's one thing to seek information and another to get it, for as James Fenimore Cooper once remarked, there is an "indisposition in the human mind to acknowledge that others have seen that which chance has concealed from our own sight" (quoted in Heuvelmans, p. 146).

The first thing that armchair skeptics do, then, when confronted with an unusual report, is to pick it apart, arbitrarily taking some statements as true and rejecting others as false, and then reinterpreting the whole observation as being a distortion of some known and comfortably familiar event. Although such a procedure is blatantly unscientific, by any definition, few skeptics hesitate to use it. Philip

Klass, the anti-UFO writer, brazenly puts it forward as a *formula* for analyzing UFO reports! His first "principle" is that witnesses may be "inaccurate" in trying to describe a new stimulus; his second "principle" is that some details will be "reasonably accurate." The armchair skeptic must then "try to distinguish between those details that are accurate and those that are grossly inaccurate" (Klass, pp. 14, 22). Although he admits this is difficult, he seems oblivious to the arrogance involved in a non-observer evaluating the "accuracy" of the report of an eyewitness! In practice this means that the skeptic attributes accuracy to whatever part of the report fits his alternative explanation, and discards as "inaccurate" any details that contradict his theory. With this formula any notion that suggests itself to him can be made to fit the report, which is then explained away as something familiar—for, needless to say, that is the thrust of all these alternative "explanations." Klass seems to feel that if he can only find some sort of commonplace object within five hundred miles and eight hours of the UFO sighting he has made his case, no matter how poorly it matches the data. As Heuvelmans observes, any explanation, however absurd, that reduces a new and surprising event to something commonplace, is seized upon by the public (Heuvelmans, pp. 304ff.). Skeptics have argued, for example, that a sea serpent described in minute detail was really a flock of birds, or a series of porpoises "swimming in Indian file." To this latter suggestion a witness indignantly asked who had ever seen fifty or sixty porpoises swimming single file, with only the first one showing his head; and who had ever seen a porpoise with a snake's head, held continuously out of water for several miles. Yet as Heuvelmans points out, this "explanation" has been offered continually from 1800 right up to the present (Heuvelmans, p. 147).

In 1877 Henry Lee, a naturalist, objected that these explanations assume that "the stay-at-home naturalist has perfect cognisance of every existing marine animal of large size, and that the sea-going eyewitness is so inexperienced

79

and uninstructed that his assertion that what he saw was none of these, is worthless" (quoted by Heuvelmans, p. 276). Fortunately for science, every field contains a few Henry Lees—would there were more.

Back in the days before Darwinian theory had triumphed over the Bible, a man found a rhino tooth and a flint weapon in the same site. This violated the theory of the day, which had extinct animals and humans in rigidly different time periods, separated by the Flood. The scientific establishment therefore disposed of the finding with the theory that the ancients had scooped ovens from the floor, allowing the weapon to get mixed up with the bones underneath. The man objected that there were no such ovens and the floor was unbroken stalagmite, but the armchair skeptics prevented him from publishing anyway (Millar, p. 25).

Still, we shouldn't be too hard on the armchair skeptics for trying to twist the unknown into the known, for this is exactly what the witnesses themselves do. The sea serpent is more often mistaken for a porpoise or a tree trunk than the other way around: One witness tried to make it look like a shoal of fish with a seal at one end. Another reported: "I just didn't believe in these things and tried to convince myself it was a flight of birds just above the water. I even thought of a miniature submarine but after watching it for some time I knew it couldn't be" (Heuvelmans, pp. 147, 171, 536). Lake monsters are first seen as upturned boats, waves, logs, otters, islands, and so on; Bigfoot is first seen as a bear; and UFO observers try to make UFOs look like planes, satellites, weather balloons, and so on (Costello, pp. 130ff., 149, 156, 218; Grumley, p. 109; Fuller, passim). The difference is that *an eyewitness can check her explanation against the facts while the armchair skeptic cannot and need not*. Thus an observer may perceive an animal as a log or boat but revise this theory when the animal moves. Or a light may be seen as a plane or star until it jumps about erratically. Yet the armchair skeptic will often give an explanation that completely ignores precisely the stimulus that forced the observer to revise her original opinion. This is simply because *the skeptics lack the direct experience to correct their conventional assumptions, to which, like the witnesses, they cling fiercely as long as they can.*

The weight an armchair expert assigns to new evidence, therefore, is a function of how much it supports his preconceptions. An eyewitness account is rigorously examined and sections of it arbitrarily rejected as implausible, but those who speak on the side of scientific convention need do little more than voice an opinion. Philip Klass tends to give a mere prejudice the weight of scientific law if it's stated by a scientist, while John Napier thinks nothing of announcing that he has a "sixth sense" that tells him when an animal "can't be real" (p. 111). In the 1860s an armchair expert announced that reports of the giant squid were based on nothing more than the remains of some sea plant. "A little reflection," he announced pompously, "will persuade the wise and especially the man of science, not to admit into the catalogue those stories which mention extraordinary creatures like the sea-serpent and the giant squid, the existence of which would be in some sort a contradiction of the great laws of harmony and equilibrium." This was science's reasoned response to 200 years of detailed eyewitness accounts of the giant squid. Unfortunately for the great laws of harmony, the next decade saw a rash of giant squid corpses washed up on the coast of Newfoundland—more monstrous in size and shape than the wildest fictions. Many people, in fact, who believed totally in the sea serpent had rejected giant squid reports as simply too bizarre (Heuvelmans, pp. 50–1, 111).

There have been many similar attempts to normalize the Loch Ness Monster—vegetable matter, gas, waves, boats, and so on. It was even suggested that it might be just a large otter, despite the vast discrepancy in size. To meet this problem Professor Burton, perhaps Nessie's most ardent debunker, offered in evidence two anonymous reports claiming to have seen otters up to six feet in length. Needless to say a six-foot otter is still far, far short of the size estimates of 99 percent of Nessie's eyewitnesses, but more important is the fact that the same scientist who summarily rejects signed statements by hundreds of reputable witnesses thinks nothing of accepting two *anonymous* reports when they fit his preconceptions (Costello, p. 100).

This is generally true in the history of science. As Napier points out, the fossil evidence for the early pre-australopithecine stages of human evolution "could be packed into a cigar box" (p. 115). In 1936 the whale shark had been seen only seventy-eight times, although it is slow, gentle, fearless, and fifty feet long, while by the same date there were over two hundred and fifty admissible sightings of the fast and timid sea serpent. Zoology texts are full of animals (including many whale species) more rarely seen than the sea serpent. Some have provided a scrap of anatomy—bone, skin, or tentacle—but others have been accepted and labeled with nothing more than the eyewitness testimony of a handful of people (cf. Heuvelmans, pp. 36–7, 325, 452). But scientists are only human, and even Heuvelmans doesn't hesitate to dismiss or reinterpret data when his preconceptions are violated (pp. 110, 301). I've also found myself doing it, for all reports strike *someone* the wrong way.

(6) *Blunted Questions.* If the evidence accumulates despite all these maneuvers, the skeptic must retreat to generalized objections. One of the most popular of these is to ask: "If what you say is true, why haven't——?" As I observed earlier in the case of UFOs, most of these questions are spurious: The skeptic asks, triumphantly and rhetorically, "Why hasn't such-and-such ever occurred?" when in fact it has. It isn't that the skeptic is deliberately misleading or deceiving the public. In most cases it's just ignorance; scientists, like the rest of us, rarely bother to inform themselves about things they don't want to believe.

We're not surprised then to find skeptics asking why "competent naturalists" have never seen sea serpents or lake monsters, although there have been many well-known instances—including one sighting by two naturalists together (Heuvelmans, pp. 332, 372–73). Another question often asked about sea serpents and lake monsters is "why, if they're real, do people never see more than one?" although in fact there have been at least a dozen such sightings of sea serpents and several of the Loch Ness Monsters (Heuvelmans, p. 144; Costello, pp. 68–70).

Not all such questions are bogus, however. Legitimate queries have been raised about how large animals like Nessie, Bigfoot, and the Yeti manage to feed themselves and remain hidden, and although I think those questions have been satisfactorily answered, they express a genuine and serious scientific concern. Some people can't imagine, for example, how a large primate could live in our own back yard and never wind up in one of our zoos. They find it much easier to believe in Yeti than in Bigfoot since North America is a "civilized" region. Yet much of the Pacific Northwest is less known and less traveled than the Himalayas. Planes have crashed in the area and not been found for years, or never found at all. Peter Byrne points out that the Tasaday tribe in the Philippines weren't discovered until 1972 although they weren't hiding, and new tribes are discovered in the Amazon jungles every now and then. Japanese soldiers hid successfully for twenty-eight years on the island of Guam in an area of 209 square miles inhabited by 87,000 people, while the Bigfoot habitat consists of 125,000 square miles, much of it completely deserted. A hermit lived for fifteen years in a *cabin* in a 149-acre municipal park in Portland, Oregon, before being discovered, although the park was full of people every day (Napier, p. 34; Byrne, pp. 108ff., 129–30).

A comparable question asks why no sea-serpent corpses have ever found their way into the laboratory. This is a little more specious, however, since, as Heuvelmans points out, there are "innumerable" sea animals whose bodies have never been washed up. Many whale species are known from only one or two beached specimens, and all experts admit that there may be others still unknown. The best-defined serpent types, furthermore, are unlikely by their nature to get stranded and could easily get off if they were. Finally, there have in fact been a great many large and strange-looking marine corpses washed up, and although most of them have turned out to be basking sharks or oarfish upon inspection, not all have been successfully explained away, despite the usual strong motivation to do so (Heuvelmans, pp. 275, 510, 569ff.). Sir Arthur Keith of Piltdown fame was one of those who rejected the sea serpent because it "never reaches the dissecting table" the way the Piltdown skull did, but Heuvelmans points out that if Keith had paid more attention to circumstantial evidence and less attention to bare bones he would immediately have recognized the Piltdown skull as a forgery (Heuvelmans, p. 26).

(7) *Theoretical "Disproof."* The major problem with the kinds of questions we've just examined is that they ignore the evidence. They answer a factual report with a theoretical objection. Suppose you say you saw a whale or a dolphin, and I say, "Impossible. How could an air-breathing animal live in the ocean without drowning?" Or you say you saw a counterfeit bill and I say "If that were possible everyone would be printing their own money." This approach is the last-ditch stand of the skeptic, and unfortunately is used rather often.

Yet such questions and theoretical "disproofs" are useful, since they often pave the way for a necessary redefinition of the event in question. The Linnaean Society of New England, for example, after studying their carefully gathered evidence on the Gloucester sea serpent, closed their eyes and concluded (apparently by pure preconception) that it was a new species of snake—a blunder that led other scientists to discredit their careful work (Heuvelmans, pp. 149–54). Questions about vertical undulation and so on, *while irrelevant to the accuracy of the observed event*, are helpful in determining just what it is that has been observed. What usually happens is that skeptics and believers alike are operating with some narrow assumption (such as, "only serpents can have an elongated shape") that breeds pointless controversy until expanded.

The literature on unknown fauna is littered with expert pronouncements that such-and-such an observed animal is "anatomically impossible." The giant squid was shown "conclusively" to be a mechanical impossibility shortly before squid corpses began to be washed ashore. The okapi and the coelacanth "could not exist" according to the experts, nor could the gorilla (Byrne, pp. 28, 103ff.; Heuvelmans, pp. 60ff., 282–3, 297). Often the experts seem unable to imagine variants of a known species: If a Yeti isn't an orangutan it couldn't be a species *similar* to an orangutan; or if Bigfoot isn't Gigantopithecus it must be totally unrelated or nonexistent (cf. Napier, pp. 178–180).

All of the phenomena discussed in this chapter are in part *like* some known category of objects and in part *unlike* that category. Experts therefore take the position that the object seen either belongs in the known category and was misperceived by the witness, or doesn't belong and hence cannot exist. *The premise underlying all theoretical "disproofs" is that nothing unknown could possibly exist.* A good example of this is Bigfoot. No known primate walks erect except a human. If a large ape is seen to walk erect the witness must be mistaken. No allowance is made for an anomaly or a new category, even though the Bigfoot evidence is internally coherent and consistent with the hypothesis of a large, heavy ape with certain faintly humanoid characteristics (Byrne, pp. 177, 232ff.). Even Heuvelmans arbitrarily rejects the possibility that a sea serpent could be over one hundred feet long, although reports of greater length are frequent and come from witnesses quite as respectable as those who report smaller specimens. When Heuvelmans talks of a "more acceptable size" he simply reveals the limited capacity of the human brain to absorb new information (see Heuvelmans, pp. 356, 398, 402).

The Wayward Gate

People let in novelty by degrees: hence there tend to be stages in the acceptance of a new species or other strange phenomenon.

I. The first stage is one of skepticism, ridicule, and abuse. Yet it's quite as important as the later ones for establishing the reality of the phenomenon. Nothing is "real" until it's noticed, and while people are saying vehemently that "it" doesn't exist, our perceptual apparatus is becoming attuned to this nonexistent "it." We have a concept for it and can now begin to see it and grasp it, whereas before it was simply inaccessible to us—we had no name for it.

Consider the opposite case. Children are always having psychic experiences and seeing things that adults don't see. But when a child asks a parent about one of these perceptions, the parent says "nothing" or "there's nothing there." The word for all these events, experiences, and perceptions is "nothing," and after a while (unless the child for some reason mistrusts the parent's word, in which case she may well grow up to be considered "unbalanced") "nothing" is exactly what the child begins to see. This is how a culture establishes "reality." Healthy, loved, well-adjusted children learn to see only what the culture considers acceptable, and become blind to all else, while those who escape the training are judged to be deranged. No system works perfectly, of course, and the slippage that occurs, combined with our knowledge of cultures with different realities, provides what we know of the paranormal realm.

II. In the second stage some scientists and intelligent laypersons begin to take the phenomenon seriously. There is heavy debate and discussion on the topic. Certain sightings by respectable persons attract publicity (and ridicule, for these people are the true martyrs of science). Hoaxes occur during this stage. Most important of all, people begin to collect reports and publish them in books. This helps to cure scientific amnesia, forcing people to confront isolated oddities as statistical regularities. In 1819, for example, Ernst Chladni wrote a book on meteorites from antiquity on, which encouraged collectors to come forward with meteorites they had previously hidden or thrown away for fear of ridicule (Heuvelmans, pp. 323–24). The books on the sea serpent by the Goulds, Heuvelmans, and others, and the various books on UFOs, have served the same function. A few scientists begin to conduct investigations during this stage, although they are usually considered a little flaky by their fraternity brothers for doing so. Newspapers begin to report "firsts" every few months, showing that scientists are mere amateurs when it comes to amnesia. For the "first time" "scientists say" the phenomenon is real, or see it themselves, or someone takes a film, or "sonar probes reveal," or whatever. Even the first of these reports isn't really the first, of course, but newspapers like "firsts," and announce them on every possible occasion. Scientific acceptance is always in the process of just beginning until it's virtaully accomplished. Hence the second stage is a long one—usually measured in decades.

III. In the third stage scientists actively assume control over the whole problem, and it becomes defined as a real and mostly dull phenomenon. But for this to happen *the data must be something being looked for because of a theory in some branch of science*. No one will definitively find the Loch Ness Monster or Bigfoot until a scientist decides it's a missing link that will verify some conceptual scheme or other. Then so much money and energy will be put into the search that we can almost say it will be found, like the Piltdown skull, whether it exists or not. Current searches are purely empirical—underfunded and underconceptualized—and probably will net very little. In any case, once "discovered," science will take all the credit, as if it had been on top of the problem from the beginning instead of ignoring or resisting it. The "discovery" will have arisen organically from a problem in scientific theory—not just a result of somebody thinking they saw something. In the last analysis scientific amnesia is always victorious. The same psychologists and psychiatrists who analyzed the public "need" for monsters and UFOs will be filling the archives with dissertations on the psychology of public resistance to new information. (Just as those who spent the early sixties writing learned papers on "Beatlemania" spent the early seventies finding hidden wonders and profundities in the music. The important thing seems to be to prove that you're smarter than the public, whatever the cost in psychic transformation).

It's perhaps a little unfair to place all the blame for resistance to new data on scientists. They behave no differently from other people in this regard. In one or two cases they have even been more receptive than laypeople—this was particularly true of the sea serpent. Even in 1827 a distinguished geologist and chemist said he didn't see how anyone looking at the mass of evidence could question the existence of the sea serpent, and at the end of the century Professor Léon Vaillant of the French Natural History Museum announced that its existence was "no longer in doubt today" (Heuvelmans, pp. 23, 143ff., 172–73, 508ff.). Throughout the nineteenth and twentieth centuries it has been scientists who accepted the sea serpent and journalists who scoffed at it. But since scientists lay *claim* to special open-mindedness this is what we ought reasonably to be able to expect, and we all too seldom find it.

Today the gorilla, the whale shark, the meteorite, and the giant squid have achieved the third stage. The other phenomena discussed in this chapter—Nessie, Bigfoot, the sea serpent, the Yeti, and UFOs, not to mention most types of psychic phenomena like telepathy, psychokinesis, and so on—are still firmly embedded in stage two. Library catalogs tell us that the marine animals are somewhat more accepted than the new primates: in most libraries, the sea serpent and the Loch Ness Monster are cataloged under "fauna," while Bigfoot and Yeti are still under "folklore." These stages of acceptance, by the way, are matched by changing views of the animal itself, which is seen as progressively less threatening (a trend less apparent in the case of UFOs, which have more often been mythologized in a benign, protective direction). Part of this is just familiarity—Norwegians seem never to have feared the sea serpent greatly, nor many Indians the Bigfoot, nor certain Tibetans the Yeti. But the sea serpent was terrifying to most other people until about the end of the seventeenth century, and was believed to be vicious and to snatch men from the decks of ships (Heuvelmans, p. 95).

The history of the gorilla is instructive in this regard, for the gorilla was long considered a mythical beast like the dragon or the unicorn. By fossil record it doesn't exist. It has been *reported* since the fifteenth century, but was regarded as a figment of fevered imaginations. In 1613 a perfectly accurate description of it was given, but to people who had never heard of or seen a large ape it sounded completely monstrous. In 1847 it was "discovered," meaning that scientists finally noticed it. But resistance was strong until the Darwinians triumphed and a strong theoretical interest in apes began to take shape. In 1861 an explorer exhibited a stuffed gorilla and was denounced by scientists as a charlatan and a liar (how little times change!). The mountain gorilla was still unknown in 1900 (Byrne, p. 28; Millar, p. 60; Napier, p. 28). After it was accepted as real it still retained for a time its "traditional monster image: horrendous, aggressive, and sexually rapacious." This diminished as it became better known, but it wasn't until Schaller's study of the mountain gorilla was published in the sixties that the gorilla became widely known as a mild-mannered vegetarian (Napier, pp. 24–5; Schaller). In this respect Bigfoot has a long head start.

SCIENTIFIC IMPERIALISM

This is the way the Fettacenzan empire used to acquire new territory: first, they accused a neighbor of being un-Fettacenzan—an irrefutable slur; second, they attacked and occupied the territory; third, they said it had really been part Fettacenzan all along, which is why it should belong to the empire now.

The Wayward Gate

Science marches in much the same way: (1) sea serpents are fictions; (2) "sea serpents" are now under scientific investigation; (3) the alleged sea monster was just a new species of mammal. Every year a scientist discovers that some old folk remedy contains a drug that "really works." And every decade someone finds evidence that some myth might "really have happened." Now it belongs to science. Scientists have recently "discovered," for example, that animals get frightened just before earthquakes occur—a fact that peasants, novelists, and other superstitious folk have known for centuries.

Translation is a form of imperialism. When Russian scientists decided that the ancient practice of dowsing had something to it after all, they were quick to rename it "the Biophysical Effects Method" (Watson, p. 101). Unlike European immigrants to America, who usually shortened their names when they changed them, scientists typically lengthen the names of acquired territories, in order to mystify the uninitiated.

If you pull pieces out of someone else's car to build your own, it's easy to prove that yours works better.

We tend to accept a "cure" as "real" if a single chemical affects some subsystem of the body in a laboratory. We tend not to accept a cure as real if a whole natural substance balances a whole organism in a natural setting. Doctors say, "This method has not been tested in the laboratory." A rough translation of this statement would go something like this:

"Bring your car around to my garage and let me take it apart and put it together again in my own way. Then I'll tell you if it really works or not. If I can get it to work *my* way, then I'll admit there was some merit in it. In fact I'll keep it and drive it myself. But if it doesn't work the way I put it together, then that will prove that it never worked before, because my way of putting things together is the *only* way to put things together. Therefore it will follow that you're a fraud and a charlatan—that your car is wishful thinking and superstition, and the fact that you drove it in here just a freak accident—a good tail wind maybe. And if you refuse to bring it in I'll *know* you're a fraud because you didn't dare submit your car to my test, which is the only test there is."

Millions of people every year feel themselves to be cured by "quacks." Other millions feel themselves to be cured by licensed physicians. But doctors have the power to define: if a man feels better after going to a doctor he counts as a cure; if he feels better after going to a "quack" he wasn't sick in the first place.

Western medicine has freed doctors from their awkward dependence on the patient's own experience by developing machines that define how ill the patient is no matter how he or she might actually be feeling. This "takes the guesswork out of medicine"—that is, it tightens up the system's self-validating process. If you can't be sure that a given drug will make a person feel better, you can be somewhat more confident that it will produce the proper reading on your apparatus. And no matter how badly the patient may feel after "exhaustive tests," the doctor can assure him or her that "there's nothing wrong with you." That is to say, if the doctor's category system doesn't include it, it isn't a "real" illness—a "real" illness is one doctors know how to treat. Conversely, an illness successfully treated by a "quack" is not "real," but only "psychological."

Many primitive societies believe in magic. When a magic spell doesn't work the benighted savages think it's because it wasn't pronounced correctly. Western doctors believe in the germ theory of disease, and when germ-killing doesn't stop disease, the enlightened doctors think it's because they haven't found the right germs yet.

In one sense the theory that disease is caused by germs was "disproven" before it got off the ground. Skeptical physicians fell all over themselves showing how absurd it was—drinking glasses full of lethal bacilli without ill effect and so on—but nothing can stop an idea whose time has come if it works half the time and seems to simplify the universe. People who didn't get sick from germs were called "immune," while people who got sick *without* germs were called hysterical or hypochondriacal. This protected the theory from all sides; at this point it would have been viable if it never worked at all.

Suppose, for example, I propose the theory that people get depressed from eating peanuts. Since there are a great many depressed folks munching peanuts across the nation my theory is an instant hit. Reactionaries object, however, that they've been gobbling peanuts for decades and live in a state of near-bliss. I *could* argue that they have "asymptomatic depression" which will only show up at autopsy, or on machines I've invented to detect it. But instead I assert that certain people are immune to the depressive effect of peanuts, for reasons that scientific research will make clear as soon as enough money is made available since, as always, we're on the verge of a "breakthrough." As time goes by, however, and peanuts are virtually eliminated from the human diet, we find that people are defiantly getting depressed anyway. But I am equal to the challenge: Any depression not traceable to peanuts I call "pseudo-depression" and pack the patient off to a psychiatrist, secure in the knowledge that the psychiatrist won't be able to do anything for it either.

The most classic example of medical self-validation comes from the field of obstetrics. Doctors have never been able to predict the date of birth: they succeed only about 4 percent of the time, which is just about as good as one could do by drawing the numbers out of hat. Nothing daunted, the obstetrician coolly places the onus for this, not on himself, but on the infant, who is pronounced "early" or "late"! Without a medical degree, the poor child can scarcely rebut the charge, and science has once more triumphed over nature, snatching victory from the very jaws of defeat. This illustrates how easy it is to create reality once you get others to buy into your category system.

Nor have the pediatricians lagged behind. Up until a decade or so ago, when it was conclusively refuted, it was an "accepted scientific fact" that babies couldn't smile until they were at least two months old. Any smiles that appeared prior to that time, therefore, were "gas pains." It's small wonder we live in harsh times: we came into the world accused of unpunctuality, and our first efforts at friendliness were greeted with Alka-Seltzer.

But doctors didn't invent the self-validating theory—it's part of every viable system of knowledge. In the movie *The Conversation* a man makes his living spying on people, bugging their conversations. In his world people have secrets, and it matters whether they're overheard or not. Since this is his way of life it bothers him when he finds he's being bugged himself. He's created a self-validating paranoid reality. It's undeniable that it matters to him whether he's overheard, and he'd be unemployed if some other people didn't care, too. So it matters because it matters. But most of the people I know don't live in that reality, since they're not involved in secrets or in presenting false fronts to the world. Many people whose phones were bugged in the sixties didn't dream of behaving differently when they found out. Being bugged only matters if you participate in the system where it matters.

Traditional nutrition experts laugh at the term "organic," since to them, "everything you eat is just chemicals, anyway." That is, since their category system makes no distinction between "natural" and "synthetic" it doesn't matter. The difference between natural and processed foods are not picked up by their category system; therefore, they're not real. The body is just a piece of machinery unaffected by everything not covered in that system.

Everybody wants their category system to be exhaustive. But if a system were exhaustive it wouldn't be a system. It would be Everything. Nothing would be irrelevant to it, and you wouldn't get to first base lugging a system like that along. You *have* to say some things are irrelevant—that's how you get to say your system is better than someone else's; it excludes more but it still works. Most scientific argument is just a matter of asserting that your set of categories includes more than some other set.

The Wayward Gate

If people who eat organic foods say they feel better, the scientist will say, "it's all in the mind." The food freak might then say, "Yes, that's what I've been trying to tell you all along." But to the scientist, "all in the mind" means "nonexistent."

Andrew Weil points out (*Natural Mind*, pp. 31–32) that since altered states of consciousness have few physiological correlates, Western science is almost totally ignorant of them. "Nonmaterial things are considered inaccessible to direct investigation if not altogether unreal." In the category system of Western science, *touching*, not seeing, is believing.

Scientists are fond of beginning their discussions with statements like: "living beings are chemical machines." Once you swallow a camel like that you're not likely to strain at any gnat they serve up to you later on. Note that they *don't* say "chemical reactions and mechanical processes occur within living beings," which no one could take exception to, but "living beings *are* . . ." Not "among other things," but "*are*," with the implication of "nothing but." Such statements, which we all make at times (this is one, in fact), are imperialistic. They stake out a territory and claim it. They're like a flag that announces possession of part of the universe by some category system. A human being is "a biological machine," or "a holy vessel," or "a nexus of physical forces," or "pure spirit," or "the product of his or her social network," or "a cybernetic message," and so on. If such a statement said "in part" we could hardly disagree— in fact it would be difficult to invent a statement like that with which we *could* disagree. But the "in part" is left out, and the "nothing but" allowed to leak in by innuendo, sometimes helped along by a firm and decisive manner. The prestige of science, in other words, rests on centuries of skillful rhetoric.

Weil observes that "there are really no significant physiological differences between a hypnotized person and an unhypnotized person." Yet a hypnotic subject who is told he's being touched by hot metal will blister, while an unhypnotized one will not. A big difference, but since the scientific category system excludes it, it effectively doesn't exist.

During the stock market collapse in 1973 a billion dollars disappeared in a very short time. One day the money was there—was *real*—then it was no longer real. It simply vanished. When people once again believed in it, it was as real as before. Every day people go to the stock exchange and clap their hands to keep Tinker Bell from dying. And as long as they do—as long as people believe in Tinker Bell or Ma Bell—she will in fact live.

But isn't a chair or table real in a different way? If I deny its reality I'll still fall over it. But I'll fall over Ma Bell, too, if enough other people believe in her. Most chairs are created and destroyed without my being aware of them, and the same may be true of many other realities that we find it convenient, useful, or even necessary to ignore.

When I was a child our bathroom floor was composed of little white hexagonal tiles. I used to drive myself crazy grouping them into different patterns—figure eights, diamonds, flower petals, and so on. Something in the mind rebels against monotony.

All seeing is in a sense a matter of grouping uniform tiles into patterns—patterns that keep slipping away. We learn with excruciating difficulty to hold certain patterns constantly in our vision. We might, for example, learn from our culture only to see flower petals when we look at such tiles, until finally we can't see them any other way. To *un*-learn this would then be harder than it was to learn it in the first place. That's what Carlos Castaneda's "apprenticeship" was all about. Without a theory you couldn't see anything. To see is to conceptualize, to conceptualize is to control. Seeing is creating reality.

THE ONE BIAS

By now it should be apparent that the biases of science are all one bias—a bias against anything that threatens the

The Wayward Gate

dominion of rational control and the power of the human ego. Myths are particularly frightening to scientists because they create reality differently from the way science does it. It's not only a different reality but a richer, more compact, more emotionally compelling one—a dangerous competitor. Science is often boring, like a speaker who drones on without expressing any feeling. (Myths can be boring, too, of course, but only when we approach them as scientists—reading an ethnographer's collection of Navaho folktales, for example. It's the difference between making love and reading about it in a foreign language.)

There's a festival going on in the street outside the lecture hall; heads are turning, people in the back are drifting out. Science has to fight to keep its audience, yet without losing its fussy integrity, which is its most endearing trait.

It's a tough battle.

There are two ways of losing that integrity: trying to out-captivate (thereby violating the rule of cautious skepticism), and trying to ignore (thereby violating the rule of open-mindedness). Science usually slips into the second one: "There is no festival going on in the street. This is a myth, and if I have time, I'll explain it to you."

One solution is to produce a facsimile of the festival, inside the hall. It's like a film review—not quite as good as seeing the movie but it gives you a feeling of superiority, which is better than nothing. The festival is translated, explained, interpreted. A myth is no longer a living narrative, an alternative reality. It's just a lie. "The festival means something other than what it says." It can be made meaningful through "symbolic interpretation," which is a way of cutting a myth into manageable pieces. It doesn't much matter how you do it—any way you slice up a pussycat it's still dead. Interpretation takes the threat away by allowing us to view the myth as a collection of disguised parts that we can then reassemble to fit our mechanized thought patterns. Unfortunately, it's all so arbitrary that we can't agree about the symbols. Andrew Lang said myths represented celestial movements; James Frazer said vegetative yearnings. Confronted with a church steeple, Freud said it was a penis. Confronted with a penis, Jung said it was God's way of saying that Carl Jung is a very special person. I'm sure that all of them are right. A tree, for example, is carbon, and photosynthesis, and branching, and reproduction, and phototropism, and sap, and wood, and a million other things. And also it's a festival dressed up as a tree.

THE DRAGON'S
VILLAGE

Once there was a village on the banks of a great river. Every few years this river overflowed and flooded the village, with great damage to property and occasional loss of life. One year a particularly bad flood completely destroyed the village and almost half the inhabitants drowned. The survivors were forced to seek higher ground and remain there for several months before the flood waters receded.

During this time the villagers became accustomed to the new site. Located on the southern plateau of a small mountain—the only high ground for fifty miles around—it was protected by the mountain from the bitter north winds of winter yet open to the cooling westerly breezes in summer. It overlooked their old home just a few miles away and was easily defended against invaders. The air was pleasant and invigorating.

Tied to the river and its fertile banks by economic necessity, the villagers had never considered an alternative site until now; but they soon realized that the building of one good road would give them access to their old farmlands, while the sunny slopes of the mountain would permit diversification in the form of orchards, vineyards, and livestock, to buttress them against the effects of future floods. After a few months they decided to stay.

The only drawback of the new site didn't make its appearance immediately. One day, soon after their decision had been made, a fledgling dragon flopped across the sky and coasted into a cave near the summit of the mountain. Apparently the dragon also liked what he saw, and decided to make his home there. Once a week he would plunge down upon the bedraggled village and seize a villager or one of the animals, which he would carry off to his cave and devour.

Meanwhile, plans were going ahead for building a permanent village. Each evening the villagers gathered together and discussed particulars: laying out streets, arranging house locations, digging wells, building a road to the river, constructing walls for defense, and so on.

There were lively arguments. People fought over who would live nearest the spring, or nearest the road, or on the highest ground. And when it came to building, some argued for permanence, others for speed, some for beauty, others for utility. Most of the debate concerned priorities, since only a limited amount of time could be spared from the desperate problem of obtaining food from the ravaged land. Some felt that the road was most important since it would provide vital access to their farms and river transport. Others pushed for defense, worried that neighboring villages might decide to follow their example, and come to contest the ground. Some felt that their temporary housing had become insupportable, and so on.

Every now and then someone would say, "And what about the dragon?"

"Look, you can't do anything about the dragon," the others would reply. "We have enough to worry about with the problems we can solve."

The villagers worked hard, and in a decade had built a strong, prosperous, and almost invulnerable hill town. Their diversified economy and invigorating environment enriched and energized them. The broad geographic out-

The Wayward Gate

look enlarged their economic vision as well, and they came to rely more and more on trade, profiting by their relative immunity from flood to reduce their neighbors to economic dependency. This was quickly coupled with political subjugation, since the villagers, in their mountain stronghold, were able to offer themselves as the "protectors" of flatland dwellers for miles around.

In the meantime, however, the dragon's depredations presented a constant threat of depopulation. Livestock were easily replaced by appropriating those of the lowlanders, but it was more difficult to replace people. The unrelenting horror of their position developed in the mountain folk a warrior mentality, and they began to devote all their time to fighting and raiding—feeling they had nothing to lose since death was inevitable anyway. This made them fearless and ferocious warriors, the terror of the land. It also added to their feeling of aristocratic superiority, already swollen by economic and altitudinal advantage. The dragon was a closely-guarded secret and the constant funneling of fresh life into the mountain's vortex contributed much to the superstitious awe with which it became surrounded.

At first the villagers took prisoners (often with some pretense that they were engaged in law enforcement), bound them, and left them for the dragon to carry off. But after a few years the dragon became bored with this effortless diet and began passing over the prisoners in favor of the more refractory mountaineers. It then became necessary to conscript a warrior from the flatlands every time one of their own was lost. This was done with much ceremony and was considered a great honor to those chosen, although they were never again seen by their loved ones. The existence of the dragon was revealed to the draftees as part of their initiation ceremony.

This situation remained relatively stable for several decades, but ultimately the forays of the dragon—whose nutritional requirements increased as he grew to adulthood—began to take their toll. The more the dragon bled the mountaineers, the more the mountaineers bled the flatlands, until the economic structure they had built with such energy became top-heavy and collapsed. The land fell into decay, the warriors into random banditry, and the population of the entire area began rapidly to decline. The dragon, sleek and splendid, soon exhausted his local food supply and was forced to fly farther and farther afield to nourish himself, until one day, almost a century after the mountain village had first appeared, the dragon, perched on the summit of the mountain and surveying the surrounding landscape, was unable to detect a single sign of life.

"Time to move on," he thought to himself, and reluctantly began to prepare his departure. Before leaving, he constructed on the summit of the mountain an enormous monument of human and animal bones, which he dedicated to the industrious villagers who had nourished him from childhood and invested so much energy in his project of renewing the earth.

Like all dragon-works, the monument still stands.

CHAPTER 4

THE RANDOM
GAME

Step on a crack,
Break your mother's back.
—Traditional

Alas for the careful sidewalk-jumper: Some say life is all cracks—that there are no free spaces where our acts don't impinge on others. "Thou canst not stir a flower without troubling of a star" (Thompson, p. 187).

Our thoughts roll along grooves provided by the culture we live in, and our culture is a road culture. The way we categorize our experience is constrained in part by the automobile. The world to us consists of roads and spaces between roads. Life moves along the roads and stands still in between. And because most of our experience in moving through space is in vehicles, following a limited number of roads, tracks, channels, or pathways, we tend to believe firmly that there is such a thing as a *non*path.

This belief in nonpaths is reinforced by the performance industry. The show is sometimes on, sometimes off. Life on stage is framed by the curtain—on television by commercials and station breaks. Outside those frames stage-life stops. There are pauses.

The Random Game

But in life there are no station breaks. What we think of as a "break" is simply a change in direction—a side path. And what we think of as a nonpath is simply one we haven't yet taken. There are no empty spaces.

Perhaps this seems frivolous. We can look at the world as having blanks, not having blanks, or being all blanks, and it won't spin any faster or slower. At this level of abstraction it really doesn't matter. Yet how we think has an effect on how we act. When we see the world we move in as seamless, all interconnected, and continuous with ourselves, we behave differently than when we imagine empty spaces, pauses, and separate compartments.

Like most middle-class Americans, for example, I've lived the bulk of my life in a family, in a couple, or alone. Being "social" has meant going out into a well-defined setting with time boundaries on it. I go out; I come home. To some extent, being out is being "on," while being home is being relaxed, "myself." I have both a public and a private existence.

For poor people throughout history most of life has been public and social. Centuries ago, most people of all classes awoke in a group and went to sleep in a group. There were few private spaces, pauses, or compartments: All passions, quarrels, jealousies, blows, caresses, and copulations were more or less in the public domain. It may be an exaggeration to say, as Philippe Ariès does, that privacy was invented by the French in the eighteenth century, but it helps put modern American experience in perspective.

In such a world one can't imagine nonpaths. One doesn't stand in isolation and then "reach out" to people—they're already there. All the world is *truly* a stage—there's no backstage, no offstage.

And there's no such thing as "random error" or "chance."

CHAOS AND COINCIDENCE

You can learn from any repetitive experience—being a cashier in a supermarket, working on an assembly line, driving a cab, or going to graduate school. It allows you to see trends that are hidden from the victim of an enriched life. Some say that graduate education merely gives you the ability to talk longer without saying what you mean, but I think there's more to it than that—I certainly learned as much in graduate school as I learned from being an unskilled laborer. One of the things I learned, for example, was the riches that could be hidden between the cracks of a computer's announcement that two variables were unrelated to each other.

The issue may seem a little technical, but it's really very simple. Suppose I want to find out the relation between affection and anger in human beings. Then let's make the unlikely assumption that I find some way—not completely fatuous—of "measuring" these feelings. What would I expect to find?

Well, first I would expect a negative relation, because we don't usually feel anger and affection at the same time. Aren't love and hate opposites? On the other hand, I would expect a positive relation, because we ordinarily get most angry at people we care about, not at the indifferent millions. Some people arouse intense feelings of all kinds, others nothing at all.

Now, if my expectations were correct, what would I get? Since plus and minus added together make zero, the well-trained social scientist would announce that there's *no* relation between anger and affection and move on to something else.

The example may seem absurd, but it points up the bias in science toward unrelatedness—for after all, the growth of science was wedded to the growth of individualistic thought. Science is like a court of law in which everything must be presumed to be separate, independent, and unrelated to anything else until proven otherwise. Students are constantly warned against finding relationships that are spurious—think how much encysted energy has been devoted to building dikes of caution against that advancing

The Random Game

sea of interconnectedness. But who worries about missing complex relationships that are actually there? In keeping with the capitalistic prejudices of science, it's taken for granted that the personal ambition of the scientist will push her to leave no stone unturned until she finds the relation she's looking for.

Since at some level we know that everything's related to everything else, why do we play this funny game of pretending that it isn't, so that we can later "prove," bit by bit, that it is? It's something children do: "pretend I don't know anything at all and you have to teach me how to crawl and walk and say everything." Wouldn't it be simpler if we started with the assumption that everything stands in an orderly relation to everything else, and then tried to prove the existence of little pockets of chaos and unrelatedness?

And how did the game of assuming a chaotic universe ever get started? Was it accidental? A random error? According to the conventions of science we have to assume that and then prove it false. To do otherwise is unscientific.

The first rule of all closed systems is that they can only be questioned in accordance with their own rules. And since their rules always force us to validate the system, the system can never be effectively challenged. But since I'm interested in putting scientific conventions in perspective, I don't feel obliged to operate within its self-validating etiquette. The chaos assumption was *not* accidental, but exists for the same reason that governments like to monopolize weapons, It's a way of saying, "There is only one order—ours; if you destroy it, you'll be left with nothing but disorder. There is no such thing as an alternative order."

I have the same uneasiness about that statement whether it's made by a police state or the scientific establishment. There are many kinds of order, many cultural systems, and many systems of reality—not just the one that scientists call the "real world."

When a WASP first encounters a new ethnic tradition he

tends to see the ethnics as failing to live up to his standards—failing to think, talk, or behave properly. He doesn't think of them as conforming to an *alternative* set of standards (liberal condescension comes only through education: a little anthropology, a TV ethnic special—a "white" paper). In other words, doing things some other way is just failing to measure up to *our* way. It's misbehavior, error.

Science uses the same device. If something happens occasionally that doesn't fit the conventions of science it's "random error." But science is quantitative—you're supposed to perk up when things repeat themselves. What happens if something unsciencelike *repeats* itself?

That's "coincidence."

What's a coincidence? *A coincidence is a trend we've decided not to take seriously.* In practice, it's evidence that threatens the traditions of science—that suggests another order. The word "coincidence" is a way of saying, "this is not another order (another etiquette)—this is merely disorder (bad behavior)."

Suppose we say, "all fruits are oranges." Every orange that comes along is then felt, tested, and added to the pile of treasures. But when plums, pears, and pineapples appear they all get tossed in the wastebasket marked "non-fruit," and are treated with contempt: "See what a hodgepodge of unorangeness we have here—no order, no trends."

Then someone says, "But look here, I see a bunch of purple things that look alike; maybe that's a trend." The reply is quick: "A coincidence. You start mucking about in that wastebasket and people will think you've gone round the bend."

Donald Menzel, the most fanatical of the anti-UFO scientists, says: "An open mind does not mean credulity or a suspension of the logical faculties that are man's most valuable asset" (quoted in Vallée, pp. vi–vii). I have a perverse affection for those statements: "Liberty doesn't mean license," "freedom doesn't mean anarchy," and so on, although I'm not sure Menzel used logic to decide that a Detroit assembly line was a greater asset than a Rembrandt. However you slice the statement it comes out, "Oranges only!"

A NEW SCIENCE

But suppose we start with the assumption that everything's related and nothing happens by chance. How would it work? We would have to accept every relation as self-evident until proven otherwise, and if someone claimed that any two events in the universe had nothing whatever to do with each other he or she would have to prove it. This may sound ridiculous but no more so than trying to reach a complex conclusion the traditional way—looking at two or three variables at a time. Conventional science starts with a silly assumption and then racks up a lot of little victories proving tiny pieces of it to be wrong. It's a kind of featherbedding. The new way would start with a reasonable assumption and have the very devil of a time proving any of it wrong.

In most ways the second assumption is as useless and absurd as the first, but it does have one advantage—it would force science to abandon its current disputatious style and concentrate on the *quality* of various influences. No self-deceiving little victories, no spurious "proofs." It would liberate science from its ruinous dependence on quantity. We would never count anything, but only look at the shape of things. This would make for a very different science—more contemplative, less frenzied and pushy. More scientists would be motivated by aesthetic appreciation—fewer by competition. There would be less concern with power, control, and manipulation. To count things you have to deal with parts, since a whole is uncountable. Parts you can manipulate, count, rearrange. Wholes you can only look at, describe, and admire.

It would also make for a different kind of technology—one less concerned with trying to push the environment around. People often say, for example, that there's no difference between the technology of the sailboat and that of the engine since both harness the forces of nature; and at one time I was swayed by this argument, although it always *felt* wrong. In recent years I've come to trust such feelings—they always tell you that the logician's category-system is leaving out some difference that matters to you, even if it doesn't matter to the logician. The difference here is in the attitude, which science usually ignores. In sailing and skiing the pleasure of mastery is balanced with the joy of being in tune with the elements. There's as much pleasure in the *dependence* on nature as there is in extracting movement from it. But the pleasure in a motor is one of pure mastery. Motors always make noise, for example, and that tells you something about the feelings and attitudes that went into it. Something was more important than sensory pleasure—nobody would invent a chair or a dish that smelled bad or made horrible noises—why were motors invented noisy? How could they possibly be considered complete or successful inventions with this glaring defect? Unless, of course, the aggressive, hostile, assaultive sound actually served to express some impulse of the owner.

The belief in randomness serves one other function, having to do with creativity and knowledge. I often find that I write or say things before I'm aware that I "know" them, and I sometimes think that "learning" is just finding out in a conscious, piecemeal way what we already know. Some people believe that in the "unused" portions of our brains is stored the means of access to all knowledge—that at some level we know everything and can perceive everything but our brains forget and our senses shut it out to protect our sanity. People clearly know things they don't know they know—most great discoveries were "known" first and only later "figured out." People seem to get a lot of information that doesn't go through the senses at all. Some of the more puzzling psychic phenomena, like clairvoyance and precognition, could be explained by assuming that some

The Random Game

people have defective valves that occasionally leak this universal knowledge. In any case, the belief in randomness is a powerful device for shoring up this self-imposed ignorance.

MAKING THINGS LOOK RIGHT

But now comes a harder pill to swallow (the image of Groucho Marx as Dr. Hackenbush comes irresistibly to mind). Suppose I think I see something—a shape. It startles me. I look again, and see that it's only a shadow, or a cat, or a curtain moved by the wind. In other words, it's an "error." The apparent plum was just an orange with mold on it.

Note that I've used a scientific procedure: I recheck my findings and they fail to replicate. The first time I see a spook, the second time a shadow. I choose one over the other and feel quite "rational" in so doing. But at the risk of encouraging anarchy I must ask why my first perception isn't as good as my second?

One obvious answer is that the second perception was more careful. A "closer look." If I look long and hard it's like looking ten times. But I mistrust that closer look. It masquerades as objectivity and empiricism and all that, but I don't think it was disinterested. I think it's a firm believer in law and order.

I look in order to "make sense out of things." That is, to make things look usual. I look *carefully*—to maintain rational control over my environment. People who want to experience other realities squint, stare, and bulge their eyes to "distort" their vision—anything to escape the overwhelming bias of normal perception.

Most people are pretty good at making odd things look conventional. Allen Funt, of *Candid Camera* fame, used to make his living presenting people with what could easily have passed for "supernatural" situations. But with dreary, sometimes comical regularity, they would "see" the contrived event in some banal way—twist it into ordinariness,

109

deny its crazy, earth-shattering, mind-boggling significance.

I don't know why we worry about people being biased *toward* the "supernatural" when it's so clearly the last thing most people want to experience. Every textbook on perception tells us that we distort what we see in favor of what we expect to see. Why don't we ever worry about the more common bias *away* from the unknown or "supernatural"—toward the "normal," the conventional, the material—when this bias is so much more powerful, so omnipresent, so suffocating?

A newspaper article (*San Francisco Chronicle*, July 8, 1976) once recorded interpretations by "experts"—psychologists, psychiatrists, and anthropologists—of the public's "need for monsters." Needless to say, the experts *don't* feel called upon to interpret their own need to live in a world in which nothing unusual can occur. Consider, for example, that one mission of the psychiatrist is to eliminate bizarre behavior from the face of the earth.

Let's go back to my "shadow." At first glance I'm frightened. I look again and am calmed. I give greater weight to my "closer look" than to my fear. Most people who see a UFO use the same procedure—it's when they look again and *still* can't make it look like something ordinary that they really begin to take notice. In some cases they will continue for hours to deny the evidence of their senses. Who knows how many UFOs have never been perceived as such at all?

The "closer look" makes good sense—who wants to go around jumpy and scared? And suppose one were to get a glimpse of another order of reality—wouldn't that be even more frightening? But if I didn't see what I thought I saw—if it was only a shadow, a mistake—my startle isn't valid. A sensible procedure. But is it science?

Science believes in mistakes. I'm a skeptic myself. "Error" is a pretty big wastebasket, and I have the feeling there's a lot of interesting stuff in it. On the other hand, I trust my fear mechanism a lot. More than I trust the idea of "mistake." Like Freud, I don't really think there *are* any mistakes, although pretending there are saves a lot of time and stupid conversation.

Why would I be frightened of "nothing"?

It may be true that what I saw was a shadow or a cat or a curtain, but it seems unlikely that that's what frightened me. Our eyes and brains tend to *ignore* familiar stimuli, not jump at them. What if something unfamiliar was riding on that familiar stimulus—something that opened "the crack between the worlds"? For everyday purposes I'm better off ignoring it. But for learning I might be better off ignoring the cat.

An objection: when Freud ruled out the wastebasket by saying mistakes were caused by wishes he was acknowledging the existence of another order of reality; but he said it was an *inner* order. His system says I saw a cat and was motivated at that particular moment to make it look like something else so I could surprise and startle myself. But who draws the line between inner and outer, and where is it drawn? Suppose I argue that it doesn't exist—that to be in touch with a strange inner is to be in touch with a strange outer? And why pick a cat or a curtain to scare myself with? Is it just random?

It all seems to rest on accidents: All of science depends on believing in the existence of accidents. Yet the progress of science depends upon denying the accidentalness of more and more of those accidents.

Perhaps next time I startle myself with a "mistake" I won't call in the "Truth Squad" to make it look all right. Maybe instead of making the first glance go away I'll follow the fear and try to make the first glance stay. Yet I know from experience how hard it is to deter my own will from its accustomed rounds. Sometimes, for example, when I'm staring absently and thinking of something else I suddenly can see the auras of objects. Yet the moment I become

The Wayward Gate

aware of this my eyes dart into focus and the auras disappear, and no amount of effort will bring them back. I have to slowly relax my vision and become inattentive once more in order to recapture them. With practice I can hold them for quite a while, but only if I can sustain a curious lack of focus. The moment I try to think about or examine the images—the mere *awareness* of a budding willful scientific urge in my body makes them flick off like a light switch.

After the "closer look" we say, "my eyes were playing tricks on me." But when was the trick played, the first time or the second time? What if saying "it's only a shadow" is the trick?

What if they're *both* tricks?

CHAPTER 5

IS NATURE HONEST?

When man yielded . . . to the mysterious temptation . . . the
universe, originally fluid and the servant of his spirit, became
solid, and crashed down upon him, overwhelming him beneath
its . . . dead mass. . . . —Arthur Machen

If we're to take psychic phenomena as we would any other
body of data we have to account for a certain capriciousness about them. They just don't seem to follow the laws of
ordinary reality. One day things "work" as a Western scientist might expect them to; the next day they don't.

Almost all major forms of psychic talent have been tested
under rigorous conditions and demonstrated successfully—telepathy, clairvoyance, precognition, psychokinesis,
eyeless sight, dowsing, and so on. Most of them have also
failed miserably, even under *less* rigorous conditions.
There have even been brilliant successes and conspicuous
failures during the same test. A person will reproduce four
pictures received telepathically and miss completely on a
fifth. Has Nature turned whimsical?

The telepathic subject Basil Shackleton provides a good
illustration of this. Shackleton had achieved very high
scores in a precognition experiment. That is, he was able to
guess, far beyond chance, what card would be transmitted
telepathically *before* the sender looked at it. He was then
subjected to another series of experiments and scored so
high that, as Watson remarks, "one could not get a result

like this by chance even if the entire population of the world had tried the experiment every day since the beginning of the tertiary period, sixty million years ago" (p. 226). These high scores were produced consistently over a year's time—not the result of a single freak event. Furthermore, a third series of tests, using a different experimental procedure, produced results almost as good. Yet there were occasions when Shackleton performed no better than chance, and this is true of most telepathic subjects. Only a few experiments in telepathy and psychokinesis have been replicated (Murphy, pp. 126–155, 181).

Some of this may be just our ignorance about the entire subject matter. We know very little about the forces that influence psychic abilities favorably or unfavorably. We know that attitude has something to do with it: not only do people who accept the possibility of paranormal events achieve higher scores than do skeptics—the skeptics actually score consistently *lower* than chance, which suggests that they're actively inhibiting their own psychic abilities. On the other hand, confidence alone is not enough: Shackleton was convinced that he was clairvoyant as well as telepathic, but his efforts in that direction were a resounding failure (Murphy, pp. 83–103, 140).

We also know that some people are more gifted than others, that boredom and fatigue take a heavy toll, that relationships are important, that mood and feelings play a major role. Most laboratory experiments on psychic abilities are extremely monotonous, for example, and J. B. Rhine found "a strange tendency to produce strings of successes whenever the subject started a new task." Even turning to a new page would start a success surge, followed by rapid decline. In psychokinesis experiments, in which subjects tried to affect falling dice, successes were concentrated in the first half of the first run of each series (cited in Murphy, pp. 158, 167–168).

Psychics have always claimed that a skeptical environment diluted their powers, but it may be a simpler matter than skepticism. A series of studies on ESP in schoolchildren found that the children who scored highest on a clair-voyance test were those who liked and were liked by the teacher. Those who had a poor relationship with the teacher scored significantly *below* chance on the tests (Murphy, pp. 101–119). Scientists are understandably scornful when psychics don't perform well under laboratory conditions, or do so only with friendly investigators, but since hostility has been proved to affect ESP scores it's hardly "scientific" to ignore this issue—or to disregard the fact that what feels homelike and safe to the scientists may not feel that way to others. How many scientists would feel comfortable at a séance?

It's not hard to understand why hostility should have a dampening effect on ESP. You don't leave your door unlocked in a high-crime neighborhood. Once the telepathic "receiver" is open to input there's no way of screening out bad ones and letting in only good or neutral ones. One out of every four persons is apparently susceptible to telepathic influence without even knowing it: concentrating on the name of a loved one at a distance will affect that person's blood pressure if he or she has this kind of sensitivity. And efforts to transmit bursts of emotion telepathically have been all too successful, producing choking fits, nausea, and headaches over great distances. As Watson points out, these data force us to reëxamine our ideas about witchcraft: You don't need to be a believer to die of voodoo death—just telepathically sensitive and in a close personal relation with someone of malevolent intent (Watson, pp. 233, 251). Scientists who keep their doors closed at all times should be tolerant of those who only try to shut out people wanting to humiliate them.

Yet scientists can hardly be expected to be attuned to such issues, since science is founded on the suppression of feeling, on the denial of motivation, and on the need to control. People who function this way themselves aren't likely to pay much attention to emotional issues in their subjects, unless these are explicitly called to their attention. This is even true with psychological researchers, who are often comically blind to any reactions and motives of their subjects other than those being directly studied.

In other words, there's a basic conflict between science and the paranormal about the importance of motive and feeling. Telepathy tends to come into play when there is high emotion and a strong interpersonal relationship, while science is supposed to take place in an atmosphere of emotional and interpersonal neutrality (spiced, perhaps, with a little competitiveness). Watson makes the point that a communication channel like telepathy is needed primarily for urgent messages. Mild feelings "can be communicated in the usual leisurely way by normal channels, such as greeting cards." Physiological measurements of Nelya Mikhailova, the famous Russian psychokinesis subject, showed her to be in a state of "controlled rage" when performing such unusual feats as separating the white from the yolk of an egg in a saline solution six feet away (Watson, pp. 138, 231). Science is hostile to emotion and the paranormal world is *all* emotion.

Indeed, psychic powers seem to be enhanced when the rational control that the scientific tradition requires is relaxed. Alcohol, sleep, meditation—anything that slows the busy, categorizing, inhibiting part of the brain seems to help. Women, who are under less pressure to stunt the emotional, spontaneous aspect of mind, score better than men on psychokinesis tests, and children are particularly gifted. But the desire of scientists to control the *external* world leads them to tighten *internal* controls as well, and this affects experimental procedure. Scientists like cut-and-dried situations with limited choices—decks of cards, numbers, dice, letters—a prescription for boredom. "The subject is not free to let his mind roam and think of anything he likes, because there is no way of scoring his success" (Murphy, pp. 60–63, 169; Watson, p. 160).

There's no malice in all this—it's just a fundamental difference in taste. Scientists want reason and order. They would prefer a world in which nothing paranormal or turbulent ever occurred, and they create one around them that minimizes the possibility of such occurrences. That some have nonetheless managed to penetrate the resistant screen of the laboratory setting is perhaps more miraculous than the events themselves. As Watson says, trying to study telepathy in a laboratory is "like trying to study the behavior of a dead animal" (Watson, p. 235).

Psychic research has also been hampered by the concessions to incredulity it has to make in its procedures. Some of the artificiality it struggles with comes from the extraordinary guarantees against fraud that are demanded—guarantees that would never be asked of the ordinary psychology student trying to get a degree, or the junior biology professor bucking for tenure. The ways in which people are imagined to be capable of faking the experiments are often more awe-inspiring than mere psychokinesis or telepathy.

Yet when all this has been said, there remains an element of willfulness about the results of psychic research. Who do things work so dramatically and consistently at times and fail so utterly at others? As Watson observes, "nobody has yet managed to produce telepathic contact that works every time and on demand" (p. 232).

SCIENCE AND REGULARITY

Einstein once said that Nature might be coy at times but never tries to fool you. This seems to be true within the game that scientists play, but when it comes to the psychic realm the great goddess often shows a sly side. In fact, when we look a little closer, the honesty and simplicity of Nature—even within the domain of science—becomes a little less certain. Our impression of Nature's candor, after all, is drawn from the annals of science itself, and as Charles Fort points out, much of that history is the purest wishful thinking—written to convey an impression of steady and certain progress, and leaving out events that don't fit that polished image (see *New Lands*, pp. 9–79).

Science, after all, is the study of regularities. It therefore tends to downplay or even discredit apparent "ir-regularities." Now behavior that's disapproved by authorities tends to become secret and hidden, so that those same authorities may come to believe it doesn't exist. To a scientist an "irregularity" is simply an untreated regularity—like a raw diamond waiting to be cut and polished. Either it's a regularity in disguise—a fact for which the explanatory theory hasn't yet been invented—or else it's just a statistical abnormality, which isn't irregular at all. According to the random theory, we can expect an outlandish event to occur every so often by chance, so we don't need to concern ourselves with it. Nature, in this view, is regularly irregular, and hence quite tame. "Irregularity" is just a name for the unknown, rapidly retreating before the inexorable advance of science. For a scientist, an event can never be more than temporarily bizarre—a horse waiting to be tamed. If you define the irregular out of existence it becomes a little hard to recognize.

Fort has an interesting discussion of what he calls "witchcraft in science"—important breakthroughs and discoveries that were announced with great fanfare and then simply evaporated:

There is scarcely an annual meeting of any prominent scientific association at which are not made, by eminent doctors and professors, announcements of great discoveries that, by long and careful experimentation, constructive and eliminative tests, and guards against all possible sources of error, have been established. A year or so later, these boons to suffering humanity are forgotten.

His examples embrace: (1) apparently successful efforts to synthesize food from inorganic materials, (2) demonstrations of the inheritance of acquired characteristics, (3) cancer cures, and (4) techniques of rejuvenation. The "deluded" discoverers included such eminent scientists as Pavlov (*Wild Talents*, pp. 165–69).

Some of these announcements faded away without embarrassment to their authors, but others were immediately challenged and in some cases led to public disgrace. One scientist committed suicide. A frequent excuse of the err-

Is Nature Honest?

ing scientists was that they had been deceived by an assistant.

Fort is skeptical of this plague of treacherous assistants, and of the ability of experienced scientists to study something for years, re-check the findings repeatedly, and still make such a blunder. His remarks about cancer research are even more true now than when he made them fifty years ago:

The story of cancer-cure announcements is a record of abounding successes in the treatment of cancerous dogs, cats, chickens, rats, mice, and guinea pigs—followed by appeals to the public for funds. . . . Look over the record of cancerous growths that, according to triumphant announcements have been absorbed, or stopped, in mice and guinea pigs, and try to think that all were only deliberate deceptions.

Fort's argument is that what scientists thought happened in the laboratory really did happen—that mice were cured of cancer, that dogs got fat on synthetic foods, that old rats became young, that Pavlov's trained mice had offspring that were more easily conditioned. All just cases of sorcery in the laboratory.

Leaving Fort's puckishness aside, we still need to pay more attention to these unique and unrepeatable events. Some of them are clearly a result of the experimenter's wishful bias, but to say this is to explain nothing at all. How can such results be obtained just by wishing?

The psychologist Robert Rosenthal has devoted his career to studying experimenter bias—showing again and again that researchers tend to get the experimental results they expect, both from human and animal subjects. Scientists like this sort of research—it supports their preoccupation with caution and control—but they pay no attention whatever to its implications. They think it just shows how rigorous you have to be with your procedure, but actually it shows nothing of the kind: the most carefully controlled studies are as much affected as the slovenly ones. Indeed, the ability of experimenters to influence their results is nothing short of miraculous—in some cases one has to assume some sort of psychokinesis—but this has attracted extraordinarily little attention. One study, for example, showed that when rats were randomly designated "bright" or "dull" the "bright" rats performed better in mazes. The same results held even for worms (Rosenthal, 1966, pp. 158–79). But how were these worms influenced? I'm fascinated that scientists can treat such a bizarre event as reassuring, since it assaults the very foundations of their discipline.

Scientific experiments done properly are always supposed to come out the same way, and laypersons assume that this is the case with "established" knowledge. But it isn't so. Every once in a while they don't. Chemical reactions, for example, "occasionally prove idiosyncratic and go off in the wrong direction or refuse to take place at all" (Watson, p. 32). Sometimes this is a result of some uncontrolled factor the experimenter has failed to take into account: lunar influence, psychic influence—Watson's book is full of examples of these unexpected effects. And sometimes the experimenter may even have ignored something more mundane. But even allowing for much that we don't know, how can we be so certain that Nature is utterly lawful? After all, the evidence we get to support this view is completely biased. It all comes from people whose whole lives are predicated on that assumption. Most scientists will insist (with rather undue melodrama, I think—science can stand on its achievements alone) that to believe anything else is to throw all of science out the window. How, then, can we trust the evidence they provide to support this assumption?

Consider, for example, what happens to a young science student who carries out a classic experiment and fails to get the "right" answer. Her first reaction, if she's properly trained, will probably be: "I must have done something wrong." If she doesn't discover a mistake she'll simply assume her own ignorance or incompetence and let the matter drop—the way we do when we lose something and never find it. Meanwhile, she'll have to keep doing it until it "comes out right."

In other words, an experiment must work every time *only until it's accepted, at which point negative results will never again be recognized as such.* The medieval alchemists used to perform the same process over and over again, with the firm and to us inexplicable expectation that sooner or later something different would happen. What they were engaged in is still unknown to us, since few of the people who know anything about the alchemists know anything about science, although respect for the alchemists has lately been increasing. In any case, they had a very different way of looking at the world, and were far more respectful of statistically deviant events.

People tend to discover what they already "know" to be true. A conversation between a modern scientist and an alchemist would probably be like the conversations that men used to have about the "true nature of women." Kindly, paternal men would say that all women just wanted to be loved and taken care of like little girls. Hostile, cold men would insist that women all wanted to be treated roughly—that they would love any man who abused and ignored them. Both were making absolutely correct observations about the women they encountered, since obviously they would only attract the types they described. Any man who makes any other generalization about women will be correct in the same way. The folly of all such statements is merely that they *ignore the effect of your own motives on the reality you experience.* And scientists are particularly vulnerable to this failing because they're *by training insensitive to their own motives or feelings while engaged in their work.* Since the idea of a completely lawful Nature is precious to scientists they aren't very attuned to data that contradict it, and as long as the theory seems to work it may be wise to stick with it.

Still, we ought to prepare the ground for disillusionment, for the history of science has not been as it's usually pictured: the slow, systematic advance of a great army, inexorably conquering more and more territory which, once taken, is never yielded. On the contrary, it's full of defeated and discredited theories that suddenly rise up and rout the conquerors a century or two later. The scorned reactionaries of one era become, in a later one, the misunderstood heroes who were wise before their time. Furthermore, as Joseph Chilton Pearce points out, "science is full . . . of cases where perfectly workable, fruitful productions have been organized on grounds later found fallacious" (*Cosmic Egg*, p. 86; see also *New Lands*, passim). Heuvelmans remarks that the history of the sea serpent "seems to have been invented by an unusually mischievous imp," since those who believed in it were wrong about what it was while those who didn't believe "ought to have been able to guess its nature" (pp. 214–15).

Charles Fort argues that astronomers "squirmed into prestige and emolument by shooting at marks, disregarding their misses, and recording their hits with unseemly advertisement" (*New Lands*, pp. 9–10). He lays waste the popular stories of planets having turned up right where some astronomer predicted, showing that (a) when such predictions were being made other astronomers were predicting various other possibilities, so that someone *had* to be right, (b) many of the allegedly correct predictions were in fact misidentified and way off the mark, (c) accidental "discoveries" were later rewritten as predicted finds, and (d) for every "correct" prediction there were dozens that came to nothing. He is particularly devastating on the subject of comets, giving pages of cases in which old comets failed to appear when expected, or new comets receded when they were said to be advancing, and so on. After reducing astronomy to a shambles, he goes on to recount the many strange sights seen by astronomers but ignored by their colleagues, using these data to underpin his own theories, which are so ridiculous we can't tell for sure whether he means them seriously (*New Lands*, pp. 9–79).

But about the sights themselves, and the ways we create

Is Nature Honest?

our own realities—putting in what we want and leaving out what we must—Fort is quite serious. *New Lands* is a compendium of the kinds of facts that scientists have gathered as individuals and pointedly ignored as a group—lights and changing shapes on the moon, dark bodies crossing the sun, UFOs, and so on. Fort points out that although the astronomer Newcomb had dismissed such events, on the grounds that only amateurs had ever seen them, while eminent astronomers never did, many astronomers— *including the very notables mentioned by Newcomb*—had, in fact, seen and reported such events (*New Lands*, pp. 102ff.). This is of particular interest since Newcomb wrote a century ago, and the belief that astronomers never see UFOs is still asserted, although it has been repeatedly refuted. For an erroneous belief to be held so long suggests that there must be a powerful need behind it—a need to hold on to a reality that excludes odd events.

There are people who are attracted to the unusual—who seek it out. Scientists, on the other hand, are attracted to regularity and order. Our culture strongly needs both kinds of people, preferably in some sort of contact with each other. Fort is valuable to us because he combined the two, for while obviously attracted to oddities he claimed that he was only interested in bizarre events that occurred with some regularity. I'd like to quote one further remark of his, since it pertains so directly to the question of a capricious Nature:

> ... in celestial phenomena, as well as in all other fields of research, the irregular, or the unformulable, or the uncapturable, is present in at least equal representation with the uniform: that, given any clear, definite, seemingly unvarying thing in the heavens, coexistently is something of wantonness or irresponsibility, bizarre and incredible, according to the standards of purists—that the science of Astronomy concerns itself with only one aspect of existence, *because of course there can be no science of the obverse phenomena* ... (*New Lands*, p. 20; italics mine).

The last phrase is worth pondering. It suggests that the blind spots of scientists are not mere conservatism, or the parochialism that afflicts all professionals, but are inherent in the very nature of science; that scientists can deal with the irregular only by co-opting it—showing that it contains a hidden regularity.

But if scientists can't afford to recognize the irregular as existing in its own right—if they have felt the need to falsify their own history to make it appear orderly and systematic—if they have felt obliged to ignore and deride facts that seem unusual or bizarre, even when reported again and again by their own colleagues over decades and even centuries—then perhaps Einstein's idea of Nature as fundamentally honest and predictable is delusional—a mental narcotic that permits us to keep treating half of experience as if it were the whole.

NATURE AS THE MODEL CHILD

The way scientists talk about Nature reminds me of the way some parents talk about their children: "She's so sweet, so good—a perfect child; she's never given me a day's trouble." It may be partly true, of course—the child might really have a mild and putty-like disposition. But it's only one part of the child's whole nature, and the nature of Nature may be just as complex. The side that scientists see is certainly different from the one psychics see—just as parents and playmates see different sides of a child.

I'd like to say that there's no harm in either of these perceptions, that each group can play happily with the side of Nature they prefer—they being none the wiser and Nature none the worse for the wear. But I'm not so sure. Those "perfect" children often end up schizophrenic, and I suspect that seeing only one side of Nature and acting forcefully on that narrow view could make Nature quite sick as well. On the other hand, the scientists' view of Nature as always predictable, honest, and manipulable is no more dangerous than the view that Nature is always dark, mysterious, and whimsical—to be approached with secrecy and devious design. There are vague hints, in the old myths of some civilizations, of devastating calamities brought about by meddling sorcerers. We treat this as superstitious nonsense, but the data are not all in, and, after all, we weren't there. As a working hypothesis I'm prepared to believe that the scientific and magical views are equally capable of ecological disruption.

I would propose instead the possibility that Nature has two faces—equally visible, equally available. One is the face scientists choose to look at: honest, rectangular, open, reliable, straight. The other is the face that fascinates poets, mystics, gamblers, and adventurers: mischievous, eccentric, droll, deceitful, malicious. I'm quite willing to believe in science's face, for it works. It gets me through the day very nicely and I appreciate its depth, reliability, and beauty. But I believe in the other one, too, for although it's a little more subtle in its appearance, it's everywhere for anyone who bothers to look. In *The Invisible College*, for example, Jacques Vallée points out the juxtaposition of sophisticated rationality and impish absurdity in UFO reports. He uses this material to argue that an intelligent species is deliberately injecting absurd messages to arouse skepticism and thereby regulate the rate of acceptance of this form of nonordinary reality. The idea is interesting—it *is* an efficient way to ensure gradual acceptance rather than mass conversion—but it's a mistake to assume that this mixture of logic and absurdity is unusual. Everyday life is full of it—we are just trained to overlook it.

In biology the word "sport" reveals some awareness of the impish side of Nature. Webster defines "sport" as "a sudden spontaneous deviation or variation from type . . . an individual organism which differs from its parents beyond the usual limits." Biologists now prefer the word "mutation" which firmly puts a fig leaf over that grinning face in the bushes. Another terminological conquest. It doesn't add any meaning but it certainly takes one away—no more visions of Nature's whimsy. A "mutation" is simply a message with a typographical error in it. No "spontaneous deviation," just a random mistake; no alternative order, just *dis*order.

Science really began to take off only when scientists stopped anthropomorphizing Nature the way I do, and it may seem like madness to start throwing all that clarity and simplicity away. But my view is that science isn't a baby any more and no longer needs all the conceptual protection it has. Children between the ages of six and ten often feel a need to avoid the opposite sex, but when they reach puberty they usually feel they can once again open their eyes to the entire population—not, of course, without some initial turmoil. Science, in the same way, seems to be on the verge of adolescence after a bland and uneventful latency. It already knows the facts of life—for example, that whenever you isolate some powerful trend its opposite usually lurks somewhere nearby. I believe in a puckish Nature partly because I believe so strongly in Einstein's vision of her honest sister. And while I admit that the theory of a dishonest Nature will make the life of scientists very difficult, I suspect the best scientists are already up for the challenge and the rest never will be.

Denying the dishonesty of Nature gets us into a dilemma much like the old problem of evil. People have always wondered how God could be good if the world—merely a part of God's wholeness—was evil. In the same way we might ask how Nature as a whole can be incapable of deception when human beings, who are a part of that totality, are quite able to bring it off? It seems the height of pomposity to attribute to humans a freedom that Life itself lacks.

It's when we enter the psychic realm that the smell of whimsy becomes overpowering—partly because Science uses so much deodorant spray that we can't smell anything until we get a little bit away from her. Psychic adventurers like Robert Monroe seem to meet countless paradoxes, strange twists and turns, and whimsical obstacles in their travels. While the psychic world certainly has its rules and regularities, the most certain generalization one can make

Is Nature Honest?

about the psychic path is that it's never entirely straight, never entirely predictable, never entirely logical, and the gate to the psychic world is never quite where it's supposed to be.

Monroe's out-of-the-body experiences exemplify this trait—particularly those that seemed to take place within our own reality. Wishing to be with a person he would rapidly find himself there, and was able at times, without prior knowledge, to give detailed descriptions of the setting, who was present, what people were doing, and so on. Sometimes he would then attempt to communicate and would often think he had succeeded. He once pinched a friend severely enough not only to startle her violently but also to produce a visible bruise. Yet other pinches were not even felt, and conversations Monroe thought he had had with people were not recalled by them, even when they could acknowledge the correctness of his description of the events. At first he thought he was fantasizing the conversations, but this hypothesis dissolved when he discovered that they sometimes brought out information known only to the other person. Occasionally some detail would be wrong—a familiar friend would be blond instead of dark. And although people usually didn't see him, someone would occasionally startle at the sight of him (or of whatever he appeared to them as). Once during a particularly clear and forthright visit to a friend—one of his most convincing evidential cases—he passed a robed and seated Oriental figure in the sky (pp. 46–7, 65–8, 127–35, and passim). No psychic experience seems to be without some such piece of unrelated nonsense—like the imperfection deliberately woven into a Navaho blanket.

Monroe himself is puzzled by this quality: "I have sat in séances with trance mediums and asked definite questions, received vague answers which were to me pure evasions . . . Yet, later, to my astonishment, in one such case I participated in a Second Body experiment that verified (to me and others) the authenticity of this medium's ability" (Monroe, p. 39).

Monroe also has precognitive visions. Twenty-one of his visions accurately predicted events that occurred minutes, days, months, or years later. Others have not, as yet, taken place. But one vision—that of a plane crash from which he survives—seemed almost deliberately misleading. For although many details of the trip were predicted with precision, they were mislocated. Most of the envisioned events of the plane trip, for example, took place on the bus *to* the plane. Furthermore, the plane did not in fact crash (nor did the bus). Four days after the trip, however, he had a heart attack (Monroe, pp. 145–54). Jane Roberts observes that "symbolism and obliqueness seem to apply to extrasensory experiences in general" (*Coming of Seth*, p. 144).

Monroe suggests that his own unconscious distorted the message and misled him out of fear, and although this theory seems plausible I'm not entirely satisfied with it. He's very quick to grab at psychological explanations for what happens to him, and I'm very comfortable myself with that sort of analysis. But in every serious account of people's struggles to understand or make personal use of psychic powers I'm impressed with the feeling of recalcitrance and contrariness in the environment. An ardent hatred of utilitarian motives seems to lurk in the psychic world. Jane Roberts's descriptions of her psychic experiments are filled with this combination of obvious direct hits and odd capriciousness: "A prediction will seem meaningless, but it will later prove so apt a description of a physical event that I am amazed, later, at my conscious inability to recognize it as valid when writing it down" (*Coming of Seth*, p. 151 and passim).

Part of the problem is language. Science dotes on these watertight compartments like "self" and "environment," and on the forced choices they lead to (science courses in college still use the multiple-choice exam, for example). But in the psychic world there is little concern with trying to divide the indivisible. Part of its confusion and mystery comes from the fact that it so pointedly ignores the false distinctions to which we've grown accustomed. In Monroe's

Is Nature Honest?

world "unconscious" and "real environment" are deeply interwoven—it's only in a maniacally individualistic society that one could think of the unconscious as a personal possession. To understand anything of what takes place in the psychic world we need to recognize that every event is in part determined by the self, but *only* in part. To say "it was just my unconscious" is as misleading as saying, "it was all caused by goblins and other demonic forces." I certainly don't mean to deny, in what follows, that one's internal conflicts play an important role in the confusion he or she may experience in psychic exploration; I stress the "otherness" of the resistance only to create a balance—to offset our more conventional ways of interpreting such things.

THE MISCHIEVOUS INTERPRETER

Why, for example, is psychic communication often so tortured? The survival material presented by Gardner Murphy fascinated me not so much as evidence for life after death, but as the documentation of some enormous self-undermining struggle (Murphy, pp. 192–270). Whether we're dealing with survival, telepathy, clairvoyance, hoax, or some unknown quirk of the psyche, the effortfulness of the process seems more inexplicable than the events themselves. Some intense communication need afflicts these "spirits," struggling with a violent resistance. Telepathic communication is sometimes quite simple, direct, and straightforward, but the norm for psychic communication is quite the reverse—allusive, elusive, elliptical, symbolic. The "spirits," "visions," "oracles," or whatever, behave at varying times and in varying combinations as if (1) violently eager to communicate, (2) restricted by some etiquette or prohibition, (3) teasingly indifferent about the message, and, most of all, (4) unfamiliar with the language. Sometimes they seem to assume communication has taken place when it obviously hasn't, while at other times they just seem not to know how to say things simply, and keep piling one metaphor on top of another.

The Wayward Gate

This is especially true of the material from mediums and is what arouses skepticism in most people—a healthy reaction when it comes to mediums. But the evasiveness that put Monroe off so much also characterized many of his own encounters in his out-of-the-body state. These "evasive" answers are sometimes a bit like those a Zen master might give to a novice still immersed in intellectual categories and dualistic compartments. They suggest that the question itself is inappropriate, an obstacle to enlightenment, and that the questioner is still preoccupied with trivia. Even to my limited and earthbound imagination the questions people are reported to have asked mediums, oracles, and sages seem provincial and stupid—reminiscent of the Pioneer 10 Plaque that scientists sent into space at great expense as a message to the future.

Frederick Van Eeden, writing about "lucid dreams"—dreams in which one knows one is dreaming and can act with full conscious agency—discusses both this sense of evasion and his occasional experience of deliberate mischievousness (in Tart, pp. 156–60). In three different dreams—all lucid ones—he meets friends or relatives who have died, and they have extended conversations. But when he asks about life after death they become vague, elusive, and hesitating, or else the dream abruptly terminates. This, of course, is quite easily explained by making conventional Freudian assumptions about dreams, but in one of the dreams he is also told of an impending financial catastrophe, which makes no sense to him at the time, but in fact occurs.

Now it's by no means unusual for the validity of a psychic prediction to be apparent only afterwards, when it's too late to influence the course of events. Somehow the person hearing the prediction forms an impression of it that causes him or her to look in the wrong direction for its fulfillment. This was the case with Monroe's plane-crash dream, for example. But in Van Eeden's case the cue that misled him was quite simple—the sum he lost was twenty

Is Nature Honest?

times greater than that predicted—leading him to expect something in the nature of a burglary rather than the plundering of a fortune. But often psychic predictions that "come true" have this quality of being incorrect in some detail.

Both Van Eeden and Monroe also speak of demons: menacing, malicious, teasing, obscene beings that seem more distressing than frightening, and that are intimidated by any bold confrontation on the part of the dreamer. But Monroe was particularly puzzled by what he experienced as "helpers" when out of his body: hands that lifted him, voices that spoke to him, figures that guided him (pp. 127–35). Sometimes they performed trivial acts—helping him into or out of his body—unbidden. Sometimes they came when he was in trouble and called for help, but at the times of greatest danger they failed to appear. They seemed neutral or even indifferent, and never acted friendly or expressed interest in him. Their attitude was more like that of a casual bystander helping a drunk. Sometimes they guided him in ways that were important and useful, while at other times the results seemed meaningless. Twice, for example, some hands held a book in front of him; once he seemed to learn something from what he read, while the second time he captured only a pointless phrase—typical of what we drag back from dreams at times, or of the great insights achieved under drugs that dissolve into gibberish on returning to everyday reality.

But again, even the gibberish isn't consistent. Scientists like to think that the insights of altered states *always* turn out to be nonsense, but this isn't so. I've experienced both myself: insights that dissolved, and insights that stayed with me—that helped me recognize our everyday reality as only one among many realities, so that occasionally I can jump outside its boundaries, much the way living in other cultures helps us get outside our own. And this is true of many people; drugs have produced both the *feeling* of illumination (without the person's carrying anything meaningful back into ordinary reality) and some true insights, in no identifiable pattern.

What happens in psychic experiences is so often unexpected that it seems willful—as if the person undergoing the experience were being teased. Much of this may be due simply to our not understanding the rules. Monroe found, for example, that he could not travel to a place, only to a person, and this led to some bewildering experiences in which he found himself in completely strange settings. He also found that his decisions were not under full conscious control—that he went where his deepest wishes took him, regardless of his conscious intent. The fact that reality was sometimes "distorted" in minor ways and that he occasionally wound up in the apartments of strangers (some of whom he was later able to identify as existing, if unknown, persons) can in part be explained by these psychic rules. If your wishes determine where you go, for example, then conflicting wishes could land you midway between two people you want to see. And if you always move toward a person rather than a place, you may be going to a reality as it's *experienced* by that person, and hence subject to minor variations from your own perceptions.

Yet even when all this is taken into account, the sense of teasing remains. Monroe once wished, for example, to see a friend who had recently died. He waited some months, fearful of what he might get into, but finally made the attempt. And although he thought at the time he had failed, his wish was literally granted: he did "see" his friend, but in an unfamiliar office, at age twenty-two rather than seventy, and hence recognized him only later from a picture. An attempt to see his dead father, on the other hand, was simple, straightforward, and successful. This impish inconsistency pervades Monroe's adventures.

One could, of course, object that all this is nonsense, that Monroe made it up, or is delusional, or whatever; but this seems unlikely to me. Out-of-the-body experiences are as old as written history, and Monroe's account is a balanced and cautious report by a man with some scientific training. I see no reason to ignore his record just because it's unconventional.

The hoax question is itself relevant to the idea of a capricious Nature. As I pointed out earlier, people are frequently excited to discover that a psychic or faith healer is a fraud, and tend to feel that this disposes of the question once and for all. But the existence of charlatans no more disproves the reality of psychic phenomena than the existence of swindlers disproves the reality of legitimate business transactions—normally a fraud can only succeed by masquerading as something real.

I can't help wondering why a hoax so often occurs just as people are beginning to take some bizarre event seriously and start investigating it. Are hoaxes *designed* to throw us off the track? An evasive action on the part of Nature? This seems like an unduly paranoid vision—more likely it's a matter of *us* throwing *ourselves* off the track. Still, it takes a lot of time and energy to bring off a hoax and one wonders where the driving motive comes from. To "prove" something is fraudulent by being a fraud oneself is a strange piece of business. Hoaxers want notoriety and enjoy demonstrating a pointless kind of power, but there's also a certain amount of fear inherent in pretending you're a monster so people won't believe in them. Charlatans, on the other hand, make money at it, and that's enough explanation for any American.

But why, then, do magicians invest so much energy trying to prove that psychics are frauds? Are they a threat to business? Magicians are themselves frauds, though openly so—do they want company? Houdini, for example, devoted much of his later life to exposing mediums. A useful activity, no doubt, but he carried it beyond the grave: he and his wife agreed on a message, to be transmitted if contact after death proved possible. Houdini died first. No message came through.

But would a departed soul, entering an utterly new plane of existence, really be motivated to send code messages through a medium? Would it care any more, now that it knew? Would it be interested any longer in such momentary trivia, or even in its former relationships? Houdini's agreement is a little like two small boys promising each other they'll still hate girls when they're twenty-five.

I remember how we used to cover up Nature's sly face when I was a social science researcher. We were interested in pluralities, and shunned the unique (which we used to call "residual"). Studies usually limited themselves to white males (unless specifically concerned with female or black "issues"), and subjects on whom raters disagreed were often just thrown out. And when it came to results, deviant cases were treated merely as "error." Of course there's nothing wrong with this approach—we were, after all, looking for trends and patterns. But it's clear that with a procedure like this Nature's impish side will always remain hidden. Those who never look, never see.

A BLACKBIRD'S DINNER

"I have here in my claw," said Rodamour, "a worm."

No one looked up.

"A worm," she continued, "that dug and struggled all through the wee hours of this morning to get to me. An early worm."

Kallakura gnawed on an elk's shoulder. She enjoyed discussions of food and its agile vicissitudes.

"A worm," Rodamour continued, "that has lived all its little life in darkness—wriggling happily in its swarthy warmth, squirming joyously in swashy mire——"

The cat under the table giggled at Rodamour's dreamy eloquence, choking a little on a pigeon wing. The recitation turned her on.

"This poor little contented and benighted worm has never seen daylight until today."

"How do you know?" objected the fox. "He may have been up dozens of times."

"Don't spoil my appetite. Bird fare isn't that varied, you know—for us, fantasy is everything. Who could eat this ugly little beast without a little romance?"

The Wayward Gate

"If you'd improve your diet," the fox snarled, waving his tail, "you wouldn't need to indulge in perverted imagery."

He left his pile of bones and feathers and went to the center of the hut to rub against the old woman's legs as she rocked silently in her chair.

Rodamour was undaunted.

"Into his life of sodden contentment a dream came—a glorious dream of dazzling light, open space, and spiritual fulfillment."

The wolf growled as the fox approached the old woman, but was too hungry to leave his own feast.

"He couldn't get the dream out of his head. Night after night he lay awake, thinking about his radiant vision. 'Oh, would that I could just once see the light—I would die happily, e'en though far from my squashy home,' he moaned, longingly."

The fox bared his teeth. "You're making me sick."

He trotted over to the cat and bit her shoulder. She screeched with pain and racked his eyes with her claws. Tottamottamio slithered up and smashed both of them into insensibility with her enormous tail. Tottamottamio hated quarreling.

"One day an angel appeared to him in a dream——"

"I thought he couldn't sleep," the wolf objected, looking hungrily at the cat as she lay bleeding. With a shiver he caught the lugubrious eye of Tottamottamio across the room.

"He couldn't sleep at *night*," Rodamour explained patiently. She hopped from the old woman's shoulder to the top of her head—fluttering her wings a little to balance herself as the rocking intensified.

"He would fall asleep early in the day and have troubled dreams—just when he should have been squoshing around and enjoying himself with all the other little worms."

The wolf realized that Tottamottamio was looking, not at him, but at the unconscious and blinded fox between them. He deliberately caught her eye and they exchanged winks.

"The angel said, 'Don't despair, little worm—enlightenment is yours, for God dwells within you.'"

With a sideward glance at the old woman the two animals sprang upon their respective victims. The fox disappeared in one crunch of Tottamottamio's majestic jaws.

Rodamour was drunk with relief at the cat's demise:

"Joy suffused the little worm's entire being, from one end of his wriggly little body to the other. His supple form arched in a spasm of delight. The vision of sunlight filled his tiny brain."

The sound of busy jaws and cracking bones punctuated Rodamour's narrative. Kallakura had finished her elk shoulder and was watching the wolf with sleepy malice.

"Unaware of what he was doing, he began to burrow upward—seeing nothing, feeling nothing, except the ecstasy within him."

Rodamour thought she heard a low sound from the old woman, and hopped nervously to the mantelpiece. The silent rocking continued. Kallakura closed her eyes.

"Huge boulders blocked his path, but he struggled on, fired by the image of the blinding sun. Day turned to night and night to day, but he never paused or faltered."

From a posture of apparent torpor, Kallakura disemboweled the wolf with a sweep of her paw. Cousinhood was avenged.

"Suddenly he sensed a softening of the dense medium through which he toiled and strained. Mad with anticipation he increased his effort, and began to feel the earth give way in a great rush before him."

Kallakura padded over to the rocking chair and with a paw on each arm laid her dripping muzzle on the old woman's breast. Tottamottamio watched them with an expression of sculptured interest.

"He was there! At the brink of paradise! Breathless with fatigue——"

"I don't think worms breathe at all," murmured Tottamottamio, "do they?"

The Wayward Gate

"*This* one does," insisted Rodamour. "Look at him now, can't you see?"

She held out the almost severed but still struggling body in her claw. Tottamottamio rotated one great eye to take in the sight.

"Breathless with fatigue," Rodamour continued, "he hesitated a little to savor the moment of consummation. Then, gathering his strength, he burst through the thin crust of earth into the brilliant sunlight!"

Tottamottamio slid under the chair so that her jaws rested on the old woman's left foot, while her tail could swish back and forth beyond reach of the rockers.

Rodamour paused, savoring the moment of consummation.

"So what happened then?" Kallakura asked sleepily, her voice muffled by the old woman's evil-smelling blouse.

"I ate him!" Rodamour announced lustfully, and proceeded to do so.

But the two large animals were asleep, and only the rocking orchestrated the worm's voluptuous disappearance.

CHAPTER 6

REALITY STYLES

A hallucination is merely a reality we normally
don't have to bother with.—Stella Denova

Every rational disquisition eventually winds up at the same
dead end: that there's no *logical* basis for assigning
importance—for deciding that one thing is more important
than another. Each philosophical system sets up some ultimate criterion: Honor, Love, Beauty, Chastity, Equality,
Spirituality, Freedom, Pleasure, Futurity—and then tries to
rank order the world in relation to it. But each system is
ramshackle, arbitrary, and of limited popularity, and
sooner or later they all collapse.

Abstract thought runs aground on the shoal of value
since a thing can only be of value *to* someone—a matter of
feeling, motive, desire. In altered states of consciousness a
frequent insight is precisely that nothing in the universe is
more or less important than anything else. The grain of
sand, the insect, the tiger, Bach, the blade of grass, the
dung heap—all are of equal wonder.

This is very confusing. Without assigning different values we can't see, we can't think, we can't act. To see, for
example, is to discriminate one thing from another. But
how can we discriminate if everything is of equal importance? Why would we look at one thing rather than
another? And if everything is equally important how can
we think about it? Thought, also, is a matter of making dis-

tinctions, and our ideas about what's important guide us in finding such distinctions. Without placing higher value on some things than on others we couldn't even detect the differences on which all thought is based. It would be like looking for a lost object that we hadn't yet missed.

There's no possible separation, then, between thinking and wanting. We can only think desirously.

Ordinarily, our biology, culture, and personal experience provide us with values and motives, so that we have no trouble choosing, thinking, seeing, and acting. But when we try to "rise above" this modest position in the universe and unhook our thoughts from our motives we either deceive ourselves or fall into despair. For thought itself cannot answer the question, "why live?" or even "why act? why move from one thing to another?" Only desire, feeling, taste, can answer such questions—modest, personal, mundane desire, based on our own provincial location in the universe. The effort to be everywhere leads nowhere. When I try to "rise above" my location and be pure, unmotivated thought it leads to the progressive evaporation of me, but not to anything else.

But the fact that everyone values some things more than others isn't much help when it comes to collective action. A community needs to *teach* importance, so that values will be shared. Some consensus about what's important is vital for people living together, and when it wobbles, or starts to unravel, people argue a lot and write books like this one. But in every community, children must be taught what's "real." They have to be taught to see only what's important.

For reality as we use it is a synonym for "important things." Absolute Reality, if we can imagine such a thing, is far more inclusive. It has things in it we've never dreamed of—that we can't see or hear with our limited sensory range. It also has things we *have* dreamed of but consider "unreal." Absolute Reality is so overwhelmingly inclusive that we can't let very much of it in—only what's "important." What we *call* reality is what we've been taught to consider important. The part of Absolute Reality we decide to let into awareness is what we choose to call "real."

"Real" means "important."

When I say, "I dreamt about a cow but the dog I saw was real," this is a way of saying that the dog event was important and the cow event was not. Cultures that think dreams are important include them in their definition of "reality." They don't say, "it was *only* a dream."

Now since movement is impossible if all things are of equal importance, all communities must build theories that say some things are more important (real) than others. These are completely arbitrary, but necessary.

I call them "reality styles." They tell us what part of Absolute Reality to attend to. Out of infinite possibility we select what we want to experience and dismiss the rest as unreal. These reality styles provide a coherent system of priorities through which we can screen our experience. They are life-and-death matters, for without them the choice of what events to select as real would be overwhelming at every moment.

Psychosis is not having a coherent reality style.

ABSOLUTE REALITY

Freud used to say that there is nothing in the mind that was not first in the senses. It was an extraordinary remark, but he hedged it for his own purposes. He said things get in and then the mind twists, distorts, and rearranges them. He said the weird creations of the mind are pearls constructed around some harmless irritant from the "real" world. With such a heavy qualification he might just as well not have bothered to say it in the first place: a grain of truth, the rest embroidery. But what if it's *all* truth? What if the mind can't create at all? What if, when I imagine a three-headed monster, there really is such a thing on some level of reality?

Men are always talking about creating. Some say they're

jealous of the biological creativity of women. But mothers don't create either. They just transmit a message. Perhaps all creation is really transmission, and all the talk about creativity just another display of that nervous narcissism that so afflicts humans. A kind of whistling in the dark: I create, therefore I am.

I'm suggesting that there is nothing imagined that isn't a part of Absolute Reality. That anything imagined in the mind is as Real as the typewriter in front of me—located in some actual temporal-spatial environment, although perhaps unfamiliar to us. Imagining or dreaming of something that doesn't exist is therefore impossible. One can only tune into different environments. To call something a fantasy is just a way of denying importance to it—a way of saying (1) that nothing has to be done about it, and (2) that it has no intrinsic meaning—only what we add to it through interpretation.

I think every serious philosopher, professional or amateur, has wondered why waking reality should be considered more important (real) than dreams. The choice is completely arbitrary, although it's been useful—the dream world, after all, is pretty sly. Yet it's also been useful to the Senoi to assign equal reality to dreams, so we can't find any solid ground by appealing to utility.

But this is only the beginning of our confusion, for Absolute Reality consists not only of every conceivable fantasy, but also of every conceivable possibility. It includes not only the events of my life as I know it, but also every alternative pathway that could have been taken. To say these alternatives did not occur is like saying that a book does not exist except when I'm reading it.

We live our lives standing on the rear end of a train, looking backward. All we can see is where we've been and a little tiny bit of where we might have gone, out to each side of us. But we don't imagine, on a train, that all the rest of the landscape is nonexistent, or mere fantasy. Why should we in our lives?

Let's take it one leap further: if every monster, goddess,

chimera, heaven, hell, or possibility in our heads is real, then it's conceivable that everything in the universe is in our heads—not in our consciousness, of course, but potentially available. In which case the senses are *not* the avenue to everything in the mind—they aren't even necessary.

Except to keep out things. The senses exist not to take in data but to restrict, sort, and censor them. Learning as we know it is solving a puzzle we invented ourselves. Seeing and hearing are just ways of finding what we've hidden from ourselves.

Clairvoyance, from this viewpoint, becomes a capability available to everyone, as experiments in psychic training seem to demonstrate. Precognition is just a matter of walking up to the front of the train and looking out. We all have that information but we block our access to it. To know everything that has happened, is happening, will happen, or might have happened, anywhere in the universe, would be a little overwhelming. Who could tolerate such awareness?

The psyches of psychics are often a little strained. And they see only fragments.

THE TINKERTOY STYLE

Reality styles help with all that. They tell us what's important. They make it possible for us to agree about which part of Absolute Reality we need to attend to. They teach us to see and hear the same things, so we can communicate about them; and they help us *block out* the same things so we won't be overwhelmed with stimuli.

For how could people communicate if everyone were paying attention to different stimuli? If would be bedlam, in every sense of the word. Reality styles keep us off the back wards. Every culture has a reality style to enable people to decide what's information and what's noise. And what we agree to exclude, and treat as noise, is overwhelmingly vast.

Remember the eye of the frog. The frog needs to make

only four visual discriminations in order to live. If he could see any more he would be enlightened. He might also get stoned on it and be eaten by a bird. When humans learn to see more it doesn't always contribute to *their* survival either.

I pointed out earlier that "reality" is a matter not of what's there but of what we need. To talk about "seeking truth" as if we'd like to have all we can get is blather. No one wants to deal with the Whole Truth—there's just too much of it. The most passionate truth-seeker just wants a viable map for navigating some little piece of experience that he or she is interested in. Absolute Reality would overwhelm and blot out that map—render it trivial and irrelevant. How could we seek the little piece of truth we want, faced with the terrifying distraction of Everything-at-Once? We just want little working hypotheses to get us through the day, and no one of these is worth more than any other, except to a particular person at a particular time. No more than a Tuesday is worth more than a Thursday. Hence a conventional scientist's resistance to paranormal material is not to be mocked; they've gotten along fine without it up to now, just as I get along without knowing a stranger's phone number. We know what we want to know. Why would we want to know what we don't want to know?

Now since reality styles have a lot to do with survival, there's a lot of overlap in reality styles around our world. With the exception of certain religious groups who consider our everyday world an illusion, the greatest overlap is about tactile things. Almost everywhere people assign reality to that which can be touched.

Beyond that, utter chaos. We believe in the reality of sound waves, neutrinos, Alpha Centauri, stock-market values, Ph.D. degrees, and a million other symbols. Some oral cultures believe in the reality of dreams, others in witchcraft and magic spells. But each style has a certain coherence—it creates a *fabric* of reality that makes sense to people.

Now a frog doesn't bother to argue that the things that

are important to him also have cosmic significance, but reality styles tend to be grandiose: They want all of nature to operate with the same style—a dreary prospect indeed. This is particularly true of our own style, which has come to dominate the earth. (As it ripples over the last free areas, however, it has begun—like all ideological movements—to decay at the center.)

I call this method of bestowing reality the Tinkertoy style, because it's based on the feeling that experience is most safely defined as a collection of little separate particles, which can be brought together into larger particles and taken apart again. The need it expresses is thus one of control and manipulation.

Western culture, science, and rational discourse are all based on the Tinkertoy style. Most of what we're willing to recognize as communication takes place in this style. I am writing in this style, trying with great effort to transcend it at the same time. Our language, or any language based so heavily on nouns, has a Tinkertoy structure. To get beyond it would take a language like that of the Nootka, which is all verbs (to refer to a table one says "it tables" just as we say "it rains" or "it burns"). In altered states of consciousness I sometimes experience the world in this verbal form—a totality expressing itself in varied ways for varying periods of time: tabling, flowering, flooring, kittening, grassing, pavementing. But in our traditional public schools every facet of the training process is an effort to inculcate the Tinkertoy style, and we're all pretty thoroughly indoctrinated with it.

The emphasis on control and manipulation—on frozen events, things that stay still so they can be combined and dismantled—betrays the extent to which the Tinkertoy style is rooted in fear—in a frantic wish to survive. But the survival is individual, not collective; it's a *sauve qui peut* style. It fosters self-aggrandizement by each organism and is an exceptionally useful system for achieving this end. But it's a poor way to filter experience when it comes to preserving the species or achieving ecological balance. The Tinkertoy

The Wayward Gate

style assumes that the life or death of the individual is of paramount importance, even if all other living things go under.

We can only speculate about how it got started. It has the desperate rigidity of a pattern learned all at once in a panic situation, yet we know it emerged very gradually. But beginnings are unimportant. Once you embrace an emergency pattern it creates its own emergencies. Reality styles always justify themselves—creating the reality for which they were designed. If you believe in money, money is created. If you believe in enemies, enemies are created. If you prepare for war, war will be created. And if you believe in particles, they'll be there waiting for you, too.

It would be helpful if we could define a reality style by the motives that kindled it, but such motives are complex and difficult to disentangle. The desire to do so is in fact a Tinkertoy trait, for Tinkertoy reality leans heavily on differentiation—on trying to see things as separate objects. Charles Fort commented on this need to separate the inseparable: the earth bulges and we say there's a mountain, as if that bulge had clear boundaries. But we, too, are only bulges in a curtain of life, and whether we treat a human being as a separate entity or a part of something else is merely a matter of taste. Tinkertoy thought is big on making distinctions, and sorting into categories, for one of its deepest motives is control: *divide et impera*.

The reality styles of many non-Western peoples have more to do with the desire to participate, although this is only a very partial description. But since I'm a Westerner I have an urgent need to find ways to contrast Tinkertoy reality with other styles, and for this purpose making a distinction between control and participation is helpful.

Arthur Deikman (Tart, p. 41) provides us with a lovely example. Writing on the mystic experience from a Tinkertoy perspective he asks whether the experience of cosmic unity—so frequent in altered states of consciousness—is a perception of "the real structure of the world" or merely of "one's own psychic structure." Such a question could only

146

be asked by a Tinkertoy realist: *either* myself *or* the world. Westerners assume the two to be *dis*united and therefore ask whether the *feeling* of unity refers to one part of the disunity (myself) or the other part (everything else *but* me)! If the mystic is correct the question is meaningless because the two structures are all one. If the world is one, so is the psyche, and if the psyche is one, so is the world. But to a Tinkertoy mind that last sentence is as meaningless as Deikman's is to the mystic.

To a mystic Deikman's question would be like saying, "when you experience the sea as salt water do you refer to all the oceans of the world or the bucket of water you just took out of the Atlantic?" But scientists are concerned with differences, and most scientists would probably argue that if we didn't *know* all the oceans were salt water the question wouldn't be so silly—that we only found it out by taking samples from all parts of the world.

But this isn't the point. The scientists are correct that you can find differences if you look for them, and the mystics are correct that you can find unity if you look for it. You can find anything else if you look for it, too, for *you can only look for things you know exist*, if my assumption about Absolute Reality is correct.

SEEING AND BELONGING

The real point has to do, not with things being *different*, but with things being *separate*. The valley is different from the foothills, the foothills from the slopes, the slopes from the peak, the cliff from the ledge, the wrist from the hand, the shin from the ankle, and so on. But they aren't separate. Nor is a human individual separate from other humans or from the entire fabric of living matter. This is the chief limitation of the Tinkertoy style (for every reality style is profoundly limiting, of necessity): it sets up artificial separations and then struggles to unite what it has put asunder. It's easy to see where all the preoccupation with control and manipulation comes from when we look at the

The Wayward Gate

Deikman example. On the one hand there is me, on the other hand the world—that is, everything else *but* me. With odds like that I'm going to need all the control I can get.

Let me give a simple example. Suppose I'm a peasant in some troubled part of the world where there's a guerilla army. If I'm not a member of that army my life is hazardous. I don't know what to expect of them—whether they'll treat me as friend or enemy. Will they confiscate my crops, loot and burn my house, injure or mistreat my loved ones, kill or imprison me? If many of them appear in my village, what should I do? How should I react? What can I expect? Life is full of questions and anxieties.

But if I assume that I'm a *member* of that army these problems evaporate. And this is precisely what happens to the mystic. Non-Western reality styles are much less concerned with control and much more willing to pay attention to subjective experience. Non-Tinkertoy peoples tend to assume that the world is reflected through their own being, and that *as long as they keep themselves clear* that reflection will be accurate.

It's a paradox that the Western concern with objectivity comes about by shutting oneself off from the rest of the world. For if I see myself as a separate entity then *I can no longer trust my own experience as a reflection of the world*. If I don't belong to the guerilla army any more I no longer know what they want or what they're going to do. Hence I have to correct for my limited vision: I have to worry about what other people think, since I don't *know* what they think. I have to find ways of understanding that world from which I've alienated myself. (Oracles and omens are thus the first stage of alienation—before that you can read nature in yourself.) I have to mistrust my own experience—become "objective."

There's no need for a referee when everyone's on the same team. But when we define every person as a separate team we feel the need for some sort of mental ombudsman who stands outside the system and tells us what is real. No one, of course, *can* stand outside the system, so objectivity means in practice that some agreed-upon form of reality is imposed coercively on everyone in the system. This is much like what happens in universities: the self-indulgent narcissism of faculty members combined with their organization into airtight compartments makes them incapable of collective action, so that their administrations tend to become fascistic by default.

We call something "objective" when it's at one remove from immediate personal experience. We're trained to believe that an "objective" datum is more "real" than a subjective experience, but this is true only in the Tinkertoy system, which defines reality that way. We're taught to believe that an experience is more real if it's filtered through some machine or apparatus before it reaches our senses.

It's a strange form of self-doubt: the guerilla army dissolves, and since we're no longer together we suspect each other's motives; and, since we're out of touch with things, we doubt ourselves as well, for our awareness has been vastly diminished. We then create mechanisms that we agree to pay more attention to than we pay to our own reactions.

In a way this is less bizarre than it sounds. When an ego detaches itself from the rest of life it discovers it has a problem with limits. A part is always bounded and balanced by the whole in which it participates, but when it detaches itself it can no longer count on that larger equilibrium. In an organism, for example, heart, brain, liver, stomach, and kidney balance and limit each other—alone each would run amok. An ego that no longer sees itself as part of a whole is in similar danger of runaway imbalance. It can't limit itself effectively, for it can no longer trust the motive behind such self-limitation, based as it is on the narrow bias of a mere part. Hence we seek some external apparatus to provide limits and controls—from the prayer beads of the holy man to the most sophisticated scientific measuring instrument. The only thing strange about all this is that ultimately it's still us, looking at and listening to our apparatus. Objectivity is just subjectivity with a middleman. Having cut myself off I can no longer trust that my own psyche mirrors the world. I therefore try to put together an apparatus that *does* reflect the world. I make it according to the laws of Nature, so that it has the quality of clairvoyance that I've lost, for although we know *we've* lost the touch we believe it still exists. A measuring apparatus is simply a nonorganic omen: we no longer believe that the entrails of a bird reveal the current shape of events in microcosm, but we still attribute that mirror-like clarity to scientific instruments.

For example: you say you feel feverish. I take your temperature, the thermometer registers ninety-eight degrees. With the entire weight of the Tinkertoy style to back me up, I inform you that you are in error. You're not "really" feverish at all.

Once again, we have two reports that are in conflict. Quite arbitrarily we choose one over the other. We say it's more real because it's "objective." Yet it contradicts your own experience. Science is supposed to rest firmly on sensory experience, but this is true only on convenient occasions. For the most part science is conceptual, imaginative, visionary.

It never occurs to you to say, "Well, the thermometer may measure something—something that relates middling well to infections and such—but it certainly doesn't measure how hot I am or how well I feel." How come? Why do you pay more attention to the numbers on a little piece of glass than to your own body's messages?

The Tinkertoy style teaches you that your body is less real than a piece of dead matter. This is important learning. In the short run it helps you survive and beat out your neighbor. But it blinds you to a wealth of experience. It's probably a safer way to live right now, but a very muted one. We should at least be aware of how arbitrary the choice is, for there's no way to decide in an absolute sense whether your body is more or less real than a piece of glass with mercury in it. The Tinkertoy style votes for the piece of glass. But which is more real to *you*?

My own vote is in. I think I'm just as out of touch with my

body as the next person but I don't need a piece of glass to tell me I'm hot. How alienated can you get? Every moment I'm flooded with information from my body—constantly changing, ever varied, an absolute riot of experience. Why should I deaden all that so I can read dials and take measurements? I might be in some danger if I don't, but I might be in some danger if I do; my life will be richer or poorer, and I'll have a satisfying or unsatisfying death, sooner or later. But as long as I have a body I think I'll trust it.

Certainly I'll trust it over the opinion of any "expert," medical or otherwise. For an "expert," after all, is merely someone who has familiarized himself with a category system—an arbitrary way of chopping the world into pieces and giving the pieces names. The only thing all experts agree on is that "ignorant" people (that is, all the rest of us) should trust the word of an expert more than their own experience.

Charles Tart's book, *Altered States of Consciousness*, is full of laboratory studies on subjective experience. The ones on dreaming fascinate me particularly. Not because they tell me anything interesting about sleep or dreaming—it's one yawn after another. The *viewpoint* is what interests me: there's an intense desire in dream research to find an EEG or EOG (electrooculogram) pattern that corresponds to each kind of mental experience during sleep. Early dream researchers were thrilled, for example, to find that rapid eye movements occurred during dreaming, and disappointed when they found that the correspondence wasn't perfect (Tart, p. 79). Scientists hoped that with machines they could tell an average untrustworthy human being whether she was dreaming or not, regardless of whether she *experienced* a dream. This is the goal of all such research: to free scientists from all dependence on other human beings—to allow them to disregard all subjective experience, all personal reports, all eyewitness accounts. Their mistrust is also expressed in the pejorative terms used to describe events that Tinkertoy reality tries to ignore: words like "regressive," "bizarre," "implausible," "hallucinated," "inappropriate," and "distorted" make it quite apparent which are the good (real) events and which are the bad (unreal) ones.

I feel quite comfortable putting down this kind of research since I've done a lot of it myself. As a graduate student, for example, I once did a study that demonstrated statistically that a group of experimental subjects had a harder time carrying out a group task when they were stoned out of their minds on acid than they did under ordinary conditions. I did a lot of computations to arrive at this conclusion, which the subjects were freely revealing at every moment.

MIXING STYLES

It could be objected that I'm behaving as if I could stand outside all this and pass "objective" judgment. You should be wondering why I'm saying all these things. Clearly I want to persuade you to abandon your exclusive commitment to Tinkertoy reality. For since I'm in the process of doing the same thing I want to have company—I want to help create a different shared reality. I also need to persuade myself, since it's very difficult to alter perceptual systems that are so basic. And there may be lots of other reasons I don't know about.

Many other people are engaged in the same effort right now—trying to open our awareness to new realities. And a great many more feel comfortable in Tinkertoy reality and are objecting to such arguments. *Together we will collectively determine the rate at which the organism to which we all belong will move.* For any organic flow is a mixture of holding and releasing, excitation and quiescence. Right now I'm working as a releaser. Tomorrow my job may change.

Exploring "nonordinary" reality is greatly handicapped by the Tinkertoy style. Not just because of its anti-subjective bias, or because it treats numbers as more real than shapes; and not just because it's linear and mechanical and all those other things we're growing tired of. It handicaps us because it insists on treating all "nonordinary" events as unreal.

Take the phrase "nonordinary" itself. Statistically, there's nothing nonordinary about nonordinary reality—it's right there all the time for anyone who wants to pay attention to it. What "ordinary" means is "comfortably accessible via the Tinkertoy style." Terms like "extraordinary," "bizarre," "weird," "unusual," or "outlandish" (that's a revealing one) don't really express infrequency. They mean, "we hardly ever get that on our receiving set." Since the set is designed to keep that sort of event out, it's "extraordinary" when one gets through—like perfume coming through a telephone.

This resistance isn't just stupidity or stubbornness—the alternative to a reality style is chaos. The power that the Tinkertoy style has—the power to remove some experiences from our awareness and shove them into closets—rests on the fact that these experiences are no longer a part of any coherent reality style. When the Tinkertoys won the last reality war they gained control over language, thought, and perception. When Castaneda finally achieves a non-Tinkertoy vision, Don Juan says: "What stopped inside you yesterday was what people have been telling you the world is like" (*Journey to Ixtlan,* p. 199).

"Secret," "occult," "hidden," "mysterious"—these words don't characterize events; they describe how we *treat* certain events. There's no change in a secret formula or ritual when it becomes public—*it's the same event treated differently.* Words like "occult" are labels given by the victors to the losers in a style war. Just as the most intact non-Western cultures survive in inaccessible jungles, deserts, and mountain wastes, so non-Tinkertoy events survive in a kind of tacky psychological wilderness.

Some people, for example, retain the ability to experience events at a distance, across space or time. Their reality is more inclusive than ours. But this ability isn't important in Tinkertoy terms, not real. People who have it are seen less as gifted than as eerie, and if not fraudulent then probably a little crazy. And crazy they may be. Other reality styles are no longer very well integrated, and people who venture outside the safety of Tinkertoy terrain often fall apart and get completely disoriented. As Don Juan observes, if we didn't keep busily creating the world with our concepts there would be nothing familiar in the environment.

Without a coherent style we simply fall into confusion and madness. If everything were recognized as of equal importance, how could we negotiate our way through the pandemonium of our moment-to-moment experiences? Castaneda had a guide in Don Juan, but the fragility of his grasp on the new style forced him frequently to run back to the familiar ground of Tinkertoy reality to avoid psychosis. Don Juan himself (assuming he or some model "exists") had retained through his own culture a reality style that allowed him to experience "nonordinary" events without losing his bearings. But by and large the supremacy of Tinkertoy reality has left alternative styles in too torn and tattered a state to provide a psychic map for the wanderer. So it's easy to call those who enter the psychic realm crazy—unless they have a coherent style to guide them they're quite apt to become so.

Castaneda's Don Juan has a vivid awareness of reality styles. At one point he says that Carlos has now experienced the world as sorcerers say it is—a world in which animals talk, and trees, and all living things. But what Don Juan wants most to teach him is to "sneak between the worlds" of sorcerers and ordinary people: "Yesterday you believed the coyote talked to you . . . but . . . to believe that is to be pinned down in the realm of sorcerers. By the same token, not to believe that coyotes talk is to be pinned down in the realm of ordinary men" (*Journey to Ixtlan*, p. 300).

Negotiating Absolute Reality without a reality style would be a nightmare of stimulation and chaos. Even with a guide and some sort of new style or combination of styles, the loss of familiar styling is always somewhat disorienting. Psychosis often seems to involve a confusion of styles.

In Euripides' *Bacchae*, for example, Agave, the bacchante queen, kills her son, Pentheus, in an altered state. Emerging from that state she realizes that what she has killed is not a lion but her son. She has "erred." The killing was "motivated," since Pentheus bitterly opposed her involvement in Dionysian rites. Agave confused the reality in which she confronted a lion with the reality in which she confronted her son, for whom she now mourns desolately. We cannot know what meaning this act had in that other reality, but we know it was calamitous for Agave in Tinkertoy reality. This happens often in psychotic confusion: acts carried out in relating to other realities are translated into acts in Tinkertoy reality that seem disorganized and tempestuous.

Yet at times it seems possible to make coherent translations from one reality to the other. This is what psychics and sorcerers occasionally do, with great difficulty and many failures. For such accomplishments require one to be completely centered in more than one world, which is close to impossible. More often people blunder in and out of different realities, always mistaking one for another and acting accordingly. We usually call them crazy when this happens, but wonder-workers who fail to achieve their advertised goals may be victims of the same confusion without displaying the more obvious signs of mental disturbance.

Our ideas about people who have special or "magical" powers are rooted in Tinkertoy assumptions. I was taught, for example, that medieval alchemists were misguided putterers trying to turn lead into gold. (Westerners have always had an exaggerated idea of the willingness of other people to engage in futile endeavors.) This belief that it was all for the sake of gold is probably a case of capitalist historians projecting their own motivations on their forebears. The Western mind can't seem to credit the idea that a person could discover something and not try to cash in on it.

The Wayward Gate

People raise the same question with the powers achieved by psychics and yogis: "If they really had such powers, they could make a fortune, or control the world." But loss of interest in worldly power and material gain is in large part the price of obtaining such skills. One way we're able to pick out charlatans is their conspicuous concern with money and power.

Out-of-the-body experiences, for example, are usually so frightening that few people think of doing it deliberately, and even those that overcome their fear are rarely inspired to use the skill for their personal benefit. For such use assumes Tinkertoy reality, and once having been "out of the body" its fate doesn't seem as important or real as it did before. It's hard for our Tinkertoy minds to imagine not wanting to advance ourselves, but leaving the body may depend on losing that desire. One of Celia Green's research subjects reports a strong determination to take some kind of advantage of his power but complains that: "Although I promise myself I shall attempt it on the next occasion I never do so because *it seems so insignificant when I am 'away from myself'* " (Green, p. 141; italics mine).

This is the crux of the incompatibility between the Tinkertoy style and psychic phenomena. Like all intellectual conflicts, it boils down to a difference in motive.

CHAPTER 7

... That which we now regard as stubborn matter was ... the Heavenly Chaos, a soft and ductile substance, which could be moulded by the imagination of uncorrupted man into whatever forms he chose it to assume.—Arthur Machen

Tinkerstyle lenses make it hard to understand events like telepathic communication, although they aren't the least mysterious in themselves. The strangeness of telepathy comes from our Tinkertoy conception of communication, which we see as a process of passing around little bits of symbolic matter: When one of these little bits gets from one mechanical or human orifice into another, and is processed, we say communication has taken place. This definition makes proximity in time and space essential. Communicators must be either physically together or linked by some visual or auditory thread—across space (telephone, radio, TV) and/or time (records, tapes, photographs, letters).

But why should we see communication as passing particles around? The word "communication" literally means to share, to have in common. Tinkertoy styling added the idea of manipulating bits—of an active sender and a passive receiver—so that what was originally a matter of sharing was transformed into a matter of power. We say, "How can we communicate with these people?"—meaning, "How can we get them to do what we want?"

The Wayward Gate

Suppose we go back to the word itself and take its literal meaning seriously: to "communicate" is simply to have something in common. That is, *communication occurs whenever two beings are in synchrony with each other*. People who feel very close, for example, often talk of being on the same "wavelength"—so much so that talk seems unnecessary. They frequently start to say the same thing at the same time, or discover they were thinking the same thought at the same time.

If we take the "wavelength" idea literally, then being connected in time and space isn't the basis of communication at all, but just a lubricating device. When we make familiar noises at each other over a phone it helps us get in tune with each other, but the noises aren't the communication—they're a *pathway* to communication, a *means*. Sometimes they're successful, sometimes not, for it takes a long time and a lot of words to achieve a genuinely shared image or experience.

Talking is to telepathy what Morse code is to speech.

Now suppose we can see each other over a two-way video system. This fosters attunement more effectively for we can synchronize our body gestures and eye movements. Films show, for example, that the rapid body motions of people talking together are in microscopic synchrony, although this can't be seen with the naked eye. Being in the same room is better still, since smells, heat, and other subtle cues are brought into play, while actual physical contact makes it hard for communication *not* to take place, given so many avenues to synchronization.

What we think of as the act of communication, then, is just a warm-up method. Communication itself is independent of the senses and doesn't require physical connection in space or time. It's just a matter of being tuned into the same channel. We talk and gesture at each other to get our frequencies adjusted.

In Tinkertoy reality communication is bridging a void, but the void is something we invent to make ourselves anxious, while at the same time patting ourselves on the back for our bravery and industry. All of life is naturally connected and "in communication." Channels may at times become obstructed or obscured, and to talk then of "establishing communication" isn't entirely misleading. But it makes a difference whether you think you're blazing a trail or opening a plugged pipeline. In one case you create what isn't, in the other you just tend to what already is.

UNITY AND PARANOIA

Normally, for example, we don't say, "My fingers are now going to communicate with each other." We assume they're in communication unless a nerve or artery has been cut. To say, "I'm going to communicate with Joe"—as if we were laying the Atlantic cable rather than merely deciding to unstop one of our many channels of connection with Joe—is part of the Tinkertoy linguistic habit of defining things as separate. *We pull them apart in our minds so we can put them together with our hands, giving us a feeling of control over our environment.* Of course we only need that sense of control because we've defined ourselves as no longer a part of our environment, which makes us quite understandably paranoid about it.

The Tinkertoy habit of pulling the world apart in our heads also creates a sense of eeriness and strangeness when we run into evidence that it's still working as a whole. Just as if we had chopped an enemy into little pieces and then saw him walking around. Much of the material in Watson's *Supernature*, for example, is strange only because it violates these assumptions of separateness. It seems astounding to us whenever invisible patterns are shown to be capable of arranging matter: that blood transfusions from a normal cockroach can give a headless one a sense of direction; or that half a million amoebae can suddenly coordinate their activities without any nervous system; or that the cells of sponges will reassemble after being shredded and pushed through a sieve; or that a colony of social insects can act like a single organism; or that the cells of a disintegrated mouse brain will regroup to form a new brain. And it seems equally mysterious that a blind chameleon can adopt a changing camouflage that always blends instantaneously with its surroundings, for this requires a connection between reptile and environment that's utterly invisible to us. Such a connection also seems necessary to account for Backster's discovery that plants react violently to the killing of other forms of life in the vicinity—indeed, that "fresh fruit and vegetables, mold cultures, amoebae, paramecia, yeast, blood, and even scrapings from the roof of a man's mouth" are sensitive to distress in other living things. And finally, it's expressed in the finding that the properties of mistletoe change drastically depending upon when the plant is picked, being affected by time, weather, the phases of the moon, and eclipses (cited in Watson, pp. 13, 153, 218–21, 244–45, 252–53, 273).

All these phenomena violate our Tinkertoy notions of reality because what happens is independent of the particles themselves. They suggest a larger unity that seems slightly spooky to us because we lack the ability to see ourselves as a *part* of that unity. Since we like to think of ourselves as separate beings the unification of all *other* life seems rather overwhelming—a huge conspiracy. Because we leave ourselves *out* of that conspiracy we imagine that it must be directed against us.

Paranoia is nothing more than that: *an incomplete perception of the unity of life*—a half-baked vision in which we become aware of everything outside ourselves moving together, but are blinded by our narcissism from the realization that we're in on the secret. This is completely voluntary: the ego clings to its sense of isolation, willing to scare itself to pieces rather than acknowledge that it's part of a whole. It blinds itself to that awareness in order to indulge its dreams of glorious detachment. Hence whenever awareness of the unity of life breaks through, the ego panics and sees the event as weird, horrifying, "occult."

Fantasies like Hitchcock's *The Birds*, in which some form

of animal life revolts and attacks humans collectively, have been popular for the past half-century or more— beginning perhaps with Arthur Machen's *The Terror*. They seem to reflect a feeling of exclusion from the web of life—an exclusion that our individualistic heritage fosters. Watson (p. 222) interprets Backster's work with plants as indicative of some kind of "all-species SOS," and believes that we are attuned to this only on an unconscious level. If we've cut ourselves off from a universal alarm system it's no wonder we're paranoid.

Watson, like Fort, sees life on earth as united into a single superorganism. He argues that the probability of life in all its myriad forms occurring by chance is infinitesimal, placing "a great strain on the credulity of even the most mechanistic biologists" (pp. 7, 280). The classic theory of evolution asks us to believe that life evolved through perfect competition, much in the way free enterprise was supposed to work in the economic theories of Adam Smith. Yet we know now that the complex forms of life we see around us evolved, not competitively, but through a process of mutual accommodation, such that both predator and prey might survive to their mutual advantage, neither one extinguishing the other.

The eeriness and uncanniness of Watson's material disappears when we accept the unity of life. Imagine if you were your thumb, for example, watching your fingers moving about. If you were a good individualist you would see each finger as a separate and complete entity, sufficient unto itself. You would wonder how they "communicated" with each other. If you were a perceptive thumb, or tripping on acid, you might suddenly get the insight that they were all moving together as a unit. And if that's as far as your insight took you—if, like the ideal scientist, you left yourself out of the equation—you'd be scared out of your wits, paranoid about the Great Finger Conspiracy. Once you see *yourself* as part of the hand the eeriness disappears.

The Wayward Gate

The mystery of telepathy vanishes in the same way when we drop our Tinkertoy notions, but scientists find this hard to do. Instead they keep trying to find some kind of familiar force—electromagnetic or whatever—to account for the strange "communication" between isolated entities. Watson argues (following the zoologist, Sir Alister Hardy) that we need to assume some form of telepathy to account for many evolutionary changes—particularly the dramatic behavioral changes in various species that have occurred in response to modern environmental conditions. He also observes that communication among social insects is often far too rapid to take place by chemical or olfactory transmission (Watson, pp. 238–44).

Nothing needs to be transmitted from one place to another if it exists everywhere already. We often use the metaphor of spatial distance to describe relations between people; we say "You're a million miles away," or "I don't feel close to him." And most of us are familiar with the experience of having this distance suddenly eliminated—a closeness instantly reestablished. But maybe we look at it the wrong way around. Maybe *all* distance is a matter of tuning. When people "get on the same wavelength" we say they've "become closer," but if I travel to San Francisco to see a friend I don't think of this as "getting on the same wavelength." Yet perhaps that's what it is. Perhaps spatial distance is merely a lack of synchrony in some dimension with which we're unfamiliar. People who have out-of-the-body experiences, for example, travel great distances very quickly. As Monroe says, there's no gap between thought and action—to want is to be there.

Electricity exists without wires, but once bound into wires it's limited and channeled by them. Perhaps we need to think of the human body in the same way—it channels us into spatial pathways and distracts us from the larger reality that communication is a matter not of bridging space but of synchronizing minds. Polygraph studies have shown, for example, that people who feel in sympathy with one another tend at those times to synchronize their heartbeats, respiration rates, and other vital signs.

Telepathic communication is most often reported between people whose lives have been interconnected for a long time. When Van Der Post asked a Bushman how his people would react when they learned that a hunting expedition had been successful he replied simply that they already knew: "We Bushmen have a wire here [tapping his chest] that brings us news," and, indeed, when the expedition arrived at the distant camp the preparations for feasting were well advanced (p. 253).

Lovers, close friends, and family members—particularly mothers and children—are the most common senders and receivers of telepathic communication. When Soviet scientists killed newborn rabbits in a submarine, the mother, ashore, showed brain reactions at each moment of death (Ostrander and Schroeder, pp. 33–4), and human mothers often show similar sensitivity. It seems magical only because we think in Tinkertoy terms—the very word "telepathy" ("feeling at a distance") betrays our preoccupation with spatial metaphors. I'm suggesting that "telepathy" is merely "sympathy" ("feeling together").

Yet it isn't hard to see why this way of looking at the world hasn't been popular in the West. Tinkertoy reality stresses mastery, distance, overcoming. One solves problems by rearranging the environment, not oneself—partly because we're so out of touch with inner feelings and partly because we don't see the environment and ourselves as part of the same unity.

I have a cube of ice in Boston and one in Detroit. My Boston cube is sitting next to a cup of boiling water. Normally we would say it's "closer" to this boiling water than it is to the frozen water in Detroit. But in terms of temperature this isn't true. Our use of "closer" is arbitrary—we attach more importance to spatial distance than to temperature distance. But if we all had the ability to leave our bodies and travel instantly to another city, and yet didn't know how to make fire, we would probably be calling the two ice cubes "closer." We use spatial distance as a metaphor for all differences, but it's only a habit—acquired perhaps because spatial distance has always seemed so great a barrier to human intimacy.

Spatial thinking makes us miss a lot of solutions to our everyday life problems. We tend always to look outside ourselves for answers—to seek remedies that involve spatial movement and search. We would rather spend an hour trying to replace a broken object than ten minutes repairing it. Or take a psychological example: a man is only attracted to submissive, dependent, and unsophisticated women, but eventually they bore him. He gets involved with one after another and devotes all his energy to educating them and getting them to be more independent. When he fails, he leaves them in disgust. When he succeeds, they leave *him* in disgust. Looking always for just the right woman he exhausts himself and dies. A second man might have the same pattern, but sees the problem as internal—realizes he has a perverse wish for something that isn't good for him. He would work out his ambivalence toward women and then easily manage to find one who's clever and sophisticated but still doesn't frighten him. Most people stumble through life with the delusion that they're in pain because they're not getting what they want. People free themselves from neurosis only when they realize that their suffering comes from wanting things that hurt them.

In other words, instead of rushing about the landscape, looking for something you can't possibly find with the receiving set you have, you might do better adjusting the receiver so you can find it all around you. This doesn't mean that adjusting the receiver is always better—they're just two different ways of doing things and each one takes you somewhere. Sometimes you *can't* adjust your tuning until you've spent a certain amount of time rushing about the landscape. I'm emphasizing tuning because Tinkertoy reality teaches us that rushing about is the only way there is, and we've just about exhausted ourselves with that approach.

I think we're beginning to move toward a reality style that depends less on this spatial metaphor. Distance doesn't have the meaning for human relationships that it used to: if we're separate, distant, detached, or different from one another it's less likely to be for geographical reasons. We can feel close to people far away and experience those nearest us as foreign. Spatial thinking also plays less part in the way we see life histories. People used to see themselves as traveling through life on a narrow track: they would say, "He's going to go places," or "I'm not getting anywhere in my life." A job could be a "dead end" or "an avenue to bigger and better things." People were assessed in terms of how much they had of some good or bad quality, not how it fit together with other qualities. Today there's a tendency to evaluate people in terms of how "together" they are, rather than by how "far" they've gone, and to look for balance and integration rather than trophies.

These changes are subtle and tentative, but they open our minds to other ways of thinking about reality. They make it easier for us to see it not just as something we can touch, but as a frequency we can tune in and out of. Knowing how much of matter is empty space, we can conceive of the possibility that a picture taken with a camera of the highest imaginable speed would show nothing at all, or at least nothing we would recognize—that it would capture the world in an "off" phase. For some people have suggested that "reality" as we know it pulses in and out of awareness so fast that it looks constant to us. We don't notice its disappearance any more than we notice that the image on a movie screen isn't constant, or that the world vanishes briefly every time we blink our eyes.

It also becomes possible to think of material reality as just one of an infinite number of frequencies that we're capable of experiencing. We're tuned to that material channel almost all the time, but we don't need to be. Some religions, in fact, go further and argue that the material world is an illusion. This kind of exaggeration is designed to shake Tinkertoy minds out of their lethargic rigidity, but it seems pointless to talk this way once you have a person's attention. The word "illusion" just means, "we don't think that's an important piece of experience—pay attention to the one we've got for you over here." Personally, I'm not ready to abandon that piece of my experience and neither are the people who say the world is an illusion. They exaggerate to counteract the exaggeration that material reality now receives, but I'd rather just say that material reality is what we pick up on one of many frequencies. It's the frequency we're taught to attach the most importance to—the only frequency we're allowed to call "real." It's very important for staying alive. And while you can be alive for a while and not be tuned into that frequency, it seems to be an extremely hard frequency to tune into while not alive.

PSYCHIC HEROISM

I once thought Tinkertoy reality might owe something to Western hero myths, which always have some individual standing above everyone else in triumph: traveling, conquering, mastering, killing, striving, penetrating, finding, stealing, returning.

But once again, reality is what you're taught to look at. Heroes are favored by the gods—helped, given magic gifts, advised, warned. Even more important, their success often has more to do with their being in a proper state of mind than anything else. Tinkertoy narrators leave those parts out because they seem to be just some uninteresting bit of magic or ritual. But still we find traces: the hero or heroine is not centered, forgets, eats the proffered food, opens the forbidden door, fails; tries again, is centered, knows instinctively what to do, is not deceived by enchantments and appearances, succeeds.

I can't help thinking again of Robert Monroe and his out-of-the-body adventures. Where he went was determined by his innermost prevailing desires, regardless of what he consciously wanted. Thought produced energy and created forms. Distance was nonexistent; emotional inhibition, masking, or hiding impossible. In such an environment, where you go depends literally on how you feel. There's no separation between your inner balance and the outside world. One arrangement affects the other. Our everyday physical world, on the other hand, is much less closely tied to inner balances. It has its own autonomous laws, and we can influence it only if we play by Tinkertoy rules.

Or so we assume.

If it were otherwise we would never know, since we're taught to think this way from birth. A child's first words, for example, are nouns—long, stable, static events. What a distortion of her world! A world in which everything is fleeting, moving, impermanent, with great rushes of feeling inside, continual movement of light, the overwhelming excitement of reverberating sensation between people, brilliant colors, and who knows what else that we've learned not to sense. And what labels are selected to summarize all this movement and feeling?

Ball. Cup. Mommy.
Not: shining, burning, loving.

Our language is one-dimensional—one thought has to follow another, all in a line—but experience is three-dimensional at least. Talking is like trying to portray the sun with a piece of string. And because experience is multi-dimensional while language is one-dimentional we have to "shut off the internal dialogue" to tune into it properly. In other words, we have to shut off the distraction of our one-dimensional receiver. Often people who have succeeded at this try to bring the experience back into verbal reality with them, but usually they fail. Words destroy the width and breadth of experience, where all the most important and magical effects take place.

I don't really know any more if the rules we're playing by are imposed by physical reality itself, or if they're just self-imposed by now and "reality" is moving on while we stay in the same place. I.Q. tests hawk a particularly stunted form of Tinkertoy reality, but the most imaginative scientists are now trying desperately to transcend the Tinkertoy style in an effort to deal with some of the more puzzling mysteries of the universe—puzzling, that is, if you try to understand them in Tinkertoy terms. Unfortunately, the rules of Absolute Reality are inaccessible to us, almost by definition. We only know Tinkertoy rules, which work pretty well. And when they don't we look the other way: "I didn't see that!" says the comic actor, confronted with some violation of "natural law."

Techniques for learning to meditate always remind me of instructions given to heroes and heroines in myths and folktales: "Concentrate on this, ignore that—let that go by." I suspect that in the earliest forms of those stories the instructions for keeping oneself centered in a tough situation were the most important and interesting part. The rest, after all, is pretty obvious: either the hero/heroine stays centered and succeeds or doesn't and fails. The action—so important to us—is trivial from another perspective: kill the dragon, steal the treasure, disenchant the lover, rescue the maiden—they follow automatically. Once the proper state of mind has been achieved these are just chores, like washing the dishes or taking out the garbage.

Remember all the stories where the good brother or sister has an adventure, brings back some treasure, and then is imitated by the bad brother or sister, who follows the same instructions but fails miserably by being thoughtless, stupid, or evil-hearted? Maybe Western folklore isn't as Tinkertoyish as we think. Things go wrong in fairy tales or myths, for example, when people lose a sense of participation in the whole pattern of life. They become self-interested and surly, they disobey instructions, violate taboos; they become ambitious and arrogant; or they give way to unintegrated impulses. Impatience is one of the most frequent causes of personal or cosmic calamity in myth and folklore. Lack of charity is another.

Success, on the other hand, comes from being attuned to nonmaterial realities, and from participating in a unity that transcends the individual. The hero or heroine is not fooled by appearances, because he or she is not restricted to Tinkertoy vision. In the same way, Castaneda's Don Juan picks out, in a crowd of people, those who are not human beings: "Real people look like luminous eggs when you *see* them. Nonpeople always look like people. . . . When you *see* them they look just like what they're pretending to be" (*Separate Reality*, p. 54).

Success also comes when the hero or heroine experiences group needs as intensely as personal ones. "Temptation" is just a trial to see whether private impulses have been successfully dissolved in the greater unity. Christian writers have made such trials seem like a moral affair, but they're nothing of the kind. The trial is purely practical: if one's ego isn't dissolved, failure, injury, or death may result. Castaneda's "apprenticeship" takes many years because he has to lose his exaggerated Western feeling of personal identity—his sense of self-importance, tragedy, and drama. To confront "nonordinary" reality as an atomized individual is too dangerous. Don Juan will allow him to confront the "ally" only when he's capable of becoming *one* with the ally (*Separate Reality*, pp. 57–8).

In a Welsh legend the hero, Manawyddan, is tempted by the gods with food, drink, entertainment, and immortality. He refuses all because he is so perturbed at a calamity that has befallen the gods, one that only a mortal can set right. He then engages in many heroic enterprises, with the usual travels and battles. But the key victories are all internal. In one case he avoids danger by keeping his mind altogether blank, in another by being insensitive to his personal peril; but above all, he achieves success by dividing the minds of his opponents—by distracting them, arousing contradictory impulses in them, and generally keeping them off center so that they can't work their magic spells. Compare this with Monroe's remark about traveling out of the body: "Let one stray thought emerge dominantly for just one microsecond, and your course is deviated" (p. 63).

Manawyddan's most serious opponent, for example, is a superlative thief, Gwiawn. Endangered by Manawyddan he starts to play a spell on a stolen harp, but Manawyddan distracts him by calling his attention to one of the magic treasures that Manawyddan carries and that Gwiawn, were he worthy of his reputation, might be expected to steal. Covetousness spoils Gwiawn's concentration and breaks the rhythm of the spell. His mind wanders into planning—just as such thoughts will intrude on meditation—and the spell is ruined. Then, as Manawyddan comes closer, the thief puts stealing out of his mind and tries another spell, only to have the same thing happen again.

Such stories are well to remember when we think about opening ourselves to alternative realities. We don't necessarily need to look to the East for all our guidance in psychic matters, for there is much that lies buried in our own heritage.

THE MAYOR'S
SILENCE

The mayor of Gelton was a garrulous man. No matter what the occasion, he always had a lot to say. Yet he was a popular politician, for he spoke warmly and energetically on behalf of the common people, and although by no means radical, he could usually be counted on to stand behind his promises. Other politicians appreciated him for his loyalty, his gregariousness, and his good humor. But his talkativeness was a joke to everyone.

As the years went by the mayor became sensitive about it. He knew that he talked too much, and he knew that the joking was affectionate. He was also wise enough to realize that a harmless human weakness in a leader was a political asset—that people loved and trusted him because they could so easily locate the flaw in his character. Yet it wounded his vanity that he could be so easily dismissed as a harmless old chatterbox.

One day he fell into an argument with a friend who had teased him about his verbosity. The friend bet him that he couldn't keep silent for an hour if there were other people in the room. The mayor accepted the bet and then vowed on his own behalf to keep silent for a whole day.

The Wayward Gate

The news traveled quickly and soon the whole town knew of the mayor's vow. Crowds came to witness the phenomenon and joke about it. Groups of friends devised temptations and engaged volunteers to test out the mayor's pet provocations.

But it was all in vain. The mayor's ego was totally involved in the effort, and the more people tried to provoke him, the more powerful he began to feel in his silence. A sense of his own dignity as a human being spread over him—he realized that we are all more complex and diversified than the stereotypes we play out to amuse others or to accommodate our own vanity. The feeling of joy and peace that this thought gave him was so intense that he wanted to tell everyone about it, but he remembered his vow and kept silent.

Hours went by. He had won the ridiculous bet with his friend and was well on the way toward fulfilling his own vow. The people of the town were getting more and more strained in their efforts to move him to speak. As they sensed the dignity of his silence their jokes began to falter. They didn't know quite how to deal with him without his flaw. It took him away from them in some way, and they felt awed, and a little angry. Some wanted to protect and honor his vow by withdrawing, others were aggravated to the point of desperation. No one felt funny about it any more.

The mayor could see what was happening and wanted to reassure everyone—to tell them that he still loved them, that he hadn't really changed, that he just needed this one day to assert his full humanity. But he remembered his vow and kept silent.

Night came and another day dawned. The mayor had not spoken a word and in another few hours the time would be up. The crowds returned to see how he was faring, but his silence continued.

As the final hour approached, the mayor began to regret the passing of his triumphant interlude. He reveled in the grudging awe of the people and in his own strength of character. He dreaded his return to the garrulous role that had won him his office. He wanted to retain the dignity for which he had fought so hard. He felt so strong, so serene—why give it up now? Why not continue a while longer?

With less than an hour to go the people noticed that the mayor was getting restless, and with every passing minute this restlessness increased. And with every fidget the people began to look more relaxed. Some began to smile. And with each knowing smile the mayor felt more and more resistant to falling back into that familiar role. Several times he opened his mouth to speak, but at the sight of the broadening grins that greeted this gesture he would clamp his mouth shut again and fidget some more.

Finally, with only a few minutes remaining, he could stand it no longer: "I've decided I want to continue my silence for at least another day. This has been a tremendous experience for me and I want to say——"

The rest of his statement was engulfed in a burst of relieved laughter.

CHAPTER 8

METAWORLDS

. . . exclusionistic science has faithfully, though falsely,
functioned. It would be world-wide crime to spread world-wide
too soon the idea that there are other existences nearby . . .
—Charles Fort

One of the strangest discoveries of our century was the finding that objects—particularly organic ones—are physically affected by the shape of the spaces in which they are placed (Ostrander and Schroeder, pp. 366–99; Watson, pp. 87–99). Perhaps all the forces we know and understand are produced by shapes, as well as many that we don't. Perhaps all shapes exert pressure to mold energy into patterns that extend and revitalize themselves. This, after all, is what organisms do—break down other shapes to perpetuate their own. Could it not be that all shapes do this as well—some less vigorously than organisms, but some a great deal more? Perhaps we just wander into one shape after another, calling them force fields when we notice them, or astrological configurations when we're not sure. Perhaps we live permanently in some, just as billions of microorganisms inhabit the human body without being the slightest bit aware of its shape or the forces that pattern its insides.

We can see our own galaxy and some others, but can't see any overall pattern to the universe. A microbe on the lining of the intestine, if it had eyes, might similarly see some surrounding tissue but wouldn't be able to see around the bend of that particular wrinkle, and could have no concept of the whole intestine, much less the whole organism.

We don't know what shapes coerce our being. If the universe is a single living entity we can no more see our part in it than the microbe. Yet some part of us is always aware that there's more to existence than meets our narrow-gauged little eyes. We know we can't hear above and below certain frequencies. We know we can't see things that are too small—and it stands to reason that we can't see things that are too big, either. Maybe all the galaxies we can see are just bright specks on a corner of a flea's bottom. But that flea may just have been resting for a second during those billions of years. Or the expanding universe may just be something someone's exhaling—someone who may at any moment start inhaling again. Scientists are too susceptible to the notion that things will go on as they have been. Too often they place themselves in the position of the historian in 1788 who discussed the future development of the French monarchy.

Imagine a little ant, trudging along, helping build a great colonial structure, doing his part to work toward a better tomorrow—part of a grand design. Then a huge human foot suddenly comes down and crushes that whole design and the ant with it. Or think of a Newfoundland dog charging through an intricate spider web in a garden. Or think of us, growing and developing, perfecting ourselves, getting in tune with the universe: there may be a huge foot coming down on our galaxy at this very moment. We never know when our part of the pattern—the part we help create—is going to be dissolved in a larger one. But it's important to remember that the dog and the foot are part of the pattern, too.

DOLLS, PETS, OR SAVAGES?

Freud once remarked that human vanity received a mortal blow when Copernicus found that the earth circled the sun

The Wayward Gate

instead of vice versa (1953). But it turned out to be just a flesh wound. For although we now realize that our planet is just a provincial byway in a small galaxy we still like to see ourselves as *psychologically* important in the whole scheme of things. We get quite uptight when faced with the possibility that we might be primitives even within our own galaxy.

Charles Fort saw us as fish in the depths of a galactic sea, puzzled when wrecked ships, bodies, and other debris from storms occasionally drifted past us on the way to the ocean floor. He suggested that we were sometimes fished for.

My own analogy makes more concessions to human narcissism. Imagine an energetic tribe of jungle people, living on clusters of islands. They have a well-developed system of trade and a lively oral literature, as well as art, music, and dance. Skilled sailors and navigators, they frequently discover and settle new islands. They have a central metropolis of some 2,000 souls where the king dwells and much of the trading takes place, and people who live there think that this is where the action is. They can't imagine that there might be other explorers. Then one day Europeans appear and "discover" them, at which point a lot of odd visions that people have had in the past—strange-looking boats with odd-looking people—suddenly make sense.

I think we're going to have to accept the role of backward primitives pretty soon, and it may be rather unpleasant. But can we be so vain, when we put a man on the moon, as to imagine that we're unique? That millions of other planets in the universe aren't also engaged in space exploration? When scientists rouse themselves to contemplate this question, it's with a curious lack of imagination. They figure out how many million planets in our galaxy might have life on them. Then they estimate how many might have civilizations "as advanced as ours." What we *don't* see is estimates of how many civilizations are so advanced that they would make us look like slugs and snails.

Our own encounters with alien explorers would fill a library, but it's simply too humiliating for a highly-trained scientist to think about. After all, other people might have some menial role to play when space explorers finally arrive, bearing the green man's burden. But our scientists will be like the witch doctors who fought the onslaught of European medicine—just obsolete obstructionists.

Then again, if we're really at a slug-and-snail level of development, maybe none of us have a role. This would explain the lack of interest in us shown by most UFOs. How many people, walking through a marsh, bother to converse with worms and frogs? Only an occasional naturalist, starving hermit, or curious child would pay that much attention. Imagine the worm's-eye view of humanity that would be acquired from centuries of living in a mangrove swamp. How many useful generalizations could you make about human culture from a couple of downed pilots with parachutes, a crazed recluse, a few naturalists, an escaped convict, and the odd hunter?

In 1917, 70,000 witnesses saw a miracle at Fátima, Portugal. Not only was it seen by a lot of people, but it had even been accurately *predicted* (hence the large crowd). Scientists say if you can predict, you're home free, but naturally this applies only to data that make scientists comfortable.

The church thought it was a miracle, scientists ignored it, many writers today think it was a UFO. What still isn't clear is the motive. People like to attach some kind of importance to an angel from the skies: that it was a delegate from somewhere—that it meant something. But so far it seems pretty meaningless—an isolated, disconnected, nonsensical interaction. I think it was a lost, neurotic, extraterrestrial schoolgirl, playing goddess with the worms in a marsh. We may smile condescendingly at those 70,000 people who thought they saw the Virgin Mary, but what would we have thought *we* saw had we been there? And what difference does it make what name we give to an event that so outdistances our primitive awareness?

Yet even an event like that is much less difficult for us to grasp than an out-of-the-body experience, or telekinesis, or precognition. A civilization that flies around in metal vehicles—even if they come from Tau Ceti and can transcend the speed of light—is only quantitatively more advanced than ours. No civilization that had mastered the psychic realm would bother with anything as clumsy as spaceships. It would just be an exercise in handicapped ingenuity—like learning to tie knots with one hand.

If there are people flying by from Tau Ceti, they're almost as primitive as we are.

The really "advanced" civilizations (and who first decided, I wonder, that evolution should be thought of as a gigantic elementary school?) have probably been here and everywhere else all along, and will continue to be, without our knowing it or being bothered by it. Occasionally, perhaps, a mischievous child might make its presence known ("Dear, how often have I told you not to tease the goldfish!") but by and large we might expect the relationship to be one of noncompetitive coexistence, like squirrels and aphids in a tree, or intestinal bacteria and body lice on a human.

Many of the great moments in myth and history might be the result of occasional breakdowns in this pattern of noninterference. Joan of Arc, for example, might have been fostered by a small group of superchildren, who gave her aid and encouragement for their afternoon amusement and then hastily abandoned her when they were called in for supper. Perhaps they were even punished for meddling with the humans. In the same way we might rearrange the pecking order of a group of hens—giving a steel beak or spurs to one we liked and then taking it back.

The best portrait of such interference is the *Iliad*, in which Olympian superbeings amuse themselves by playing with live soldiers instead of plastic ones. Their emotional involvement in the game is given exaggerated emphasis by the human narrators—for understandable reasons—which makes it hard to detect their real motives. Their biggest problem seems to be boredom—just what we'd expect from a small group of people forced to be in each other's company forever, sick of each other's hang-ups and longing for diversion and fresh blood. But this, too, could be a human projection.

Another possibility is suggested by domestic experience: humans may provoke interference only when they become noticeable in some way, like vermin in a human kitchen. Perhaps some superbeing periodically gets annoyed that the planet has become infested with parasites and attacks them. A few escape and reproduce, as chronicled in the universal myth of the flood survivor (Noah, Deucalion, and so on). The notion that all these Noahs were chosen people, of course, is sheer vanity. They were just the lucky ants or roaches that survived the insecticide spray, stamping foot, or whatever.

We consider something a pest when it appears in large numbers (or when we fear that it will). It's those prolific species that collect in groups or industriously build some sort of ugly dwelling that attract human attention and get exterminated. We might similarly imagine that human cities, roads, and other signs of our presence could eventually attract the attention of beings who would see our presence as an infestation—a violation of their notions of beauty and order. One species' home, after all, is another species' nuisance, and the frantic industry of ants, termites, moles, beavers, gophers, and humans rarely yields a beauty to match the casual flowering of forest and field.

On the other hand we might be serving some useful function. Perhaps the earth is part of a laboratory experiment for some eager teenager's Science Fair Project: "Species Evolution on Three Atmospheric Planets Under Contrasting Experimental Conditions—A Longitudinal Study."

In any case, it seems plausible to me that beings in any really advanced civilization could (a) assume nonmaterial form, and (b) transcend time and distance. What they would do with these capabilities is almost impossible for us to imagine, since our ways of looking at the world are so totally determined by our being encased in material form. While I think it puts a damper on life to view the body as a prison, it does tend to limit one's perspective. How could we conceivably imagine what it would feel like to be utterly freed from mortality fears and all their egoistic derivations: wounded pride, hurt feelings, unrequited love, squelched rage, stage fright, humiliation, failure, ambitious striving, abandonment and loss, pressures of every kind? Not to mention the more reasonable but insistent demands of the body itself?

What does seem clear is that any nonmaterial beings who would involve themselves in a personal way with the lives and goals of humans would have to be a frivolous, disturbed, or decadent segment of that advanced civilization. What kind of human being, for example, would play games with insects or frogs: trying to alter their relationships, supporting and abandoning certain favorites, setting tasks, punishing the unloved, and so on? The gods of Homer and the Bible are portrayed as cockfight enthusiasts, bear-baiters, and little boys pulling the wings off flies. Their motivation rarely seems to transcend the ten-year-old's level of moral development—alternating between sadistic frivolity, sanctimonious enthusiasm, and punitive brutality. Theologically speaking, I think we got in with the wrong crowd. Western deities seem to have a prurient interest in the affairs of humans—seeking human followers and human admiration and enjoying their power over human activities. Zen Buddhism, by contrast, simply offers a transcendent state to those who seek it; although it must be admitted that few religions, East or West, are free from all taint of divine interference in human affairs.

The idea of an advanced, nonmaterial civilization existing invisibly side by side with our own, with only an occasional rip occurring in the Corporeal Curtain, finds an interesting echo in the readings of Edgar Cayce on Atlantis. Cayce describes nonmaterial beings—"thought forms"— projecting themselves into matter and then becoming trapped in it, unable to doff their materiality (*Edgar Cayce on Atlantis*, pp. 56–83). Experimenting with a variety of forms, apparently for amusement, they create and propagate a variety of hybrid monsters and give themselves over to a hedonistic lifestyle, using the knowledge and power of their spiritual existence to further their decadent pursuits. They produce organic slaves, harness vast material forces, and ultimately bring about the destruction of the continent, forcing them to flee to South America, Egypt, and the Pyrenees. In all of this they are opposed by a group who seek an escape route to their original spiritual and collective existence.

This conflict between baser and more exalted (though "fallen") beings appears in the Bible and other creation myths. Genesis speaks of "the sons of God" and "the daughters of men" (6:2, 6:4), and one of the Dead Sea Scrolls has Noah being suspected by his father of being one of the "sons of heaven" and not his own child. The flood itself is made by God to "make an end of all flesh" (Genesis 6:13). Von Däniken uses this material to support his theory of a superior race of astronauts, worshipped as gods by the beings they had created through manipulation of the genetic code—beings who continued, in the face of severe punishments, to mate with the animal species from which they had been separated (*Chariots*, pp. 34–44; *Gods*, pp. 26ff., 143–62).

Choosing among various unorthodox theories of human origins can only, at this stage of our knowledge, be a matter of taste. But it's at least worth noting the frequency, in many traditions, of certain themes: the division between a spiritual race and a material race; the iniquity of the latter and the punitive anger of the former; a series of efforts to destroy the material beings; widespread human copulation with animals (and "gods" with humans) and the creation of hybrid monsters; the existence of subhuman slaves, some of them giants, others inorganic; the story of a fall, usually associated with loss of immortality; and a period of time in which people lived for hundreds of years—a time felt to be the golden age of a superior civilization. Whether all this was the work of a decadent race of spirits or of flesh-and-blood astronauts is up for grabs, like the rest of prehistory.

Actually, there's no reason why both couldn't be true: the discovery that Vikings visited the western hemisphere didn't negate the later voyages of Columbus. It seems likely that alien astronauts have often appeared in the history of our planet and left some sort of mark. If I incline a little more to the Cayce version it's only because it seems to tie more threads together: particularly the tension in almost every cultural tradition between material and spiritual existence. Where would such a tension come from? Why would anyone seek a bodiless state if it weren't a potentiality? People who have out-of-the-body experiences—once they recover from their initial terror—seem to find flying rather natural, as if flying were the proper condition for humans. There's a sense that bodilessness is "the way it's meant to be"—all energy, movement, flow, and feeling. Not in the cold, dead, cerebral way that some "spiritual" or highly intellectual people represent "liberation from the flesh," but in a way that celebrates and accentuates the best and most joyous feelings that the body itself offers.

In Cayce's reconstruction of Atlantis, the embodied and power-hungry inhabitants harnessed some very explosive forces with their technology and destroyed both themselves and their continent. Only a few escaped, presumably in the airborne and submarine vehicles they are said to have developed. Thus the "gods" of Von Däniken need not have been extraterrestrial astronauts at all, but could instead have been Atlantean refugees, carrying their superior civilization to primitive peoples.

Scientists and scholars are most resistant to the idea of a superior civilization existing in the remote past. They're quite willing to believe that Plato's Atlantis existed if they can play down its age and achievements and stick it on a small island in the Aegean. Jacques Cousteau, the explorer, carried this to its ultimate absurdity by searching the Aegean seabed for thirteen months and then announcing that Atlantis was just a fantasy of Plato's, since he had been unable to find it there. We could just as well decide Rome was a myth by searching for it for a year along the Mississippi River. But this is quite typical of the arbitrary revisionism of armchair skeptics. Plato said Atlantis was a continent and was quite explicit about its geographic location, great age, and cultural superiority. Why take *any* of what he said about Atlantis seriously if not this?

Before dismissing all these ideas as fanciful we should remind ourselves that science is rooted in tenets that can at best be described as provincial. Modern astronomy rests on the premise that the entire universe is just like our little corner of it, while the theory of uniformity, on which so much of geology, biology, paleontology, and evolutionary theory is based, makes pretty much the same assumption about history. Imagine how we would smile if a primitive tribe, living on a dormant volcano, thought that the whole world was just like their peaceful little island, which in turn had always been just as it was now! *Yet a startlingly large portion of our most sophisticated scientific "knowledge" rests quite explicitly on these two utterly ridiculous propositions.*

THE GOLDEN AGE

When I was in college, for example, it was fashionable to point out that the ancients, in their profound simplicity and pessimism, had thought the Golden Age to be in the past, whereas we, gifted with a twentieth-century perspective, knew it to be in the future. (Apparently no one has ever thought it was in the present.) And while I doubt that any historian today would have the effrontery to advance such an opinion of the future, the idea of a past Golden Age is still thought to be an ancient superstition.

I'm beginning to have a lot more respect for ancient records, and if they all say there was a time in the distant past when civilization reached a peak of peace, prosperity, and cultural elegance, I'm prepared to pay attention. Why should they all invent such a notion? Where would they get the idea? Psychoanalysts argue that it's a metaphor for the

The Wayward Gate

bliss of infancy, but in that case why didn't people have it in 1950? It wasn't so long ago that psychoanalysts treated the flood myth in the same way—water meaning "womb," or "unconsciousness," or whatever. It sounded rather natty until geological evidence accumulated that all those primitive peoples the world over had simply been describing something that actually happened. How many times are we going to have to be surprised in this way?

Scientists think that everyone else in the world is addicted to believing nonsense, and their favorite example is magic. Now we've seen how quick all of us are to ridicule observations that violate our basic assumptions, and no one who claimed that a magic spell actually worked would survive with an unblemished reputation for sanity. Yet we know that most of the acts that people are taught to perform for survival in the world are things that have worked. The longer people have been doing them, the more practical they usually are. Imperialistic countries have had a hard time understanding this because they've seen Third World peoples doing things that looked impractical by Western notions of the good life, in which everyone has their own automobile, hair dryer, and machine gun. But it's a bit arrogant to assume that a tribe of people could live for centuries under arduous conditions cheerfully investing energy in things that never worked. *We* may enjoy the luxury of believing utter nonsense, but they do not.

On the other hand, we also know that people hang on to things that *have* worked long after they've *stopped* working. And we know that when people don't understand which of a complex series of acts is the one that works they usually continue to perform the whole lot. What's absurd is to assume that someone could *invent* a magic spell that didn't work and get everyone to keep using it for centuries under conditions of extreme practical necessity. If we want to assume that primitive magic is ineffectual (an assumption that is universally made and almost never tested) it seems more reasonable to view it as a remnant of something that once worked than to see it as a primitive invention. As Von

Metaworlds

Däniken points out, the cargo cults that sprang up in the South Pacific after World War II show how an apparently meaningless ritual can come about through imitation of a more sophisticated and poorly understood civilization.

In one sense primitive magic and religion aren't primitive at all, but a great cultural advance, for they transcend our biological limitations in a way that technology doesn't. Tinkertoy reality is mired in survival needs, like the eye of Ornstein's frog, while magic and religion stretch beyond these limits and explore functions that have little to do with biological survival. Hence they may be the decadent form of a culture more "advanced" than our own. The conservatism of many "primitive" tribes also suggests decay rather than emergence: hanging onto the remnants of a great civilization, almost forgotten.

Parts of our own culture share this trait—the parts that scientists keep trying to stamp out. Luckily they haven't succeeded, for what seemed irrelevant in the industrial era may well be the foundation of the era to come. It usually turns out that way—what's scorned on Monday is adored on Saturday, and vice versa.

Many people have predicted disasters and calamities for our planet between 1980 and 2000. I'm still skeptical about this—the earth's demise has been predicted so often I suspect it's only a kind of cosmic death wish. Yet the sense of crumbling institutions amid the chaotic stirrings of new life is hard to escape. If nothing is plunging in on us we're certainly plunging outward—not into space so much as into a total transformation of our minds. The changes of the future will have very little to do with technological development, which isn't change, after all, but more of the same. They will involve a drastic revision of the way our minds work—a new reality style. In particular, three popular eighteenth-century ideas will recede into the background to await the next Dark Age, several millennia hence.

The Wayward Gate

MATTER

The first is the idea that matter matters. In Tinkertoy reality matter is of the foremost importance. The tiniest bit of matter—a virus for example—makes the scientist feel he or she is dealing with something "tangible" (a key word in Tinkertoy science). Physics has slowly been moving beyond this point: it's now fashionable to consider very tiny amounts of energy as "real," although this opens a Pandora's box that few scientists are ready to deal with. They've been saying for some time that we should pay more attention to relationships and less to things, but so far the effect of this statement has been on a par with Jonathan Peacham's wish that human beings could be good. Once you take the statement seriously the bias against psychic phenomena can no longer be maintained, and this is too threatening for most scientists, who would have to apply their advice to their own work.

Tinkertoy reality maintains that two people cannot occupy the exact same physical space at the exact same time. We know, of course, that they can occupy the same space if they do it at *different* times. It doesn't seem to require any great burst of imagination to go one step further and suggest that two people could occupy the same space at the same time if they were separated on some fifth dimension not yet accessible to us, given our constricted sensory range.

TIME

A second notion that will probably fall into disuse is that time is linear and moves. Time to us is like a book, or music: you start on a narrow track and stay on it until "the end." Books, music, movies propel us through time, unlike paintings and sculptures, which are just there all at once. Of course, you don't *have* to read a book in the order it was written, and a great many people never do. But reading words backwards or randomly is futile. Books are *meant* to be stretched out in time.

The thing that most certainly moves on a linear time track is normal consciousness. Perhaps it's the only thing that does. What we *call* time—the thing that passes—is an illusion of consciousness. I would argue (as others have) that all time exists simultaneously—that consciousness consists of playing a tape of one part of it.

Think of it this way: time is a huge valley and we're standing on a hill looking over it. It's nighttime and we have a powerful flashlight. We play it over the valley, trying to see what we can see. Thus we're following a moving point of light—making a narrow little ribbon of awareness. We're only seeing a little bit of the valley, and what we do see we see as a moving line. If the darkness is complete and someone else is holding the flashlight the line may actually look straight to us, even when it zigzags all over the valley. Furthermore, we can only see one point at a time, although we can remember, with middling accuracy, what we've already seen.

Now the sun comes up. The valley is enlightened and so are we. We see the whole valley at once and it takes no time at all. We can, of course, keep our narrow perspective and follow a little path around the valley with our eyes, but it's harder to do with the lights on.

This metaphor says two things about consciousness: first, that it's wrong to say we're conscious of what's actually there—consciousness is only the little bit we bother to look at. An oft-stated point but one we need to keep saying until we believe it. Second, the metaphor says that the illusion of time requires a surrounding darkness. If our consciousness were expanded to take in the whole valley, time as we know it would vanish—past, present, and future would coexist— just as it sometimes does for mystics.

When I drive from New York to Boston, for example, I say that Hartford "comes after" New Haven. What I'm suggesting is that when we say the Russian Revolution "comes after" the French Revolution we should think of this as having exactly the same meaning. That is, if we weren't traveling this particular route, the Russian Revolution might come before the French Revolution, or at the same time, or not occur at all. If I drive from New York to Washington, Hartford "does not occur."

Time, then, could be thought of as a large spatial area, which doesn't move but just is. It appears to move because *we* are moving, just as the landscape appears to pass by when we drive from New York to Boston. It seems linear because we're moving in a line through one segment of it. Time isn't "happening"—we're looking at a part of it from the rear end of a moving train.

Think of a huge sphere, like our planet. Somewhere on that sphere (or in it) draw a line an inch long. That line is human history, and the moving pencil is us, experiencing time. We follow the flashlight as it moves, but the valley just sits there. Consciousness moves, we move. That's what consciousness is all about.

This way of looking at time illuminates two confusing phenomena: psychic prediction and ghosts.

Take ghosts first. Ghosts are of course the most suspect of all psychic phenomena. The available evidence contains more hoaxes, more frauds, more publicity-seekers, more credulous and suggestible observers than any other type of psychic event. The ghost literature is largely deserving of the scorn that scientists heap indiscriminately on all psychic phenomena. Watson wants to dismiss the whole idea of "ghosts" on the grounds that so much of the data can be explained in terms of telepathy (p. 274).

This is certainly true. Most apparitions coincide with the moment of death, and could be interpreted as an urgent telepathic communication from a still-living person. Even the best ghost cases have the peculiarity that they're not always seen by everyone present, while those who see it one time may not be the ones who see it an hour later and vice versa.

Still, I'm not yet willing to dismiss as "suggestible" or "collectively hallucinating" the thousands of highly-intelligent people who have had such experiences. If they're suggestible in the afternoon, why don't they remain suggestible in the evening? If they're faking it why don't they do it more efficiently? And if they're hallucinating why don't they hallucinate anything else, or at any other time? The fact is, we have a huge literature reporting visions of nonmaterial entities that seem related to persons who are dead. Usually they're connected in some way with violence, although the death itself need not always have been violent. The apparitions themselves usually behave rather aimlessly and stupidly, as if they were "stuck" in some event.

Now suppose we have the latent capacity to see all of time at once—that the information is available to us, although unconscious (as in the valley metaphor). Normally we screen it out to protect ourselves from overstimulation, but occasionally something leaks through. What kind of information would be most likely to permeate that screen? Watson, talking of Backster's work with plants and the sensitivity of all living matter to murderous impulses, proposes a universal, cellular SOS signal, to which most of us have somehow managed (fortunately) to deafen ourselves. But for those who retain any sensitivity to such signals, it seems to me that this is precisely the kind of information that would penetrate the time screen we've erected in order to confine our awareness to the present.

It was violent *intent* that freaked out Backster's plants, not just the acts of violence themselves. While their reactions registered on the polygraph we obviously have no way of knowing how the stimulus was *experienced* by the plants, or how it would be experienced by us. It could well be through an apparition in our case. This is to say, a violent emotion, intent, or act in the immediate vicinity breaks through into our awareness because we're responsive at some level to danger signals, even when they transcend time. (Just as strong emotion close to us in time can transcend space telepathically.) The aimless stupidity of the ghosts may be due to the fact that they're not engaged in any significant instrumental act but merely reverberating with some impulse. Their very aimlessness might be a result of their breaking into vision at a moment of intense preoccupation: a vivid murderous fantasy entertained while mechanically lighting the lamps or doing the dishes.

Psychic predictions present a more complex problem. Obviously the self-professed psychics that make newspaper predictions are mostly charlatans engaged in educated guesswork—given the shotgun quality of the predictions and their plausibility, some of them *have* to be right. On the other hand, the Bulgarian Vanga Dimitrova, a state-supported psychic who has been repeatedly investigated by panels of scientists, has an 80 percent record in predicting highly specific and unique events in the future. She seems particularly accurate in predicting the date of one's death and in locating missing persons. Apparently Vanga Dimitrova has the ability to see the whole valley, although imperfectly (Ostrander and Schroeder, pp. 265–88).

Furthermore, there are indications that this is not a special "power," but rather an ability available to all humans—a channel of communication that most of us prefer to keep blocked. Dr. Lozanov, a physician who has studied Vanga Dimitrova, tried the first time he saw her to foil her by imagining himself as another man. Although she identified him correctly, as well as his motives and his effort to block her, she was not able to give an accurate reading, as she acknowledged herself. Since, on the same occasion, she accurately foretold future events for a colleague, Lozanov concluded that her ability was merely telepathic—that somewhere we carry a knowledge of the future within us (Ostrander and Schroeder, pp. 276–77).

Yet the picture is more complicated than that. It isn't just that not all of her predictions come true—whatever channel of awareness we use, it sometimes seems more blurred than others. But all psychics, even the most palpably gifted, occasionally make *confident* predictions that are inaccurate. That is, while any psychic tends to be more certain of some statements than others—feels clearer, more aware, more attuned or whatever—even the most certain assessments are occasionally wrong. Is this more of Nature's whimsy?

Many of Edgar Cayce's predictions have not come true, although his record is extremely good and his medical readings seem to have been almost infallible. His more global predictions, furthermore (such as wars and earthquakes), were rather broadly stated—he would give a range of dates rather than a specific one. Even more important, his life readings were often couched in contingency terms: if the person does so-and-so then such-and-such will happen, while if she moves in the opposite direction another outcome can be expected. In other words, some predictions seem completely deterministic, while others seem to assume free will (Stearn, 1968).

The valley metaphor helps clear up this confusion. To be psychically open is to know what lies "ahead" of us in the valley—to know what the flashlight would pick up next if it continued in the same direction. But it may *not* continue in the same direction. Our consciousness may *change* direction, in which case the prediction will be inaccurate even though it correctly located an event "ahead" of us. Just as we can reasonably predict that we're going to encounter New Haven on our way from New York to Boston, although we might decide to take a detour on the spur of the moment. In the same way, I can tell you what you're going to encounter on the last page of this book, but I can't predict with certainty that you'll get that far, or, if so, when.

One puzzle remains. I know why I'm going from New York to Boston. But I don't know why we're traveling through time on the particular route we've taken.

LADDERS

The third obsolete idea is that life is a stairway to paradise—for individuals, cultures, or species, in this world or the next. In other words, that anything grows or evolves or develops to some point of perfection and is then finished. We've lived for a century and more with the idea of progress or evolution—some sort of ascent, triumph, climax: all of life just racing to get to the victory banquet.

But victories and grand finales are created by cultures. Nature just comes and goes, and every race is like the caucus-race in *Alice in Wonderland*. When you get to the top of the mountain you just have to come down again. People grow up, mate, grow old, die, are born again. Who saddled us with the idea that life is a test of skill with a trophy at the end? It certainly can't be blamed on us Westerners, since it infests many reincarnation doctrines, including the concepts of karma and nirvana. I've always been uneasy about the idea of nirvana—it has the ring of "When I *really* get to the top I'll be able to retire and leave this whole rat-race behind."

I think I mistrust any religious system that features numbers and hierarchies of prestige. The minute people start talking about the Ten Commandments or the twenty-four levels of enlightenment my reverie is shattered by the recognition of a familiar mundane voice. Virtually all religious ideas have been funneled through pedagogues by the time they reach us, and we know all too well the exquisite refinements of professorial devotion to prestige and order. When you hear a recorded symphony it's useful to know which is the symphony and which is surface noise. Whenever a guru talks of numbers and hierarchies I hear a scratchy needle.

Life is movement—circling, going out, changing, returning changed, going out again changed, and so on. And the changes themselves cycle and alter. Life isn't a Parcheesi game ("You have landed on the mass-murderer square—lose forty-seven karma points and return to square one as a moray eel"), or going up an escalator and getting off at the top after you've made the right moves. What's so wonderful about the top? If you're climbing a mountain going up is good, but if you're skiing the best part is going down. Flying is a beautiful feeling but if you want a little human contact it's nice to land.

Metaworlds

You can't go toward something without going away from something else. To focus is to lose context, while to see the whole picture is to see very little. In Zen the goal is non-attachment, but is it wisdom *never* to say: "This is my home, or country, or loved one, or community—I can't live without it, and if it goes, I go with it"? There's something humanly frail and humanely modest about attachment.

There's great pleasure in letting go, and great pleasure in hanging on. All of culture—art, poetry, music, drama, literature, ritual—is a kind of hanging on, clinging to things, unwilling to let them pass on. Culture is a great effort—sometimes it isn't worth it and then letting go is ecstatic. But without all that hanging on, letting go would be boring and vice versa. Sometimes it seems that everything I see is the center of an elaborate pattern—like a magnetic field—that radiates out to infinity. And each of those patterns is formed around a conflict, like a whirlpool formed in a stream by opposing currents. Every shape we see is such a whirlpool—an interruption in the flow of energy, a hanging-on. Some ambivalence makes an elegant little disturbance in the stream—a little eddy—and each has a unique fantastic pattern that radiates and reverberates through the whole universe in an exquisite dance.

In my valley metaphor, I talked about seeing the whole valley at a glance. Distance helps us do that. But being farther away doesn't allow us to see any *more*. It just allows us to see a larger configuration. Imagine, for example, an infinite series of concentric circles. The farther out we get the fewer small circles we can see—more and more of them blur into a black dot at the center. But the closer we get the more outside circles are lost, because they fall outside our field of vision. *Close or distant, we always see the same number of circles.* By the same token, wherever we stand, whatever position we take, whatever viewpoint we adopt, no matter how we move or what tools we use: we always see the same degree of complexity around us. Never more, never less.

CHAPTER 9

HANDS OFF

If now, affairs upon this earth be fluttering upon the edge of a
new era . . . all of us will take on new thoughts concordantly, and
see, as important evidence, piffle of the past—Charles Fort

Is it the prolonged infancy of humans, or is it the burden of
consciousness, that has us searching the heavens? People
have been asking, "Are we alone?" ever since humanity became literate. Perhaps writing things down is the
problem—writing is a very unsociable medium. I don't
think people fret as much about the existence of God in
oral cultures.

In the last chapter I discussed the strong likelihood that
the universe contains beings who would seem like gods to
us. This doesn't mean, of course, that we need to swallow
any of the religious visions that have come down to us, for
all of them are corrupted by human misperceptions. We
need to be particularly skeptical when people start having
their deities behave like parents: parents are so
projectable—why should extraterrestrial beings be any less
likely than teachers, bosses, or therapists to have that pa-
rental cloak thrown over them? When gods start reward-
ing, punishing, and telling people how to behave I take it as
more surface noise.

It's fashionable just now to reinterpret all the epiphanies
of religious history as visiting spacepersons—Ezekiel's
wheel as a flying saucer and so on. The earthlings kept be-

lieving the visitors would return some day and save the world, but they haven't; hence the theory that God is dead. (Better He should be dead than just to have lost interest in us.) Or, alternatively, the visitors were superseded by a completely nonmaterial civilization, giving rise to the suspicion that "God is everywhere."

The "God-wears-a-space-suit" theory is interesting and plausible and probably correct, but it doesn't really solve the cosmic uneasiness it pretends to solve. The thrust of the argument—popularized by Von Däniken—is something like this: "Poor, funny, primitive ancestors—they thought the spacepeople were gods, and worshiped them!" But what exactly *is* a god? If we were and still are as primitive to them as monkeys are to us, then "god" might be an appropriate term to use. Maybe we shouldn't feel so condescending toward our ancestors until we know for sure exactly what they were dealing with.

Suppose we discovered that the biblical God was after all just some minor flunky in a huge celestial civilization, but did in fact do all the things he is said in the Bible to have done, including the Creation. Where would that leave us? Our vanity would be injured yet again, but he'd still be God to *us*. I've always been too caught up in the obvious fact that all of our information about such beings has been filtered through dull-witted pedants, charismatic egomaniacs, and self-serving professional cliques; ignoring the equally obvious fact that there must be beings vastly "superior" to us in the universe and that people have always sensed that.

The orderliness of the universe has often been advanced as an argument for the existence of God. I've always thought this was silly. Orderly compared with what? Others have used the *disorder*, or evil, in the world as an argument *against* the existence of God, which seems even sillier. Evil compared to what? But it strikes me now that using Plato's technique we can find points of contrast *within* our world that are quite relevant to the question. It's actually technology, of all things, that suggests an answer—an answer the exact opposite of the usual one: If we and our natural world are to some degree orderly and predictable, how much more so are the machines we create; this suggests the possibility that *as the machine is to us, so are we to less orderly beings.*

Order is predictability, and predictability has value only when we want to control something. Scientists want to predict because they have an emotional investment in manipulating and mastering their environment. (Other people avoid predictability on the grounds that it takes all the fun out of life.) Machines are predictable because they're instruments of our control. We might serve in a similar capacity to another race of beings—a more playful, less anxious race requiring less predictable machines. Science-fiction writers have always been fascinated with the idea of androids or cyborgs—manufactured organic beings designed for tasks of various kinds—grown in a laboratory like chickens on a modern chicken farm; but it rarely occurs even to science-fiction writers that earth might be an experimental laboratory for breeding a sophisticated species of semi-predictable androids. On the other hand, our predictability might serve no useful purpose whatever.

What makes us orderly and predictable is primarily our concepts, for our instincts are not very specific about the multitude of stimuli we encounter in our daily lives. Our predictability comes from the way we conceptualize our experience—our tendency to group events and respond to them as a category or class: A, B, and C are pleasures; D, E, and F are painful; G, H, and I are sins; M, N, and O are humiliations; J, K, and L are boring; W, X, and Y are "a trip," and so on.

The richest source of predictability is our tendency to form concepts of ourselves and then try to live up to them—to be a "good," "strong," or "together" person. This means we never respond clearly to any situation or stimulus, because we interpret it in terms of what it means for what we want to be. Even the effort to respond clearly founders on itself: trying to be a person who lives in the here-and-now is merely another self-concept. A fair chunk of clarity can be recaptured if I'm not trying to *be* anything in a given situation—if I can allow myself to look as joyful, miserable, awkward, graceful, silly, stupid, weak, powerful, soft, spiteful, dull, mean, helpless, sentimental, swinish, prudish, fussy, obtuse, plodding, whining, insensitive, cruel, or uninteresting as I feel. Most of us find this impossible even when we're completely alone.

I can predict the behavior of someone who wants to be cool, kindly, sexy, strong, nurturant, *macho*, or spontaneous. I can't predict the behavior of someone who responds cleanly to the event. Events are too specific, too unique, and the feelings they arouse too dependent on the details of one's personal history, combined with current bodily conditions. This suggests that it's our egos that make us into androids. A superior, less ordered race of beings would seem as chaotic to us as we would seem to conscious machines.

Volumes have been written about the unconscious, about dreams, myths, hallucinations, and psychic experiences (conceived as error)—all trying to reduce these phenomena to some kind of simple Tinkertoy order. If machines were to undertake to analyze human thought processes they would run up against the same problem. (In fact, what they probably would come up with is pretty much what experimental psychologists have been doing for the past fifty years). For how can something simple and predictable analyze and understand something unpredictable and complex?

We all assume that we're of a higher order than our machines. But by the same token you should attribute divinity to what emerges from what you like to call, in good capitalistic tradition, "your" unconscious, since it's far less ordered and predictable than you are in your conscious life. To "primitive" peoples a touch of chaos suggests a superior being—a spirit, a god. We Westerners aren't so insightful about this, even though we have the machine to teach us: We tend to look down on chaos, just as a computer might feel superior to its programmer because she was slower at adding figures and had an imperfect memory for details.

One of our handicaps in thinking about these things is our inability to separate our heads from our hands. We think of superiority as greater control. For us, mind is grasping. "Do you grasp my meaning?" Our thought is dominated by our hands. We wonder: "What do dolphins *do* with all that brain power? Why don't they protect themselves, save their environment, *run* things?" The great brain of the dolphin seems mysterious because most of our fantasies of superior civilizations are just exaggerated imitations of our own: bigger, more cerebral, more power-hungry, more ego-ridden, more lethal. The fact that we can kill or capture dolphins and they can't kill or capture us is what makes us see them as an inferior, less intelligent species.

Yet the history of human culture is one long series of civilized peoples being overrun by barbarian hordes who absorb the conquered civilization, become civilized, and are in turn overrun by another horde of unlettered savages. Mesopotamia, Greece, China, and India provide many examples. Dolphins are probably the closest model we have for what a truly "advanced" civilization might be like— highly social, responsive, pleasure-loving, indifferent to personal death. Perhaps we'll have the capacity to "conquer" such a civilization one day, so that we too can learn, in the only way we seem able to learn, the futility of power.

MAKING IT

As a species we're unique in our manual dexterity. What we use of our big brain is largely geared to touching, handling, and manipulating the world around us. Watson observes that "if human proportions were determined only by the nerve supply, we would have hands the size of beach umbrellas" (p. 171). Expressive people can't talk without their hands, but as a species we find it hard to *think* without our hands. Our brains are all snarled up in our fingers.

Hands Off

We're so used to thought being tied to control, to "grasping," that we seldom notice how fundamental it is. Gardner Murphy, for example, comments uncritically on the fact that scientists are never satisfied with spontaneous material: "even if [the scientist] should work in a field in which nature permits little or no control of her performances—a field like geology or astronomy—he *reaches out* to find something which he can *take apart*, examine closely, *cause to happen* over and over again." In short, he tries to "get experimental control over his phenomena" (Murphy, p. 51; italics mine).

There is, of course, an elaborate rationale for this procedure, but in fact manipulation is not vital for the acquisition of knowledge. Or rather it's essential for only one branch of knowledge—the kind that leads to technology, to control over nature. Experimental science might best be called "Manipulative Science," for it's founded on, expressed through, and directed toward the manipulation of the environment, human and nonhuman. Such a science may be necessary and desirable but need not present itself (as it does today) as the only science worthy of the name.

Sometimes it's in petty things that we can see a character trait most clearly. For thousands of years people have been dowsing for water with forked twigs. When scientists started to take dowsing seriously one of the first things they did was to substitute a manufactured steel rod for Nature's own (Ostrander and Schroeder, p. 191). Reasons were given, naturally, but even without those reasons, can anyone imagine scientists investigating dowsing *without* making such a change? Manufacture is for the scientist what pissing on a tree is for a dog—a way of marking a territorial claim.

Manufacture ("hand-making") is so fundamental to us that we can't imagine a superior civilization without it. But brains and hands are intimately linked only for species that *have* hands. A species that didn't have hands would be far less concerned with manipulation ("handful-ing") and far more concerned with communication ("sharing in common"). There's a lot of our brain that we don't use and no one seems at all clear what it's for. Maybe it's for the same thing that the dolphin brain is for, except that our consciousness—the hand-ridden part of our brain—is so dominant as to force the rest into the background.

Our brains are running on manual.

Perhaps the unconscious is more than the chaotic manure pile suggested by psychoanalysis—rich in impulse and life, poor in meaning and direction. Perhaps it's a latent resource—a biological time bomb waiting to be triggered by some external, even intelligent, force. Perhaps it's an entirely different kind of mind, free of manual obsessions.

Tinkertoy thought is resistant to psychic phenomena because they challenge the rule of thumb and threaten to transfer dominance to the less handy part of the brain. It's because dolphins have no hands, for example, that their big brains seem so mysterious to us. The accepted notion is that a lot of the dolphin brain has to do with communication, yet they can't even write things down. Since our own communication system is based so heavily on technology and the manipulation of visual symbols it's hard to imagine dolphins doing much more with communication than we do.

This leaves us with three possibilities. One is that the big brain of the dolphin is just Nature's way of being cute. Another is that the big brain is a hangover from some primeval time before the dolphins decided to go back to the sea and goof off. A third is that it just enables the dolphins to play some elaborate chess game with each other by calling out signals. So long as we assume a purely material existence, there just doesn't seem to be much sense in the dolphins having that big brain. If they're just going to groove on the ocean, why all the heavy intellectual equipment?

If, on the other hand, we allow for the possibility that nonmaterial forms can exist, the mystery disappears. If humans can leave their bodies, why not a dolphin? If John Lilly can explore all kinds of strange psychic spaces, what's to prevent his former subjects, whom he treats with such admiring condescension, from doing the same?

A manual brain sees the material body as the beginning and end of life. Hands deal with matter, and are made for hanging on to things, not for letting things go by. But without hands, life is just an unguided tour to one location. When it ends, something else comes along.

Until I read the literature on out-of-the-body experiences I could never take seriously the idea of immortality—particularly the various theories of reincarnation. There was just too much patent wish-fulfillment involved. People's "past lives," for example, always seem disproportionately prestigious—one wonders who cut the wood and hauled the water in the old days, since there seems to have been no one around but kings and queens. Edgar Cayce, it's true, produces a reasonable proportion of ditch-diggers and haberdashers, as does "Seth," but by and large the purveyors of past lives, for all their clairvoyance, can't seem to see past the elite. I guess I'm always skeptical when the nonmaterial provides too much fuel for narcissism in this life. John Lilly's "guides," for example, sound a bit too much like fond teachers with a star pupil—always grooming him for something better—and one can't help thinking that this is a role he's probably played all his life. He would expect to be chosen by the gods to help enlighten humanity.

But this is a very tricky point. Suppose John Lilly went to the Himalayas and wrote a book saying that mountain climbing is where it's at; that he, John Lilly, had mastered it in double-quick time and was now the best in the land; that nothing was happening in the Himalayas *but* mountain climbing; and that he, having been taught by the greatest masters, had developed a system for learning the art which he was passing on to humanity so that we, too, could pass through the twenty-seven levels of attainment to the pinnacle on which he now stood. We might have some doubts that life in the Himalayas was as he presented it, or that he was as proficient as advertised, or that he had The Way. But would we therefore doubt that the Himalayas exist?

In any firsthand document there is coloring and distortion. Every narrator is telling a story of which he or she is the hero. What adventurer or explorer, writing of his or her exploits, comes off looking bad (intentionally at least)? We expect this, take it for granted. We know that the conquerors of Mexico and Peru missed a lot, misunderstood more, and were outrageously pompous in their understanding of what they did. But we still take their documents seriously as an ignorant perception of something real.

The more unusual and unprecedented the experience the more it will necessarily be distorted. Monroe understood himself as "seeing" and "hearing" events because these were the labels he usually applied to incoming information, although later he realized that the way he sensed things was quite unclear. A new experience is difficult to portray accurately because we may have only old and irrelevant categories for it—both Monroe and Lilly, for example, used spatial metaphors to describe their "journeys." People who have unusual psychic experiences are as limited by their own preoccupations, motives, and perceptual categories as anyone else. When something extraordinary occurs the devout person will describe it in conventional religious terms, the science-fiction enthusiast in terms of space travel, the child in fairy-tale language. All three will sound absurd to a scientist, used to applying his *own* conceptual tools to data for which they're tailor-made. As Charles Fort remarks, "all reports upon such phenomena are colored in terms of appearances and subjects uppermost in minds" (*New Lands*, p. 145).

People see something extraordinary and do what they can to make it familiar. Fort has several cases where multiple witnesses saw "mirages" in the sky—usually cities or marching armies. He effectively demolishes the conventional "explanations" (auroras, or "reflections" of armies and cities on the ground), leaving the puzzle intact. Something extraordinarily complex was seen in the sky on those days and nights, some by sophisticated observers. We may never know what. But when we hear that a Frenchman in 1871 saw a procession of objects in the sky, moving very fast but capable of stopping in midair, we immediately suspect UFOs, since this capability is what first attracts the attention of so many twentieth-century observers. Our suspicion is confirmed when he says that one of them "fell, oscillating from side to side *like a disc falling through water*" (Fort, p. 146; italics mine), for this metaphor appears repeatedly in modern UFO sightings. In other words, as an event recurs it builds up its own categories and images. We suspect we're seeing the same kind of event when the same metaphor is used to describe it. In time we can even distinguish subcategories and correct early misperceptions. We know, for example, as Fort did not, that the vehicle didn't "fall," but was just approaching the earth in a characteristic but as yet inexplicable manner.

But let's return to the material body. Matter might be defined as ambivalent energy: two opposing forces create a stasis, the same way two opposing impulses do, like love and hate, or anger and fear. Release one, and the other one pops out, too. (The metaphor may be objectionable to scientists since energy is supposed to be unmotivated, but that, after all, is more than we know.) Certainly most human energy is trapped in internal conflicts—people who have few of these knots seem full of available energy. Some energetic people, of course, are just driven—energetic only as long as they can turn everything they do into a task (since they're unconflicted about tasks); but others seem to have natural energy—full of joy and enthusiasm. Sometimes we call them flighty and use airy and insubstantial adjectives to describe them.

Perhaps there are degrees of materiality that reflect the amount of ambivalence. Perhaps a being that had *no* preoccupation with self—the source of most such ambivalence—would consist of pure energy. The size of the ego is the weight of the anchor, dragging our beings down into substance, binding it into matter. Self-consciousness makes clods of us all.

I suggested earlier that matter could be thought of as ambivalent energy—like a whirlpool caused by an ambivalent current—becoming a "thing." It could also be argued that three-dimensional space itself is created by the word "not." So long as everything is One, then everything is everywhere and nowhere at the same time. The moment we say that A is not B we create a separation between them, a distance. The whole of three-dimensional reality is an arrangement of such distances, differences, "nots." For to the degree that A and B are not the same thing they are in different locations. We use physical space as a metaphor for all kinds of distance—psychological, temporal, thermal, and so on—but fail to notice that physical space might itself be a metaphor, as Jane Roberts' voluble spirit, Seth, so often points out.

Now I've represented humans as predictable, orderly, and hence inferior beings, weighed down with self-consciousness and repetitious internal conflicts. This is a little unfair, since we also dream at night, and in dreams space becomes recognizable as the metaphor it really is. Our dreams suggest that we share at least some of the capabilities of less orderly, more advanced beings: non-manual thinking, intelligence without control. This is why dreams are so important to non-Tinkertoy traditions. And this is why so many psychic careers begin with an effort to introduce consciousness into the dream world.

SIXTH TALE

PASSION IN PARMA

Once at the court of Parma there lived two powerful courtiers, Ugo and Paolo. Year after year they plotted and intrigued to improve their positions at court, both with considerable success. But most of all they plotted against each other, for as time went by, each became the other's only serious rival.

One day Ugo went hunting, his mind so distracted with schemes and counterplots that he scarcely noticed where he was going. As he wandered aimlessly through a thick wood he came upon two foxes copulating in a small clearing. Quickly he drew his bow and in a moment had impaled the couple on a single shaft.

When Ugo inspected his double kill satisfaction turned to astonishment, for the male fox was familiar to him—an old and crafty specimen who had eluded him so often in the past that Ugo had long since abandoned hope of ever catching him. The effortlessness with which he had finally succeeded, after so many years of futile sweating through tangled thickets, made a deep impression on Ugo. Was the call of love so compelling that it could blind this shrewd old fox to mortal danger?

Ugo turned the event over in his mind all the rest of that day and long into the night. When he finally fell asleep he dreamt he was himself a fox, trotting up a hill toward the setting sun. Suddenly, framed by the sun's hemisphere, he saw the outline of another fox, its head pointed directly toward him. Inflamed by the noble bearing and dignity of the other animal, Ugo snarled and charged. But as the sun sank, so did the silhouetted fox, and by the time Ugo reached the crest of the hill, both had disappeared. Then Ugo realized that he was on the edge of a towering precipice overlooking the sea. But instead of water, the sea held the fallen sun, flaming and bubbling in a vast, deafening, molten confusion. And in the midst of this volcanic brilliance was the vanished fox—leaping, writhing, diving, and twisting—whether in ecstasy or agony Ugo couldn't tell. Almost blinded by the dazzling light, Ugo turned away to soothe his eyes on the peaceful landscape he had left behind. But as he did so another light struck his forehead and he saw the sun rising in the East, although he could still feel the heat from the molten sea behind him. Perplexed by the apparent contradiction he stood immobile, and as he sought to resolve the dilemma the scene faded until he was aware of nothing but the warm light striking his forehead. This proved indeed to be the morning sun coming through his window, and Ugo awoke.

Ugo couldn't get the dream out of his head all day. His schemes seemed to have lost their usual savor, and he found himself playing his parts abstractedly—although he was too gifted a courtier for a day's preoccupation to affect his performance very noticeably. Late in the afternoon he was walking in the garden with the rest of the court when he noticed his rival Paolo in private conversation with the Prince. A familiar anxiety suffused his stomach until the strolling pair reached the balustrade, behind which the setting sun suddenly framed Paolo's head and shoulders. Ugo finally realized the significance of his dream.

From that moment on Ugo's plotting took a completely new tack. All his current schemes were instantly demoted to diversionary tactics, designed to distract attention from his new master plan. He even contrived to lose one or two important contests, as a way of enticing Paolo to relax his vigilance.

Meanwhile he studied his rival's sexual preferences with minute care. He began to understand almost better than Paolo himself the kind of woman that attracted Paolo, that moved him, that enchanted him, that excited him. He talked endlessly with Paolo's ex-loves, and came to realize not only what Paolo wanted, but what he needed, and what he prevented himself from getting. He discovered that Paolo shied away from those women who were likely to fulfill him in any permanent way, being drawn instead to those who initially aroused but ultimately frustrated or bored him. The secret, Ugo decided, was to create a situation in which Paolo would be tricked into mistaking the kind of woman he could really love for the kind he was attracted to; or perhaps to force him into intimacy long enough to break down his usual barriers.

But where to find such a woman? And how to create such a situation? And what if the woman didn't care for Paolo? Ugo felt at times that the task was insurmountable. Yet he knew Paolo well, with the kind of intimacy that can only come from spending all one's days trying to read an opponent's mind. He almost felt that he could experience Paolo's psyche as his own—he knew he would recognize the right woman instinctively if he saw her. And if she was right for Paolo, would not Paolo be right for her? He was handsome, intelligent, gifted, gentle—most women were attracted to him—wouldn't the suitability be mutual? And what if it weren't? An unrequited love would simply be a different kind of fire. And as for creating the situation, that kind of arranging was child's play to Ugo. It might take months, but he knew he could do it.

As it turned out, it was only three months after the birth of his plan that an opportunity arose to carry it out. Word came from France that the eminent and aged Comte de la Rêve had died, and that his young widow, Francesca, a native of Parma and a distant cousin of Paolo's, was returning in another month. Paolo, as her nearest relative of suitable rank, would be expected to travel to Geneva to escort her back. Ugo made this easy for Paolo by devising a pretext for being away from court himself during that period.

Ugo had met the Comtesse in France a year or two before, and had been deeply impressed with her beauty, brilliance, and warmth. He realized immediately that she was precisely the woman he sought. She had left Parma scarcely more than a child and Paolo had not seen her since. Ugo felt lucky, and seized the opportunity without a moment's hesitation.

Thus it happened that a few weeks later Paolo found himself and the Comtesse taken prisoner by a small army of mercenaries and held for ransom in an obscure mountain castle in Lombardy. Ugo had chosen the setting with care—the castle was small, poor, and isolated, with a charming little garden and a spectacularly beautiful view. The prisoners were confined together for three weeks and then allowed heroically to escape and wander in the wilderness for several days before being rescued.

The strategem was successful. Paolo and the Comtesse returned to Parma madly in love and fatuously happy. But this was only half of Ugo's plan. While Paolo and his new love were confined in Lombardy Ugo had been preparing the foundations for the other half.

Months went by, and the passion of Paolo and the Comtesse remained undiminished. When Ugo had made all his preparations, bribing allies and informants both in Parma and in France, sowing suspicion and planting misinformation, he finally struck. A letter from Francesca to powerful relatives in France was twice intercepted—the first time by Ugo in Parma, who had a page inserted by a clever forger and then smuggled it back into the Comtesse's household where it was resealed with her own seal. The second interception occurred in France and was made by a forewarned agent of the Prince. Since the letter now contained information that would have sorely embarrassed the Prince had it come to the attention of the French court—information known only by Paolo, Ugo, and one or two more of the Prince's closest confidants—the Prince had no choice but to banish the couple from his kingdom.

Sixth Tale

A vigilant Paolo would have sniffed out so bold a plot. His own spies would have anticipated at least one of Ugo's, somewhere along the line. A counterbribe, a false informant, a treacherous servant—with so many involved, so close to home, discovery would have been assured. But Paolo was too contented, too joyous, too enraptured to care.

Fortunately for Paolo, Ugo had played his cards so deftly that even the French believed Paolo had betrayed the Prince for their benefit. It wasn't the first letter of the Comtesse's that Ugo had amended, and he had also planted rumors at the French court suggesting that Francesca detested Parma and the Prince and longed for her adopted country. The French king, therefore, delighted to recapture this jewel for his court, invited the pair to return to France, where they were married in honor and awarded a magnificent estate. While they were loved and welcomed at court frivolities for their beauty and charm, the couple spent most of their time at their own estate, where they reveled in the sunshine of each other's company and patronized the arts.

Ugo, in the meantime, grew to a position of unchallenged eminence in Parma, until the Prince was ruler in name only. Under Ugo's direction the state attained an unprecedented degree of prosperity, peace, and security. Honors, titles, lands, and riches poured into Ugo's hands and his family became one of the most powerful in all Italy.

Twenty years passed, and one rainy November Ugo had occasion to visit the French court. On the third day of his journey he was traveling through a deserted region when darkness began to fall. He had passed by one inn in his haste to reach his destination, even though the next inn was several hours away, and no sooner had night fallen than he found himself in the midst of a raging storm. His driver, blinded by wind, rain, and darkness, promptly took a wrong turn and lost his way.

After hours of aimless wandering they saw a light in the distance and hurried toward it. It soon proved to be a large chateau and Ugo sighed with relief. Leaving the driver to see to the weary horses he leapt from the carriage and rang the bell. A sleepy servant let him in and informed him that the chateau belonged to Paolo and Francesca. Torn between dismay and curiosity, he slept fitfully that night in anticipation of the morning's encounter.

His fears proved groundless. Francesca and Paolo greeted him warmly and plied him with questions about Parma. Remorsefully he confessed every detail of his plot against them but they only smiled and reached for each other's hands at the memory.

"Should we be angry at you for bringing us together?" Francesca asked. "A plot so thoughtful has more in it than hate. Your scheme succeeded because it was so close to the truth: You were just a little bit ahead of our own wishes."

From that day on, whenever he journeyed to France Ugo always stopped to visit the couple at their chateau. He experienced a delicious relaxation in their company and basked in their warmth and contentment; while Paolo and the Comtesse feasted avidly on news and gossip from their homeland. All three were the same age and died on the same day, in their eighty-ninth year.

CHAPTER 10

THE MAGIC

OF THE WEST

> The difficulty of moving from Germany to France, say, or from
> competition to cooperation, or from March to April, is created
> by our entertaining the notion that there is a gap or barrier
> between Germany and France, between competition and coop-
> eration, between March and April. If we stop believing in that
> gap or barrier the difficulty ceases to exist.—Ugo da Parma

Scientific theories never quite fit all the data around, but
since they fit most of the data that people care about, we're
justifiably reluctant to change them. The things that don't
fit seem trivial at first, but as our understanding increases
they seem to come nearer, and therefore begin to look bigger, until the theory starts to seem inadequate and a new
one emerges. The theory that the earth was flat, for example, fit most of the data that mattered to people until the
great voyages of discovery in the sixteenth century. Only
astronomers needed a round earth—for others the dis-
crepancies could be handled with makeshifts.

Changing a theory because of a few deviant events is like
junking a car that has always run well and never needed
repair, to buy a new, unknown one—it's wise to do these
things slowly. Our Tinkertoy world wasn't built in a day
and a new one won't be either. Tinkertoy reality is the only

The Wayward Gate

one we really know, and to many of us the others seem strange and repugnant. I still have to overcome a slight feeling of embarrassment, for example, when anyone talks about acupuncture meridians and "energy flows" and so on. Some internal voice mutters "unscientific nonsense" and I feel a touch of shame to be taking it seriously. It seems alien, looked at through the Tinkertoy lenses I still wear; it just isn't my style.

Yet all such systems are potentially useful maps, and although fragmentary and confusing, they relieve the emptiness of uncharted spaces. We can't afford to be snobbish while wandering in unknown seas: every traveler has something to tell us, even though many have annoyingly self-important ways of distorting their experiences. Any frame of reference helps us see more—no matter how fallible, it provides a ground against which we can see a new figure. Without it we could see nothing but chaos and would be blinded by confusion. Pearce's observation, noted above, that science has made great advances with mistaken assumptions is an example of this.

Furthermore, we seem to be in need of a more radical alteration of our scientific premises than we have ever had to have before, which is perhaps why we find so many Westerners gazing round-eyed at the decayed wisdoms of the East—wisdoms hopelessly corrupted: the mumbled and garbled rituals of a ceremony whose meaning has long since evanesced, contaminated for centuries by the social systems in which they were preserved, riddled with hierarchy, social callousness, and elitism, preaching selflessness but full of subtle arrogance.

Must we take the decadence of the East along with its wisdom? The West has its own mysteries: democracy, passion, commitment, openness. And change, after all, is just a matter of new combinations. It's always the same old Unity, but its great richness is created by dissolving and recombining its elements. Suppose we junk East versus West and make a North versus South arrangement? Or Northeast versus Southwest?

The Magic of the West

Democratize enlightenment? Popularize the Mysteries? It's been tried before. Usually it winds up as the worst of both worlds: Western arrogance combined with Eastern superstition. Maybe the whole idea is Western arrogance. And maybe the resistance to it is Eastern decadence and passivity.

One thing that makes synthesis difficult is that Eastern religious traditions demand complete commitment. A religious system, after all, isn't a supermarket. You can't just sift through it like a prospector, looking for some nugget to cash in. It's a living fabric—to experience it you have to put in on whole, like getting inside the body of an animal to see what it feels like. Westerners often don't understand this because Western thought assigns so little value to subjective experience. Yet to approach Eastern religions with a Westerner's critical dilettante style is like trying to understand time by taking a clock apart.

Actually, no real synthesis ever came from sorting things out critically. Critical thought tends to compromise rather than to synthesize. But how can you synthesize two systems and be totally immersed in one of them at the same time? This seems like an insoluble dilemma, but like all such dilemmas it exists only because we look at the world from the ego's narrow crabbed viewpoint. The question is, what is it that's being immersed? It can't be just a mind—it has to be a whole person, carrying a whole culture, so that there's a meeting of two real forces. Otherwise you just get OM-on-the-range. Synthesis isn't a logical process—*it's created by the immersion, not by the bather* (despite what our Western arrogance would like us to think). I don't do the synthesizing, I'm just one of the *ingredients* of it.

To generate a synthesis, then, you can't be detached from your own culture—you have to be really immersed in it for your new immersion to have impact. You may recoil from that immersion or end up just another expatriate. But sooner or later, through someone, a new synthesis will come from that genuine collision.

The altered states that Eastern mystics achieve, the powers that Yogis have mastered—these are hard to come by. There's a strange Western notion that every journey has a shortcut somewhere. Yet there's a strange Eastern notion that only by submission to an authority can you ever learn anything. This is good for curbing the ego but it means that the old routes to enlightenment are never questioned— they're just passed down from master to disciple. Most Eastern religions are elitist, and tend to mystify enlightenment to discourage the uneducated. It doesn't take a lot of study to realize that there are almost as many paths to enlightenment as there are people—that the achievement of it is utterly unpredictable. The various religious traditions are just calcifications of how one person managed to get there—inflicted on disciples who struggle vainly with an alien strategy.

Perhaps this is the point where Western input can trigger a new jump in human evolution. Eastern "wisdom" has been imprisoned in authoritarianism and elitism like a butterfly in a cocoon since time immemorial. Western democracy has been equally trapped in Tinkertoy materialism since its inception. Perhaps as power goes to the people in the East, simpleminded materialism will lose its grip on the West.

TAMING THE TYRANT

As one small example of how Western culture might contribute to Eastern wisdom let's take the complex case of the rational mind or ego. In virtually every tradition the path to enlightenment begins and ends with the overthrow of the human ego, with its Tinkertoy chatter, anxious preoccupations, and romantic self-dramatizations. Yet this is an extraordinarily difficult task, for the ego is in charge of our individual survival, and its overthrow seems like suicide. Most of us make no distinction between our ego and the core of our being—we tend to think that the noisy ruler that continually talks to himself inside our head is the "real me." But my ego is no more "me" than George III was Eng-

The Magic of the West

land, or George Washington was the United States in the late eighteenth century. It's only a part, not the whole.

Our confusion comes from the fact that the ego tends to be a dictator instead of a democratic pilot. Furthermore it's a slave to Tinkertoy assumptions, since the Tinkerstyle was developed, as we've seen, to meet the ego's needs for security, control, and flattery, and fears of death or overthrow. Our entire culture can be viewed as the creation of a kind of "Ego Mafia"—a collection of dictatorial egos huddling together in a smoke-filled room trying to extend, through concerted action, their stranglehold over their respective territories. Each ego tries to deny its humble origins and dependence on the masses. Together they plot to surround themselves with a manufactured environment that will give the impression that the egos created themselves. When we move from the subtle curves of nature into a rectangular room we know we're in the presence of the Ego Mafia. Those right angles betray the despot's fear—his need for total control and constant reminders of his power.

The ego's tyranny, of course, may wax and wane, You know your ego is being tyrannical whenever you hurry, whenever you strive against your feelings, whenever you push yourself, whenever you fight yourself, whenever you feel self-conscious, ashamed, guilt-ridden, proud. Psychic growth comes from balance, not from "achievement," and while stretching yourself feels good, wholeness is a natural desire of your being and you don't have to force yourself to attain it. Nor *can* you. Striving against yourself—using your will to "better" yourself (by going on rigid diets, for example, or forcing yourself to meditate every day)—is useless since it strengthens merely the ego, not your whole being. Ideas of how the self *should* be are almost always ego-noise. The ego is a specialist and a utilitarian; it can tell you how to make money or buy groceries, but it isn't competent to tell you how to live.

Consider the problem of fear: Explorers like Monroe and Castenada have much to say about fear and the importance of overcoming it. At the same time, they're very responsive to their own fear signals and are not at all ashamed to flee from a dangerous situation. What they seem to be saying is that: (1) terror can prevent you from ever getting into the psychic realm far enough to discover anything; and (2) you can't overcome that terror by locking up your fear in some emotional prison and walking about like a zombie ever afterward. You can only flee, and return to confront it again and again.

The ego complicates this issue. Some of our fear is a response of the whole organism, telling us our life is in danger. But the ego has its own alarm system—like the dictator who has a palace guard. Dictators always try to equate their own survival with that of the nation, arguing that chaos and national collapse will follow their overthrow or resignation, and the ego plays the same game. When its own palace alarm goes off it calls out the national guard, puts the military on "red alert" and declares a state of national emergency with martial law.

Since exploring other realities demands that the ego be demystified and cut down to size, this surplus terror presents a major obstacle and must be overcome. But the ego is very tricky. People often respond to this obstacle, for example, by trying to abolish fear through discipline, stoicism, or reckless valor. We will not be deceived by this maneuver, however, having already detected in it the fine Machiavellian hand of the ego itself. Striving against feelings, pushing yourself—these are the earmarks of the sly fox, cleverly pretending to join the opposition.

Think again of the political analogue: the dictator knows his overthrow is being planned. He's on guard all the time. The populace has declared itself unwilling to equate the dictator's uneasiness with national security. The dictator says, "Fine! Let's abolish all warning systems, all military defense, all police departments. I'm with *you!*" Popular panic at the prospect of total anarchy quickly restores the dictator to his old position of power.

The Magic of the West

The ego's attempt to abolish fear is just a trick to prove you can't get along without a dictator.

Fear is not something to abolish. Fear is a friend. So is the ego when it renounces its dictatorship. And so is the ego's fear when you can recognize it for what it is. Most fear is an organismic response to be respected. There's no hurry—one can always return to a dangerous situation. No one's giving out medals for bravery—that's another system altogether.

But fear isn't the only bodily sensation that needs to be respected. For while some traditions, like Christianity, scorn the body altogether, the wiser ones acknowledge the paradox that the road to spirituality leads *through* the body. In part this simply reflects once again the fact that the ego is the main obstacle to enlightenment; to scorn the body is to inflate the ego even further. Ego-dominated spirituality is not enlightenment but cold-blooded, schizoid megalomania—the kind of malady that has afflicted so many religious, political, intellectual, scientific, and industrial leaders, leading to rigid ideologies and (in one form or another) mass murder. It's what Wilhelm Reich called the Emotional Plague (pp. 248–80).

If we view the body as a prison, in other words, we'll never get to know it well enough to learn where the key is. We know that is isn't through the ego, for the ego is like a turret: from it we can *see* out, but we can't *get* out. We have to turn our backs on the ego and its turret visions and go away from it, into the more down-home visions that the body provides. That's why genuine spirituality is so hard to achieve: like flies on a window pane, we're baffled that we can't fly straight ahead when we can see so clearly. We keep bashing our head on the pane, blinded by our clear vision to the fact that escape lies only a few feet away, through the darkness.

Joy is the only reliable sign of freedom from the ego's tyranny. Depression, or absence of feeling, is a clear indication of a despotic ego and a personality ruled by arrogance.

The Wayward Gate

In a truly unassuming person, emotions come and go freely—nothing is hidden or masked out of affectation and pride. And only if all these are available for easy expression can true joy emerge.

True joy centers you and keeps you connected with other people. This is how you distinguish it from elation, which does neither. Elation is a sensation that occurs when the ego feels flattered. Unlike joy it makes people feel detached from you. Joy is not only affectionate but genuinely responsive to and interested in other people. The elation of a puffed-up ego may be jovial and exuberant, and even generous in a condescending way, but it doesn't really see other people because it fears reality. It doesn't want to be "brought down," because it knows it will stay up only as long as it can spin in its own private orbit. Joy doesn't worry about being "bummed out" or "brought down" since it knows it has the freedom to bounce up again. But elation is like a balloon artificially filled with gas, doomed to expire in a dump somewhere as soon as all the gas has escaped.

The Eastern approach to the dictatorship of the ego is extremely complex, and any summary statement is bound to oversimplify. For thousands of years teachers and disciples in a hundred different traditions have been developing creative solutions. They have used techniques that trick the ego, confuse it, ignore it, seduce it, surround it, overwhelm it, or batter it into submission. Each tradition uses several of these techniques in varying degrees, while the individual master may tailor them to suit the peculiarities of a given disciple, often with the same kind of subtlety that a gifted psychotherapist might display.

Almost all traditions, however, assume that the only way to dethrone the ego is by transferring its functions to the master. The disciple submits to the master in the hope of achieving enlightenment—a kind of voluntary authoritarian contract. The master becomes the disciple's ego until the disciple is capable of dethroning his or her own ego—living by mobile balance rather than rational control.

This technique makes very good sense—even though it

218

offends our democratic values—and I feel somewhat hesitant to criticize it. I don't share the kind of knee-jerk, "what-about-freedom" response that these techniques arouse in many Americans, whose sense of their own integrity is so fragile that they're unable to entrust themselves to another person's direction for even a few minutes. A lot of what passes for "freedom-loving" in America is just the vigilant self-indulgence of people who have never experienced necessity.

Yet when all that's been said, the master-disciple approach to enlightenment has problems: One can't be sure that replacing one tyrant by another will lead to a permanent solution. There is often an implicit elitism in the contract with the guru: "I will become one of the chosen few—as he is, so will I be." The eye is on a future gain, and in this vision the cagey ego can quite easily make a secret dwelling. In the possibility of one day serving as the ego for another the ego has a future refuge, and the knowledge of that refuge may lead to a more willing but quite deceptive abdication: "I can surrender now because one day I'll not only rule myself again but also another as well."

Most traditions are well aware of this danger, and have various ways of guarding against it. But the East has never known anything but authoritarianism (unless we go back to primitive tribal democracies), and this limits the range of their thinking on such matters. A Westerner, inexperienced in Eastern ways but for some unaccountable reason moved to seek the same goals, would tend automatically to think of a more democratic approach to the problem—revolution, collective reform, or electoral repudiation rather than outside military help.

This is certainly a slower and more difficult path, but it's also a more certain one. Merely replacing one tyrant with another—no matter how loving and benign—tends to serve the people only as long as the benign despot lives, or remains benign. It doesn't make the people strong in and of itself. Were the old tyrant to return—no matter what democratic reforms the benevolent one had forced through—

things would tend to regress to their original condition. The old tyrant must somehow be reconciled to the new state of affairs—not just sit brooding on Elba. As Seth argues, the ego may have "been allowed to become a tyrant," but "it is much more resilient and eager to learn than is generally supposed. It is not natively as rigid as it seems. Its curiosity can be of great value." He also points out that a strong ego is a necessity during any act of creativity or psychic exploration. The ego's tyranny comes from the fact that it is adapted to manipulating external "reality" and is extremely uneasy about the inner sources of its power—the portions of the self from which it originates and over which it has no control. It needs to be maintained but softened, so it will acquire the flexibility to grow along with the rest of the organism (Roberts, *Seth Speaks*, pp. 15, 364, 367, 384–85).

BOURGEOIS MYSTICISM

Western egalitarianism also has a special view of our responsibility to others. Eastern traditions allow the disciple to see himself as a member of a deserving elite. Should he elect to serve the people it's just a way of advancing his own development, for the poor have earned their misery and are unimportant in the larger scheme of individual enlightenment—to help them is to engage in virtuous condescension. The Western tradition on the other hand (however disregarded in practice), says that people suffer from malformed institutions, that we are all brothers and sisters, that our destinies are linked, that insofar as one suffers, all suffer. To work for the poor is an act not of condescension but of solidarity. This way of thinking makes it more difficult to turn one's back on the world for the sake of a personal spiritual benefit (even although Western individualism has always encouraged it) without at least a twinge of guilt. In the East, such self-indulgence is traditionally a perfectly acceptable prerogative of any elite and needs no justification; in the West we tend to fall back

uneasily on some kind of strident social Darwinism or Cal-
vinistic piety to justify such behavior. In the East one can
even delude oneself into saying, "First I'll save myself, then
I'll return and save the others." In the West we've had too
much experience with social climbing to entertain such an
absurd fantasy. We know that the act of ruthless detachment that precedes "saving oneself" is irreversible—that a
man who has successfully gone through such a bitter struggle alone rarely retains the generosity to bestow its rewards
on others. The social climber says, "Let them buckle down
and do it the hard way, like I did," and the successful guru
almost always adopts the same stance.

If we accept the teachings of Eastern sages there is only
now, and one cannot help but look askance at postponed
enterprises. To save oneself before others is not a strategy,
it's a priority: it says others are less important. The usual
argument is, "How can I enlighten others until I myself am
enlightened?" But enlightenment is a matter of degree like
everything else, and the decision that one is enlightened
enough to "pass on it" must always be suspect, even if
affirmed by a master. An equally valid position would be
that there is no reason at any time not to pass on whatever
one has. Or rather, that there's only one reason—the same
reason that one becomes a social climber rather than waiting for the revolution—it's a lot slower for you if you try to
take people with you. That's why there are so many social
climbers and so few revolutions.

Why does one withdraw from the world, live in a
monastery, or hide in the wilderness? Perhaps just because
it feels right at the time. But if it's *in order to* achieve enlightenment then how does it differ from the many Western ways of planning for future profit by delaying gratifica-
tion? One gains a vision of the greater light by blinding
oneself to the distractions of the lesser ones. But if that
greater light is everywhere, then it's also here, among the
lesser lights, and what's the point of the withdrawal? Isn't
that postponement ("First, withdraw from the world, then,
when you return, you'll be able to see it for the first time") a

message from the ego—a capitalist message, saying, "Forget your friends and invest your money, when you get rich you can buy them all presents"? I guess I can't help but be suspicious of a revolutionary strategy that comes so blatantly from the dictator himself. I wonder if it isn't this latent capitalism in Eastern religion that makes so many Eastern gurus so vulnerable to Western corruption.

This raises another question: doesn't "enlightenment" disable a person for complete and passionate participation in the here-and-now? If you can see the whole, see that none of it really matters, just watch yourself unfolding— then in one sense you're not really *here*. You may be here as an onlooker—as one who experiences the world more clearly and vividly than anyone else—but it's just like going to a movie stoned: you may experience more than others but it's still just a movie. You're not *in* it. You can walk out any time.

Let's put it another way: If life is just a kind of psychodrama for working out karma, why bother to clean the stage or change the sets? You can't have a good drama without oppression, and one can play *any* part "mindfully." One could be a mindful mass murderer. If the earth is just an irrelevant stage, why not just pollute it and move on?

The question of motivation can't be ignored: If you're after personal enlightenment then this world's suffering doesn't matter. There's no way you can intellectualize a political or socially concerned life out of that motive. You need to be "endarkened" enough to think that all of that matters. And you need to be *willing to remain in the dark*—to sacrifice your own progress—to facilitate the movement or well-being of others.

Now the objection is usually made that an unenlightened person can't very well be of any help to others— that your efforts will only end by being destructive and self-deceptive. The question is asked, "Who are you to think you can be of use to others?" But one can also ask, "Who are you to think you can separate yourself from the destinies of others and rise above them?" Or, to put it another way, "Who are you to think you can be of use to yourself?"

In other words, the dilemma can't be resolved through any appeal to reason. You have no way of knowing if your efforts either on your own behalf or on behalf of others will be of any use. There's no way to reason your way into one position or the other. You can only do whichever you want to do most, or try to combine them in some way. What I would like to do now is to express some of my own concern and ambivalence about the problem and to rally you in support of my own very partial resolution.

What distresses me about the quest for personal enlightenment and growth—spiritual, psychological, physical, or holistic—is the callousness toward the rest of the world that almost invariably accompanies it. This elitist indifference toward the masses was roundly attacked by Peter Marin in a review of the human potential movement called "The New Narcissism," which, although somewhat undiscriminating in its criticisms, was a devastatingly accurate portrayal of the principal weakness of that movement—a movement of which I consider myself a part.

The problem is that our culture colors all that we do, and our quest for enlightenment is as tainted as everything else—as filled with (in this case) middle-class self-indulgence, simpleminded individualism, and ignorant class bias. It all smacks of rich adolescents who know their parents will be pleased with them if they spend a lot of money educating themselves and having a happy social life in college: "What's good for Junior is good for the country."

The most serious and sophisticated attempt to cope with this dilemma is an article by Ram Dass entitled "Advice to a Psychotherapist." If you want to be convinced of the rightness of the individualistic path it will convince you. It will also provide you with many fine and beautiful thoughts that will help detoxify that path as much as it's possible to do so. Despite what follows I admire most of what it says. There are only four statements that disturb me.

The Wayward Gate

The first is that "anything that man does in order to increase his consciousness relieves human suffering by bringing more consciousness to bear" (p. 88), which resolves all too easily into "whatever benefits me will benefit humanity." It may be true in part that my enlightenment will benefit others, but the statement is meaningless unless it's also reversed in various ways—anything I do that relieves human suffering will increase my consciousness, and anything others do to increase *their* consciousness will relieve *my* suffering. The flaw in the statement, in other words, is the one-sided phrasing—this characteristic American need to deny one's dependence on others while imagining oneself conferring grandiose boons on humankind.

The second statement is that "as long as you have certain desires about how you think it ought to be, you can't hear how it is" (p. 85). But this again involves detaching oneself from the rest of the world. My desires are *a part* of "how it is." When Ram Dass decides we ought to be free from "oughts" *he* isn't hearing how it is. Why is this part of existence less valid than all others? Why is human attachment—wishing, daydreaming, complaining, guilt, regret, longing, and all the other there-and-then passions—less valid than other forms of experience? I realize that this is a cheap kind of argument—one that can be turned against many of my own statements throughout this book—and I share with Ram Dass a strong belief in the value of stripping away as much as possible of all that noisy debris that distracts us from the here-and-now. Yet I can't help wondering why I'm trying to "rise above" the ordinary run of human being: I may in one way be getting closer to the here-and-now, but in another I'm getting farther away. It's easy to plunge myself utterly into the present if I'm pretending it's only a movie. But am I really more *here* than those who believe completely in the importance of their personal reality, even though their minds are filled with plans and analyses?

This brings us to the third statement, in which Ram Dass talks of seeking "total involvement in the physical plane," except that he's "not attached to how it comes out." In theory such a combination is possible: I can involve myself passionately in a revolution or some other project, but if it fails I laugh, like Zorba the Greek, and turn to something else—or smile at the firing squad through my cigarette smoke. But while I would be happy to have Zorba the Greek on my team in such an enterprise, I would be obliged to exclude Ram Dass, except as a kind of peripheral consultant. I don't mind having people with me who can laugh when we fail, but I don't want them to know ahead of time that such laughter will be at their disposal. I want passionate commitment to the cause right up to the end. If I'm playing for keeps, I don't want my comrades playing for laughs. I don't like games where I use real money and others use counterfeit. Nonattachment is a wonderful thing, but *if you know ahead of time* that you're not going to be attached to the outcome then you're not really involved. And to be quite frank, I don't think any American, with all that cultural training in uninvolvement and noncommitment, can distinguish emotionally between nonattachment and schizoid withdrawal.

The fourth statement is that "you can just sit inside and see your own life unfolding . . . you are not necessarily identified with the doing of it." The problem with all these statements is that they take the individual human being as the point of reference, as every good, educated American upper-middle-class affluent liberal is trained to do. But what about being or not being identified with the unfolding of a community or society or all humanity or all of life? Most of the people who dominate the human potential movement began as psychologists, and tend to see the world as a collection of unrelated individuals. It's quite easy to resolve these dilemmas if you only take one human atom at a time, but this isn't the way the world is. Ram Dass is giving advice to a psychotherapist—someone engaged in a conventional individualistic service. But what about advice to a community organizer or commune member or any of a hundred careers in which one can't even pretend to be able to act independently of others? What about *collective* interests and goals? One can't begin to change a social structure without planning and coordinating efforts, and this requires attachment, and many departures from the here-and-now. Ram Dass's advice amounts, in fact, to an endorsement of the status quo through default. Most Eastern systems are quite explicit about this: the oppressor and the oppressed must always exist in a sufficiently extreme form to allow for the working out of individualistic karma.

I think this is a serious defect in Eastern thought and I see no reason for perpetuating it. Eastern "wisdom," like Western "science," was perverted and warped by the cultural milieu in which it grew—a milieu saturated with privilege and aristocratic detachment. Why should our thought be bounded by these archaic limitations? To act out dramas in a fixed stage setting is, to be sure, a very fine thing to do; *but to act them out on a shifting, evolving stage is even finer*. Sometimes the sets get dirty or drab and need refurbishing, and sometimes we need new ones altogether. To ignore the stage, or to treat it as fixed or static, is not to be whole, for we are a part of this Earth—our stage—and it is part of us.

Suffering may always be with us—certainly death, loss, physical pain, unrequited affection, and many other deprivations seem here to stay. But oppression—though it has weak analogues in the animal kingdom—was largely invented and wildly elaborated by humans, mostly in conjunction with the invention of agriculture. If it ever had any usefulness it's certainly invisible today.

Jane Roberts's spirit, Seth, has several interesting things to say about this issue. First, he claims that the conventional EST or Gestalt attitude that "the poor are poor simply because they chose poverty, and therefore there is no need for me to help them" is likely to "draw poverty to you" in another lifetime. Furthermore, he insists that growth and development are not an individual process—that every apparent individual is only a part of some more complex personality. He also has much to say about how we involve ourselves in material reality, using the analogy of a rich man who wants to try being poor for a day: if the rich man knows he can return to his mansion at the end of the day he can never really experience what poverty is like. In any given lifetime, Seth argues, you hide the knowledge of immortality to insure "that the present reality is not a pretended one" and can be fully and deeply experienced— "you forget your home so that you can return to it enriched." (*Seth Speaks*, pp. 200ff., 205, 258ff., 346ff., 484–85, and passim.) Hence if we're enlightened, and know that all this "doesn't matter," our enrichment is correspondingly diluted: the fruits of enlightenment may be simply a pale and wishy-washy lifetime—blissful but empty. If life is just a drama, then to be aware of that fact is to dilute the experience and render it pointless. Why bother to live in this reality if we're not going to take it seriously? We might as well pick up our marbles and go home.

A case could be made that this was the essence of Christ's message, garbled by centuries of professionals with their own preoccupations. It serves as a kind of antidote to the more aloof religions of the East—encouraging passionate commitment to material reality in the form of love and generosity toward other humans. It scorns individual achievement in favor of collectivism, and trashes all forms of aristocratic detachment, for Christianity is perhaps the most explicitly proletarian of all major religions. This is the real meaning of the suffering on the cross, and the mysterious, doubt-provoking cry, "Why hast thou forsaken me?" As Seth says, if you know it isn't for real—if you know you can return to your safe mansion in a little while—then your day of slumming is meaningless. If Christ were a god, he would have to disbelieve his immortality at the end, since for life to have value it must appear "real." Hence the paradox that the more one's life is devoted to otherworldly religious activity, the less religious value it has. Charity performed to acquire Brownie points in Heaven is worthless compared to charity performed for its own sake. A life lived in relation to a vision of immortality is not a here-

and-now life. The person who lives in the here-and-now believing that this life is all there is, is clearly more enlightened than one who meditates all day trying to achieve the same goal.

Detachment is a strategy: I retire from the world, achieve inner clarity, and return. But strategies are often self-deceiving, for they pretend that the strongest motive is the one to be acted on last. Yet every animal, even the human one, tends to act on the strongest motive first. Strategies are a piece of arrogance—the ego proclaiming confidently that the impulses are all in check and lined up in proper order according to the master plan. What the ego never realizes is that his master plan was drawn up in secret by the impulses themselves, in accordance with their relative strength, and cleverly smuggled into the ego's awareness disguised as his own idea. As the impulses line themselves up in accordance with the ego's instructions their smirking docility betrays the fact that those instructions are already suspiciously familiar to them.

What usually happens is that what I do now is what I want most, and what I do later—the supposed goal of all my efforts—is actually just a weaker desire, one that can be postponed almost indefinitely. Withdrawal from the world, then, is in reality the very simple thing that it looks like on the surface: people withdraw from the world to get away from the world.

The detachment strategy is an individualistic one, and comes from seeing people as disconnected particles, rather than as segments of a complex living fabric which grows and changes as a unit. Each corner of the fabric may grow in a different way, just as the parts of the human embryo develop in unique ways and at different speeds, but the process is either a collective one or the embryo dies.

We tend to overlook the fact that Eastern religious disciplines are as much an individualistic corruption of primitive collective re-

The Magic of the West

ligion as Western capitalism. Pre-monarchic religions are utterly unconcerned with the individual or her "enlightenment." They don't *seek* a sense of oneness with the
universe—they're an *expression* of that oneness. Eastern disciplines represent a fall from that state of grace. The cor-
rupt elitist tries to return to it by withdrawing still further
from the masses and submitting his ego to the discipline of
still another elitist. He believes that through detachment he
will find participation, and seeks a purely *personal* enlightenment through discovery of his oneness with the universe! Small wonder he so rarely succeeds, weighed down
by so much ambivalence. It's true, of course, that you can
get from Nevada to California by going East for a long
time, but it seems a little roundabout—and the longer the
journey the more apt you are to miss your target.

I said that strategies are self-deceiving, since they pretend that what is done first is less important than what is
done last. The Dictatorship of the Proletariat in Marxist
theory, designed to facilitate the "withering away of the
state," is a good example of such self-deception. We usually
do first what we like best, and the later stages of such
strategies are often unavoidably detained. Some people,
for example, like to accumulate facts and analyze data before acting. Others like to experiment with life—acting first
in order to produce feedback which can *then* be analyzed.
Both strategies are quite reasonable and utterly self-
deceiving. The intellectual keeps on accumulating and
analyzing and never does take the plunge. In fact he accumulates so much information that he can never unravel
it, or even successfully relate it to the proposed action. The
impulsive man, meanwhile, never digests any of the experience he has, and, in fact, prefers irreversible actions so
that the feedback he gets is of no use anyway.

In any group of people engaged in a task these two
strategies are likely to come into conflict. Proponents of
each strategy want to impose it on everyone, leading to the
usual tedious political arguments. The fact is that in any
group some people want to gather facts endlessly while

others want to act, and both of these things need to be done. A group succeeds when it recognizes this and is able to maintain a dynamic communication between the two wings. The issue is not which strategy is "correct," but whether the two parties can maintain an awareness of the whole in which they participate. If they can, the product of such a group will be (as it always is) a metaphor of the process: It will contain real feedback loops and real flexibility.

Most philosophical and political conflict results from individualistic thinking, for Nature is not deterred by what the human ego calls "contradictions." It's like a finger arguing about which side of an object should be grasped. The problem dissolves when it realizes that one finger can grasp one side while another finger grasps the other. In individualistic America this solution, like other solutions, tends to become corrupted—appearing as "every finger just grab whatever it feels like." Awareness of the whole is the first necessity, for it's what we have most deeply lost. It's true that the world finds its way best through different people doing different things. It's also true that people seeking radical change often waste untold energy trying to get everyone to pursue the same strategy. On the other hand, the tolerant, pluralistic approach that everyone should do his or her own thing is equally a creation of the Ego Mafia, for it gives each ego free rein to run its territory dictatorially.

Let's take a specific example, close to home. I'm now engaged in writing a book in which—no matter how sophisticated and pluralistic I may try to be—I'm fundamentally trying to persuade everyone to follow the same strategy, or at least move in the same direction. It could be argued that I'm going counter to my own argument in so doing, but this depends entirely on what my assumptions are about this effort. If I see myself as attempting to convert everyone by degrees—that so many people will see the light today and tomorrow they'll convert others, and so on, until everyone "understands"—then I'm ignoring my own words. On the other hand if I take no position at all, believing that everyone should do their own thing and not bother anyone, then I'm operating on exactly the same assumption: that is, that it's *possible* to convert everyone. If I'm really attuned to the immensity and complexity of human life and experience, however, then I realize that it might be useful to try—to express the energy I have around some issue, since in any case the hugest effort on my part will make only a tiny change in the arrangement of things, and that the interplay of such changes allows for creative evolution. To argue that everyone should pursue their own path, in other words, is a piece of tolerance that masks the most outrageous grandiosity—the belief that if I try to make some impact on people I might suddenly succeed in creating the whole world in my own image.

Not to be involved is not be alive. If you don't struggle to improve the stage even your spiritual mission will fail, for where should you work on yourself if not here? And who are you to separate your development from everyone else's? Many traditions emphasize the here-and-now, but to concentrate all energy on the immediate moment—to zero in narrowly and cut away all surrounding tissue of past memory and future plans—is a form of withdrawal in itself. To live utterly in the moment is to cut away context and hence lose all connection with those who are tuned to a larger unit of time.

There are two ways, in other words, to detach oneself from people and assume an aloof posture. One is to take a broader overview than other people—seeing the long-range trends and smiling at the intense passions of those who involve themselves in the struggles of their time. The other is to take a *narrower* view than other people—living in the moment, letting everything go by, clinging to nothing, and smiling at the attachments, the wishes, the regrets of those who involve themselves in the struggles of their time. Both express an elitist refusal to be swept up in the things of the world—to work out one's issues in this life.

This raises a perplexing question. I've quoted "Seth" a number of times, and there are now several books full of his teachings. Seth talks frequently about "speakers"—the great religious figures of history who come to tell us the world is not as we see it—and Seth himself functions in this role. But what is the motive of these speakers? Our narcissism blinds us to the oddity of their bothering to tell us these things.

Let's assume for the moment that Seth, Jesus, Mohammed, Buddha, and other religious leaders are all inspired prophets telling us the truth—that while we think our three-dimensional reality is of the utmost importance they are revealing to us in one way or another that it isn't. They say that it's transitory, or illusion, or purely symbolic, or a theater for working on our personal development. But then why, if it's so unimportant, do they bother to tell us? It's like reminding the actors in a tragedy that it's only a play, just as they're getting into it. What's the motive? It has a discordant feel to it, as if someone wanted all this kept a secret and someone else wanted to give the secret away. One thinks of the "knowledge of good and evil" that cost Adam and Eve the Garden of Eden.

Perhaps the battling deities of certain religions express this cosmic ambivalence—the elegant tension of the secret, the explosive release of giving it away. Is "Seth," then, a kind of Satan? Are the "speakers" just muckraking reporters trying to give the game away? One thing alone seems clear—if three-dimensional mundane experience were entirely trivial in the grand scheme of things *there would be no reason for anyone to bother to tell us that fact while we were still enmeshed in it*, since such information would only have impact on mundane reality itself, which is supposedly unimportant. Furthermore, there seems to be a certain amount of consensus among these "speakers" that upon leaving mundane reality this unimportance becomes known anyway. Why tell people when they're *still in it*?

Like all conflicts, this cosmic one about the secret of life seems to be just a way of achieving balance—one must believe in mundane reality enough to make it seem important, but not so much as to lose perspective entirely about

The Magic of the West

its modest place in the larger universe of realities. Seth says that life is continually developing in all spheres, including this one. All I know is that I'm in this sphere now, playing on this stage, and I want to grow with it as best I can, and that means, in part, making the stage habitable and the drama meaningful. To trash it in favor of a dream is to create on a cosmic plane the miseries of our mutilated environment.

But to vote for participation in this life is not to close one's eyes to other realities. The world we live in is not a fixed entity: the stage changes, evolves, expands. To opt for this life is not to turn one's back on the "paranormal"— the psychic realm—for "this life" includes much that we don't see. We can live in the world and still be aware that it includes a vast array of events to which Tinkertoy reality blinds us. Our future stage may not only be one in which the few no longer oppress the many, but also one in which everyday "reality" includes all those psychic events of which we now speak but in which we still largely disbelieve. Nothing stands still, especially our ideas about what's "real."

PLAYING FOR KEEPS

Theologians and poets have often suggested that the world begins with a bored deity. Since the deity includes everything and is all Oneness and Perfection, it becomes bored and lonely. Hence it divides itself for diversion and company. God and Devil emerge and play hide-and-seek—God representing the original unity and the Devil expressing the separation—the illusion of breaking away. We have many myths that celebrate this game, from *Paradise Lost* to *Bonnie and Clyde*. We glory in the elation of freedom and feel satisfied with the tragic climax—the hail of bullets, the morning after. This illusion of separateness serves to expand and complicate living forms, for which every breaking out ends in a return, each cycle creates change and variety.

233

The Wayward Gate

The variety of living forms is impressive even on our tiny planet alone. Even more awesome is the variety of their adaptations. Some species live in the relative stability of ocean depths, arctic tundra, mountain tops, or deep forests—secure in environments that have remained substantially unchanged for thousands of years. Others make their home in the incredible chaos of the intertidal zone, exposed intermittently to cold water and hot, dehydrating sun, and periodic assaults by the unquenchable violence of wave battering against rock. Of these species, some cling to a fixed position, like the dogged limpet, while others hide in crevices or pools, or bury themselves in the sand, while still others are swept about by the ungovernable ocean. None of these lives is more or less valuable than another. We may have sentimental favorites, just as we might be more interested in one or another organ of the body—the heart more than the kidneys or the lungs more than the brain—but to have all of them trying to do the same thing would mean death to all. Every life, however trivial, is a sacred drama. But each also plays some part in a larger and more significant drama, and has the option of playing that role intensely, with passion and commitment, or self-consciously, with cold abstraction.

BIBLIOGRAPHY

Ariès, Philippe. *Centuries of Childhood: A Social History of Family Life*. New York: Knopf, 1962.

Blum, Ralph, and Judy Blum. *Beyond Earth: Man's Contact with UFOs*. New York: Bantam, 1974.

Brown, G. Spencer. *Laws of Form*. New York: Julian, 1972.

Byrne, Peter. *The Search for Bigfoot: Monster, Myth, or Man?* Washington, D.C.: Acropolis, 1975.

Castaneda, Carlos. *Journey to Ixtlan*. New York: Simon and Schuster, 1972.

———— *A Separate Reality*. New York: Simon and Schuster, 1971.

———— *Tales of Power*. New York: Simon and Schuster, 1974.

———— *The Teachings of Don Juan*. New York: Ballantine, 1969.

Cayce, Hugh Lynn, ed. *Edgar Cayce on Atlantis*. New York: Hawthorn, 1968.

Costello, Peter. *In Search of Lake Monsters*. New York: Coward, McCann, and Geoghegan, 1974.

Cronin, Edward W., Jr., "The Yeti: The Abominable Snowman." *The Atlantic* (November 1975): 47–53.

de Mille, Richard. *Castenada's Journey: The Power and the Allegory*. Santa Barbara, California, Capra Press, 1976.

Dinsdale, Tim. *The Leviathans*. London: Routledge and Kegan Paul, 1966.

Donnelly, Ignatius. *Atlantis: The Antediluvian World*. (Rev. Ed. by Egerton Sykes). New York: Gramercy, n.d.

Fort, Charles. *The Book of the Damned*. New York: Ace Books 1972. (reprint of 1919 ed.).

———— *Lo!* New York: Ace Books, 1973. (reprint of 1931 ed.).

———— *New Lands*. New York: Ace Books, 1973. (reprint of 1923 ed.).

———— *Wild Talents*. New York: Ace Books, 1973 (reprint of 1929 ed.).

The Wayward Gate

Fox, Oliver. *Astral Projection*. Secaucus, N.J.: Citadel, 1974.

Freud, Sigmund, "One of the Difficulties of Psycho-Analysis." *Collected Papers*, Vol. IV. London: Hogarth, 1953: 347–356.

Fuller, John G. *The Interrupted Journey*. New York: Dell, 1966.

———— *Aliens in the Skies: The New UFO Battle of the Scientists*. New York: Berkley Medallion, 1969.

Gould, Charles. *Mythical Monsters*. London: W. H. Allen, 1886.

Gould, Rupert T. *The Case for the Sea Serpent*. New York: G. P. Putnam, 1934.

Green, Celia. *Out-of-the-Body Experiences*. New York: Ballantine, 1973.

Grumley, Michael. *There Are Giants in the Earth*. Garden City, New York: Doubleday, 1974.

Heuvelmans, Bernard. *On the Track of Unknown Animals*. New York: Hill & Wang, 1959.

———— *In the Wake of the Sea-Serpents*. New York: Hill & Wang, 1969.

Hynek, J. Allen. *The UFO Experience: A Scientific Inquiry*. Chicago: Regnery, 1972.

———— and Jacques Vallée. *The Edge of Reality: A Progress Report on Unidentified Flying Objects*. Chicago: Regnery, 1975.

Jung, Carl G. *Memories, Dreams, Reflections*. New York: Vintage, 1963.

Klass, Philip. *UFOs Explained*. New York: Random House, 1974.

Lilly, John C. *The Center of the Cyclone: An Autobiography of Inner Space*. New York: Bantam, 1972.

Machen, Arthur. *Tales of Horror and the Supernatural*. New York: Knopf, 1948.

Margalef, Ramón. "Perspectives in Ecological Theory." *Coevolution Quarterly* (Summer 1975): 49–66.

Marin, Peter. "The New Narcissism." *Harper's* (October 1975): 45–56.

Menzel, Donald H. *Flying Saucers*. Cambridge, Massachusetts: Harvard University Press, 1953.

Michel, Aimé. *Flying Saucers and the Straight-Line Mystery*. New York: Criterion, 1958.

Millar, Ronald. *The Piltdown Men*. New York: St. Martin's, 1972.

Monroe, Robert A. *Journeys Out of the Body*. Garden City, New York: Doubleday, 1971.

Muldoon, Sylvan, and Hereward Carrington. *The Phenomena of Astral Projection*. London: Rider, 1969.

Murphy, Gardner. *Challenge of Psychical Research*. New York: Harper Colophon, 1970.

Napier, John. *Bigfoot, the Yeti, and Sasquatch in Myth and Reality*. New York: Dutton, 1973.

Bibliography

Ornstein, Robert E. *The Psychology of Consciousness*. San Francisco: W. H. Freeman, 1972.

Ostrander, Sheila, and Lynn Schroeder. *Psychic Discoveries Behind the Iron Curtain*. New York: Bantam, 1970.

Pauwels, Louis, and Jacques Bergier. *The Morning of the Magicians*. New York: Avon, 1968.

Pearce, Joseph Chilton. *The Crack in the Cosmic Egg*. New York: Pocket Books, 1973.

Plato. *The Dialogues* (translated by B. Jowett). New York: Random House, 1937.

Puharich, Andrija. *The Sacred Mushroom: Key to the Door of Eternity*. Garden City, New York: Doubleday, 1974.

Ram Dass, "Advice to a Psychotherapist." *Journal of Transpersonal Psychology* (1975), 7, pp. 84–92.

Reich, Wilhelm. *Character-Analysis* (3rd Edition, translated by Theodore P. Wolfe). New York: Farrar, Straus & Cudahy, 1945.

Roberts, Jane. *The Coming of Seth*. New York: Pocket Books, 1976.

——— *The Nature of Personal Reality: A Seth Book*. Englewood Cliffs, New Jersey: Prentice-Hall, 1974.

——— *The Seth Material*. Englewood Cliffs, New Jersey: Prentice-Hall, 1970.

——— *Seth Speaks*. New York: Bantam, 1974.

Rosenthal, Robert. *Experimenter Effects in Behavioral Research*. New York: Appleton-Century-Crofts, 1966.

Ruppelt, E. J. *The Report on UFOs*. New York: Ace Books, 1956.

Schaller, George B. *The Mountain Gorilla: Ecology and Behavior*. Chicago: University of Chicago Press, 1963.

Stearn, Jess. *Edgar Cayce: The Sleeping Prophet*. New York: Bantam, 1968.

Stewart, Kilton. "Dream Theory in Malaya." In Tart, Charles, ed. *Altered States of Consciousness*. Garden City, New York: Doubleday, 1972, pp. 161–170.

Tart, Charles, ed. *Altered States of Consciousness: A Book of Readings*. Garden City, New York: Doubleday, 1972.

Thompson, Francis. "The Mistress of Vision." In *The Poems of Francis Thompson*. London: Oxford University Press, 1937.

Vallée, Jacques. *Anatomy of a Phenomenon*. Chicago: Regnery, 1965.

——— *The Invisible College*. New York: Dutton, 1975.

Van Der Post, Laurens. *The Lost World of the Kalahari*. New York: Pyramid, 1966.

Van Lawick-Goodall, Jane. *In the Shadow of Man*. Boston: Houghton Mifflin, 1971.

Velikovsky, Immanuel. *Worlds in Collision*. New York: Dell, 1950.

——— *Earth in Upheaval*. New York: Dell, 1955.

The Wayward Gate

Von Däniken, Erich. *Chariots of the Gods?* New York: Bantam, 1971.

———— *Gods from Outer Space.* New York: Bantam, 1972.

Watson, Lyall. *Supernature: A Natural History of the Supernatural.* New York: Bantam, 1974.

Weil, Andrew. *The Natural Mind.* Boston: Houghton Mifflin, 1972.